Mind in Character

University of Missouri Press / *Columbia, 1987*

Mind
in
Character

Shakespeare's
Speaker
in the
Sonnets

David
K.
Weiser

Library of Congress Cataloging-in-Publication Data

Weiser, David K.
    Mind in character

    Bibliography: p.
    Includes index.
    1. Shakespeare, William, 1564–1616. Sonnets.
    2. Sonnets, English—History and criticism. I. Title.
    PR2848.W44   1987   821'.3   87–5845
    ISBN 0–8262–0647–6 (alk. paper)

∞™   This paper meets the minimum requirements of
the American National Standard for Permanence of Paper
for Printed Library Materials, Z39.48, 1984.

For my wife, Rina

hat record could with a backward look O that

'n of five hundred courses of the sun Even of

ow me your image in some antique book Sho

ce mind at first in character was done Since

O that record could with a backward look O

Even of five hundred courses of the sun Eye

Show me your image in some antique book S

Since mind at first in character was done Si

that record could with a backward look O the

en of five hundred courses of the sun Even

ow me your image in some antique book Sho

nce mind at first in character was done Since

O that record could with a backward look O t

Even of five hundred courses of the sun Even

how me your image in some antique book S

Since mind at first in character was done Sin

that record could with a backward look O tha

en of five hundred courses of the sun Even

ow me your image in some antique book Sho

ce mind at first in character was done Since

O that record could with a backward look O

Even of five hundred courses of the sun Eye

Show me your image in some antique book S

Since mind at first in character was done Si

—sonnet 59

Preface

This book is about poetry rather than theory. Shakespeare's poetry, I find, remains more relevant and more rewarding than any theory, however elaborate, as to who, if anyone, should read a text and, if so, how they should do it. In other words, I do not intend another prolegomena for future studies of the reader in the text and/or the text in the reader. I simply have written what I think the sonnets are about, what they say and how they say it. I do not attempt to speak for "the reader," as I know little about him or her, but only for myself. What interests me especially is the behavior of Shakespeare's sonnet-speaker, the coherent psychological entity projected by the speaking voice in these poems. I do not identify that speaker with the historical William Shakespeare, knowing scarcely more about him than about "the reader." Some biographical circumstances and thirty-seven plays are not enough, I feel, to warrant generalization about the man. Nevertheless, I cannot deny having made inferences about the purely literary, not historical, personality that I think underlies both the sonnets and the plays.

Perhaps these poems, having been read, reread, and misread for nearly four centuries, can no longer provoke new and worthwhile responses. In that case, readers like myself who claim to be interpreting them may merely be repeating our predecessors. I have endeavored therefore to avoid well-trodden ways by including many of the less fully annotated sonnets or by reaching conclusions different from those I have read. I find that the exhaustibility argument does little credit either to poetry or to its critics. The chessboard, with sixty-four squares and thirty-two pieces, has yet to be depleted of all its possibilities. Standard gambits and strategies do exist, but gifted players still devise endless variations. If that ancient game contains more things than are dreamt of, even by the computer, perhaps we ought not to give up so quickly on Shakespeare and ourselves. There are 154 sonnets, most of them packed with enough complexity to inspire a dissertation. And there are infinite ways of combining them into meaningful patterns.

The sonnets thus make good their promise to endure "so long as men can breathe or eyes can see." The real difficulty, as the sonnet-speaker discovers in himself, is that our eyes do not always see clearly. When one reviews the annals of commentary on these poems, what emerges is an exemplum of the extent to which literary judgment can become arbitrary. Their endlessly suggestive power has generated enough turmoil to justify

Stephen Dedalus' well-known quip: "Shakespeare is the happy hunting ground of all minds that have lost their balance." Appropriately, Hyder Rollins quoted that epigram in the preface to his *Variorum* edition of the sonnets, which attempted to reduce aberrant criticism to absurdity. More than forty years later, his efforts seem to have largely succeeded; we hear little about the search for a historical "Dark Lady" and can easily resist contradictory theories about "Mr. W. H.," while the Baconian heresy has been safely neutralized. Nevertheless, criticism today might well pause to consider whether its methods and findings are really any more balanced than those of earlier days. Once again, the sonnets are being used to illustrate what they themselves call "new-found methods" and "compounds strange." The new theories are psycholinguistic rather than historical; for all their seeming rigor, they often provide readings no less fantastical than those that amused James Joyce.

Most nineteenth-century scholars were well versed in historical research. Their errors lay not in method but in specific conclusions: each claimed more for his hypothesis than the accumulated evidence could bear. Their readings of the poetry tended to be overly literal even to the point of inventing facts. Thus traveling "without my cloak" in sonnet 34 means to Samuel Butler that Shakespeare had been "surprised to a preconcerted scheme and very probably roughly handled." In sonnet 37 Butler insists that the lameness mentioned is "literally true for this period of Shakespeare's life."[1] The fault of such readings is their restrictiveness; other inferences based on the same evidence are simply overlooked. What Edward Hubler called "the sense" of Shakespeare's sonnets, their intrinsic forms and meanings, yields to a fiction that is essentially non-sense.[2] Now, by an edifying paradox, the very insistence on analysis of the text urged by Hubler and other "new critics" has led to new misreadings often more eccentric than the whimsical assertions of the past. The current trend is not to delimit meaning by an arbitrary theory but to foster infinite expansion of the texts until they mean everything and nothing.

One link with the older type of misreading is that the generalizations still lack sufficient evidence while contrary inferences go unconsidered. Stephen Booth's useful and influential edition, including over four hundred pages of commentary, is crammed with interpretations of the kind

1. As cited in Hyder E. Rollins, ed., *A New Variorum Edition of Shakespeare: The Sonnets*, 1:98, 106. This work will hereafter be cited as *Variorum.*
2. *The Sense of Shakespeare's Sonnets.*

that have become prevalent today. Booth habitually mocks those predecessors who supposed the sonnets had some palpable connection to the external world. On the matter of lameness, he wryly refers us to the *Variorum* for "orthopedically literal readings of this metaphor." He simply glosses "made lame" in line 3 of sonnet 37 as "rendered ineffectual" without citing any other contexts for this image. Yet Booth's remarks are sometimes as diverting as those of Samuel Butler and hardly more substantiated. Citing "as a decrepit father" in the same sonnet, he comments: "a metaphor of sexual impotence is dimly apparent throughout quatrain 1."[3] Dimly indeed. One finds "deeds of youth," "active," and of course "lame" in these lines, but they do not create a sexual overtone that would modify the dominant theme of "thy worth and truth." Citing "any of these all, or all, or more" in line 6, Booth reminds us of "the possible sexual innuendo in *all*." Dimly possible (because of the homophony between "awl" and "all") but not probable at all. Booth inflicts this feeble pun relentlessly; are we to hear *awl* in every use of *all*? As a sophisticated rather than naive misreader, he grants that "verbal side effects *cannot* displace or substitute for the clear expository intentions that are ordinarily obvious in the sonnets."[4] The trouble is that his professedly "irrelevant" associations, once legitimized, multiply in chain reactions of impertinence. In other words, there are no criteria for determining why some irrelevancies are more relevant than others. On line 4 of sonnet 1, for example, we are told that "bear his memory" has "logically inappropriate suggestions of 'bearing fruit' and 'bearing young' which are pertinent to the previous botanical metaphor." If this is so, then why not consider the pun on *bear* and *bare* that would link up with the fading rose? Why not recognize that *bear* also means "suffer" and thus implies a fine ambiguity: the heir who will not "bear" posterity does so because he cannot "bear" the memory of his father? To use Rollins's well-worn summation, "the foregoing are mere specimens that could be multiplied indefinitely."

Most of the more recent studies of the sonnets have indeed been multiplying the type of insight that Booth provides. These efforts do have a peculiar value within the context of rarefied, academic speculation. By causing us to examine some of our preconceptions about these poems, they break down a consensus that may not have been justified. Undeniably,

---

3. *Shakespeare's Sonnets: Edited with an Analytical Commentary*, p. 195.
4. Ibid., p. 372.

when a familiar picture is turned upside down we get to know it better. But there are some serious limitations to the newer critical approaches, particularly when they neglect to replace the picture right side up. First, a problem of intelligibility arises from the sheer mass of detail that is required to substantiate any sophisticated argument about structure. A pioneering example in this respect is the study of sonnet 129 by Roman Jakobson and Laurence Jones, a pamphlet whose thirty-three pages are filled with detailed information about fourteen famous lines.[5] On the level of minute description their study is quite satisfying, yet it does not help us deal with the problem it has unwittingly created: what, if anything, can be done with all the data collected here? To argue that these phenomena are perceived subliminally by the reader, as I. A. Richards does in his intriguing review, may be the only solution, but a rather contrived one.[6] It is difficult to suppose that a reader who has not been prompted to look for "three kinds of binary correspondences" will ever see them, least of all unconsciously. What is more, a loss of perspective is inevitable when so much attention is bestowed on microscopic effects. Part of what is known to be an apple can become a cross section of cellular tissue when mounted on a slide, but it would be a strange form of science to take that part for the entire fruit. Similarly, when close reading yields to a subtle analysis of constituents, we are likely to lose sight of what the text as a whole contains.

A second flaw in the newest criticism emerges in its shift of emphasis from explication to theory. Here we encounter a level of abstraction so high as to preclude ordinary comprehension. For example, we are told in a recent, representative article, "The sonnets . . . dramatize not only their contemporary agon of *verba* and *res* but also the very historical confrontation of Renaissance and Romantic poetics out of which has grown the crux of their interpretation. They solve the particular problem posed by their erotic rhetoric, but they also propose a solution of the more general hermeneutic problem created whenever we try to make a richly correspondent and yet reasoned sense of the literary text."[7] A host of philosophical and historical generalizations, some of them dubious, are interwoven here. One wonders whether an "agon" of words and content ever really

5. *Shakespeare's Verbal Art in Th'Expense of Spirit.*
6. Reprinted in *Poetries: Their Media and Ends,* ed. Trevor Eaton, pp. 39–49.
7. Adena Rosmarin, "Hermeneutics Versus Erotics: Shakespeare's Sonnets and Interpretative History," p. 27.

existed, whether the sonnets do dramatize such a conflict, and whether any body of poetry can of itself "propose a solution of the more general hermeneutic problem." Without pursuing these arguments, which the writer develops with much erudition, we can observe that the poems have become ancillary to larger issues; they are no longer being read as poems but as paradigms. A rather misleading perspective is again the result. Shakespeare's sonnets are now being viewed as if through a telescope, a bright spot discerned among vast drifts of cultural history. They become interesting only because they happen to deal with the very same issues that concern the critic: "By taking artifice and sincerity as their topics, the sonnets remake themselves into a more difficult kind of writing, a poetry that is more properly and usefully termed philosophic as well as—or, even, rather than—amatory."[8] Once again, the foregoing passages can be easily multiplied (or should one say "generated"?) by any reader of current literary journals.

Thus, by means of overwhelming detail and inordinate generalization, modern criticism has begun to render the poetic text obsolete. The virtuoso interpreter replaces the poem as the source of our intellectual experience. One senses that certain leading practitioners could perform as well with Barnabe Barnes's *Fidessa*, or even the telephone directory, as with Shakespeare's sonnets. The danger involved in such a triumph of criticism as an end rather than a means is easily apparent. Professors of literature and their students today seem to be repeating some of the excesses that Jacob Burckhardt pointed out in tracing the decline of Renaissance humanists: "They are the most striking examples and victims of an unbridled subjectivity."[9]

The present study is based on a set of assumptions quite different from those that appear to be dominant now. Pluralism, I take it, is a function of the community rather than the individual; as many men, as many minds. In expounding my own reading of the sonnets, I have tried to avoid the exclusiveness of earlier commentators who equated their opinions with objective truth and the inclusiveness practiced today when critics grant that all statements about a text are equally valid. However, I do not claim immunity from the two critical distempers mentioned above. Some of my explications of the sonnets I consider to be neglected or especially signifi-

---

8. Ibid.
9. *The Civilization of the Renaissance in Italy*, trans. S. G. G. Middlemore, p. 165.

cant are quite protracted. I have also found it impossible to avoid theorizing, albeit for pragmatic purposes, in making a distinction between those sonnets that are soliloquies, "speaking of," and those that are dialogues, "speaking to." Believing in an informed subjectivity and in personal knowledge, I cannot presume to supersede other readings—only to supplement them with an analysis that is as coherent and readable as I can make it. My specific thesis is that we identify with the sonnet-speaker as a well-defined dramatic character, not with a set of structural patterns. I also maintain that the 1609 Quarto, despite its surface inconsistencies, reflects a steady pattern of growth and final disintegration in the speaker's personality. The youth and the woman, whoever they might have been, define two distinct areas in the speaker's experience. The same quest for self-knowledge, through a relation with others, remains the essential subject of both.

Chapter 1, "Ironies of Awareness," introduces the sonnet-speaker as a dramatic character very much akin to the Eiron character of comedy. His vivid awareness of impermanence in nature and society leads to the formation of three modes of irony that are intertwined throughout the sequence. First, the irony of natural process is set forth in sonnets 1 through 17. Then rhetorical irony begins to mock the false values of other poets and lovers. Finally, beginning with sonnet 29, the speaker employs a form of dramatic irony to point out his own flaws and contradictions.

Chapter 2, "Soliloquy Sonnets," demonstrates how the speaker's leading traits, his detached irony and tolerance of contradiction, are expressed through the techniques of "speaking of" rather than "speaking to." A relatively small number of sonnets are defined as soliloquies in that they do not explicitly address any "you" or "thou." Traced through the Fair Youth section, these poems constitute a progression toward deeper levels of introspection. The speaker thus applies his ironic temper to the development of personal values. His final affirmations—sonnets 116, 121, and 124—are the culmination of that search.

Chapter 3, "Dialogue Sonnets," deals with implied dialogue as opposed to soliloquy. In quantity and quality, Shakespeare's sonnets are distinguished by their use of dialogue, their reiterated address to "thou" and "you." The changing relationships between speaker and auditor in sonnets 1–126 create a dramatic framework that transforms the conventional themes of time, love, and poetry. These relationships become meaningful in themselves as the idea of reciprocity is reflected in structural patterns that coordinate the speaker and his beloved.

Chapter 4, "Awareness Lost," focuses on sonnets 127–54, traditionally the Dark Lady group. The speaker's previous growth from observer to participant is now extended and even threatens his sense of selfhood. Simultaneously, there is a change in emphasis from seeing to feeling that results in a breakdown of the personal integration achieved before. A division between soliloquies and dialogues shows that introspection is reduced in range and coherence while the ability to sustain dialogue has also been impaired. Images of sight and seeing, continued from the Fair Youth section, are most indicative of the speaker's final breakdown. Shakespeare's sonnets thus conclude their dramatic enactment of a universal pattern: personal growth, conflict and decline.

* * *

I should like to thank the editors of several journals who have kindly permitted me to include revisions of work that originally appeared in their pages. These are the *Shakespeare Newsletter, Neuphilologiche Mitteilungen, Cahiers Elisabéthains, Studies in Philology,* and the *Journal of English and Germanic Philology.* As I have tried to keep bibliographical notes to a minimum, I wish to acknowledge a general indebtedness to past and present commentators on the sonnets, including those who may not be cited and particularly those with whom I have disagreed.

D.K.W.
New York, N.Y.
1 May 1987

Contents

1 Ironies of Awareness

The coming on of his old monster Time
Has made him a still man; and he has dreams
Were fair to think on once, and all found hollow.
. . . . his lark may sing
At heaven's gate how he will, and for as long
As joy may listen; but *he* sees no gate,
Save one whereat the spent clay waits a little
Before the churchyard has it, and the worm.

—E. A. Robinson,
"Ben Jonson Entertains a Man from Stratford"

At the end of Plato's *Symposium,* Socrates is holding forth to his sleepy companions on the subject of drama. He argues that "the genius of comedy . . . [is] the same as that of tragedy, and that the writer of tragedy ought to be a writer of comedy also."[1] Aristophanes and Agathon unfortunately are too weary to take up the argument, which, in any case, would not get its best support until two thousand years had passed. The writings of Shakespeare exemplify most fully that the genius of comedy and tragedy is the same. What links both aspects of that genius, I believe, is the common factor of irony.

Curiously, although the word *irony* is used by writers as early as More, Coverdale, and Puttenham, it never appears in Shakespeare. Its absence may come as somewhat of a surprise in view of the poet's innovative and wide-ranging vocabulary.[2] Yet irony, as a rhetorical and dramatic technique, is ubiquitous in Shakespeare's work. It can be isolated as a central idea that creates multifarious types of ambiguity and dissimulation; it is a willingness to tolerate (and exploit) customarily opposed meanings. In the early comedies we find varying forms of intrigue and connivance, ironies imposed from outside; these gradually yield to more flexible patterns. In *As You Like It* and other later comedies, character no less than plot determines the shape of events. Those characters who have ironic insight into themselves and others will best survive and prosper. In the tragedies, too, there is a steady deepening of ironic meanings. *Hamlet* shows that "purposes mistook" may still

1. *The Works of Plato,* trans. B. Jowett, p. 357.
2. See Otto Jespersen, *The Growth and Structure of the English Language,* pp. 224–48.

dominate the world, but the hero's ironic disposition has also helped bring about many of those reversals. In *Othello, Macbeth,* and above all *King Lear,* the protagonists themselves trigger their downfalls, gaining too late an ironic recognition of their flaws.

The sonnets, therefore, can be approached as a microcosm of Shakespearean irony. They condense many of the ironic attitudes, habits, and resources that are more fully developed in the plays. Thus the love triangle involving poet, friend, and mistress closely resembles the situational intrigues of early comedies, especially *The Two Gentlemen of Verona.* Frequent verbal parallels between the sonnets and such plays as *Love's Labour's Lost* and *The Merchant of Venice* are yet another link. The sonnet-speaker himself adopts an Eiron role with elaborate self-disparagements that scarcely mask his confidence, as many leading characters do in the later comedies. As we move toward the concluding section of the sequence, concentrating on the speaker's involvement with his lady, his plight acquires an undeniably tragic resonance. He undergoes a greater disappointment than that of Troilus, being deceived not by a Cressida but by his own mind and heart. Self-knowledge, or the impossibility of attaining it, becomes an obsession to him no less than it is to Othello and Lear. In this way, the sonnets afford us an opportunity to explore Shakespeare's irony most directly; the mediating element of dramatic characterization has been reduced though not eliminated.

A study of the opening sonnets in the 1609 sequence will show that irony as a poetic technique is bound up inseparably with our awareness of irony as a complex of ideas. These sonnets, numbered 1–17, are usually referred to as the "Marriage" or "Procreation" group. The latter title is preferable, for marriage is mentioned only as a means of begetting children. Few themes, it is safe to say, could be less appealing to readers of poetry today. Changes in the social fabric, as well as biological innovations, have loosened the old bonds of marriage and the family. It is no longer necessary to marry in order to have children, and statistics suggest that to many people having a family may no longer be desirable. Perhaps for those reasons, and because of a surface repetitiousness, these seventeen sonnets tend to be underestimated today. They are rarely anthologized and receive relatively little attention from the commentators. Yet the Procreation group defines the sonnets' thematic center, locating it in the cosmic process of change. These poems yield a rich harvest of ironic perceptions and introduce us to some of the speaker's most important characteristics. Here we encounter his typically ironic attitude toward the physical universe, so that three distinct levels of irony gradually unfold: the cosmic, rhetorical, and dramatic.

I. *The Cosmic Dimension*

The opening of sonnet 1 at once reveals an ironic view of the world:

> From fairest creatures we desire increase,
> That thereby beauty's rose might never die.
> But as the riper should by time decease
> His tender heir might bear his memory.[3]

Conventionally enough, beauty is represented by a symbol that also involves the concepts of time and death. The rose embodies only the perfect moment that intervenes between fulfillment and decay. Describing it, Shakespeare makes no attempt to speak in a biographical voice, or in that of a dramatically defined persona. It is simply "we" who speak, as the voice of consensus, and our desire for preserving the flower's beauty is no less natural than its coming decline. Such a confluence, using "we" to unite temporarily speaker, reader, and the ordinary world, has a justification of its own. Even when the sonnet-speaker becomes a recognizably dramatic character, the universality of his experience lends it a wider scope. Nevertheless, one is tempted to see the internal rhymes in the opening quatrain as summarizing much of the speaker's personal vision: "fairest," "heir," and "bear." These words denote transient beauty, followed by death and bereavement, leading to remembrance and rebirth. The cosmic irony they imply derives from one all-pervading idea, the speaker's vivid awareness of impermanence. He never forgets that all living things must change, more or less predictably, according to the dictates of time. That initial awareness leads him to embark on what will become a far-reaching search for permanent value. Yet the ideals that he will later propound—procreation, idealized love, and poetic immortality—never cancel his ironic and essentially pessimistic vision of natural process.

Having announced a purely temporal perspective, sonnet 1 does not convert that way of seeing into a fully developed irony. The speaker's concern is with the youth, addressed as "thyself thy foe," because he is opposed to conventional opinion and, therefore, to his own self-interest. Being "the

---

3. Stephen Booth, ed., *Shakespeare's Sonnets: Edited with an Analytical Commentary,* p. 4. All references to the sonnets are from this edition.

world's fresh ornament," he ought to "pity the world" by bringing it an heir. Not to do so would be "to eat the world's due, by the grave and thee." So mundane an argument actually lacks some of the breadth required for cosmic irony. It acknowledges time and death but seems overly secure as to how they can be circumvented. Only as the Procreation sonnets continue do we find the speaker's emphasis shifting to an account of change as an over-whelmingly dynamic process that admits no easy solution. Sonnet 2 offers a series of contrasts between the youth as he is and as he will become:

thy brow	forty winters
thy beauty's field	deep trenches
proud livery	tottered weed
the treasure of thy lusty days	thine own deep-sunken eyes

Further images of reversal or decline will be added by the sonnets that follow, transforming familiar aspects of natural process into icons of mortality. Our place in the world, sonnet 4 explains, is transient because "Nature's bequest gives nothing—but doth lend." Sonnet 5 relates that time "leads summer on / To hideous winter and confounds him there," adding further antinomies:

sap	frost
lusty leaves	quite gone
beauty	bareness

Sonnet 6 retains the image of "winter's ragged hand" ruining summer's beauty, whereas 7 depicts "strong youth" and "feeble age" in terms of the rising and the setting sun. In all these images, human life is not dissociated from vastly different units of time, such as days and seasons, nor is it dis-tinguished from the brief life span of leaves and flowers. Quantitative dif-ferences, it is implied, matter nothing compared to the purely qualitative distinction between mortal and eternal. Sonnet 12, compiling other instances of decline, does not pause to distinguish between "the violet past prime, / And sable curls all silvered o'er with white." The same principle of mortality established by both images is then reinforced by "brave day sunk in hideous night," "lofty trees . . . barren of leaves," and "summer's green" being sheaved and carted away.

The patterns of reversal established in these sonnets do not entirely lend themselves to the procreation argument. For example, the meaning of the flower imagery is by no means confined to short-lived beauty. Sonnet 1, after introducing one such image, turns the flower into an emblem of arrested development. "Within thine own bud," the youth is told, he has buried his "content," his essential substance as well as his happiness. In sonnet 2, "t-ottered weed" has a similarly double meaning. In the archaic sense, it is the worthless garment that "youth's proud livery" will become; in the more modern meaning of "weed" as an unwanted plant, it is the very symbol of "small worth." When we reach sonnets 5 and 6, flowers are linked to the distillation process as a metaphor for procreation:

> But flow'rs distill'd, though they with winter meet,
> Leese but their show, their substance still lives sweet.

The youth is urged to "make sweet some vial," preserving his biological essence through the act of generation. Sonnets 15 and 16 then refer to engrafting as yet another symbol of continuity. Not child-bearing but a new idea, the writing of poetry, is now expressed. Finally the flower symbol, introduced as a conventional reminder of mortality, comes to convey precisely the opposite quality: sonnet 16 claims, "many maiden gardens yet unset, / With virtuous wish would bear your living flowers." If we have been attentive to the speaker's oft-repeated arguments, we cannot ignore the ambiguity of those lines, even though they still insist on prodding the youth toward fatherhood. All flowers are "living" until they die; that event, we have so often been told, is never far away. What the speaker apparently intends must be an identification between flowers and children, something like "animate flowers." But this argument for procreation now becomes equivocal: flowers, whether animate or simply living, cannot serve as durable weapons against time.

Such inattention to their own implications occurs often in the Procreation sonnets. They argue so single-mindedly for "breed" that on the surface very little likelihood of irony appears. These poems do nevertheless provide a basis for irony throughout the sequence. Although they insist that the youth should propagate his beauty by marrying and having children, they raise larger questions that are only partially answered. They show that the fundamental irony, for which no remedy exists, results from time itself. In the process of nature nothing can pretend to stability, let alone permanence. The instability of a world whose elements are incessantly changing creates a host of double meanings. No person or object can remain the same from minute to minute, since each segment of time defines a new reality.

Not only the flower and vegetal imagery but also the frequent references to the earth itself show a pervasive and only partly controlled dualism that results from cosmic irony. The first sonnet concludes by coupling "the grave and thee" in order to label the youth's self-love (being confined to his own "bud" or body) as life-defeating. In the same way, sonnet 4 threatens that "thy unused beauty must be tombed with thee," and 6 warns of making "worms thine heir." These three warnings tightly bind up earth and death; all of them appear within the couplets, so that their finality in ending the poems corresponds with the physical facts of death and burial. Yet as the Procreation group progresses there is no further imagery of that ominous sort. Instead, an opposed aspect of earth imagery emerges, evoking life and growth. That second phase begins with the archly rhetorical questions of sonnet 3:

> For where is she so fair whose uneared womb
> Disdains the tillage of thy husbandry?
> Or who is he so fond will be the tomb
> Of his self-love to stop posterity?

The rhyme of "womb" and "tomb" exactly renders the two antithetical aspects of earth as a poetic symbol. Between those extremes lies the neutral ground of sonnet 7, whose perspective is that of "each under eye" looking up to heaven, and of sonnet 15, which dispassionately surveys the world as "this huge stage." But if the two concluding poems are any indication, the tendency of the entire Procreation group is decidedly toward the positive, life-giving sense of earth as "womb."

Sonnet 16 revives that forgotten connection with fertility when it speaks of "maiden gardens yet unset." And in sonnet 17 the imaginative argument comes full circle so that the "tomb" image has been reversed; ignoring the youth's self-love, the speaker now applies that image to his own artistic failure. His poem "is but as a tomb / Which hides your life, and shows not half your parts." Instead of flowers that fade and die, this sonnet envisages "my papers, yellowed with their age . . . scorned, like old men of less truth than tongue." Time the destroyer now feeds on art; neither the speaker's poetry nor the portrait previously called "your painted counterfeit" can long survive. The earth has been revalued as the source of life, not merely its burial place, while the tomb image reflects the limits of art rather than those of bachelorhood.

These ironic complexities of image and idea force us to think more carefully about the reiterated case for procreation. What Shakespeare is urging through his speaker differs radically from the biblical command to "be fruitful and multiply." He supposes that increase will not be desired for all things but only for "fairest creatures." Sonnet II explicitly makes that point:

> Let those whom nature hath not made for store,
> Harsh, featureless, and rude, barrenly perish.

So selective a view of generation could never have peopled the earth, having as its criterion beauty rather than life itself. But a further and more serious flaw of this argument lies in its purely vicarious triumph over time. It grants that each generation will return to dust, but insists that having offspring will compensate, at least partially, for that fact. The youth, as a conscious egoist, might well have challenged such vulnerable logic. What is it to me, he might have asked, to be survived by others even if they bear my features? Having resolved only to live as handsomely as possible, he could consistently maintain a total lack of interest in posterity.[4] Furthermore, supposing that the young Narcissus had been persuaded, his acquiescence would be due to the very self-love so vehemently censured by the speaker. Rather than beholding his image in a mirror or pool, he would continue to admire it no less in his children. The child gets no more intrinsic worth than the sweet "vial" that bore him; he will merely be an ornament to his father's vanity.

Procreation, therefore, is a questionable strategy for the defeat of time. It offers a vicarious triumph by substituting the survival of future generations for that of the individual. What Shakespeare's speaker demands of the youth is actually a submission to the natural sequence of generation and death. The first of many paradoxes in this deceptively simple argument is that collaboration with time proves to be a method for defeating it. Irony as an intellectual construct thus resides in the speaker's vision of a complex, ever-changing existence. Many details in the Procreation sonnets reveal his habit of seeing a

---

4. An interesting parallel occurs in Chapman's *An Humourous Day's Mirth* (1597), when Lord Dowsecer is urged by his father to marry and have children, "the ende of marriage, and the ioye of men." The young lord replies:

> O how you are deceived, you have but me,
> And what a trouble am I to your ioy?

Dowsecer continues by mocking the idea of procreation; he concludes:

> But for the ioyes of children, tush tis gone,
> Children will not deserue, nor parents take it:
> Wealth is the only father and the child,
> And but in wealth no man hath any ioy.

The Plays of George Chapman, the Comedies: A Critical Edition, ed. Allan Holaday, p. 90.

dynamic physical reality. But more than anything else, the insistent mentioning of family relationships creates a twofold irony that both supports and subverts the case for procreation. Only three of these poems, sonnets 5, 14, and 15, actually fail to mention either father, mother, or child. The first of these is a cryptically impersonal account of natural process, using distillation as its central metaphor. The other two shift away from the procreation theme; sonnet 14 briefly mentions "store," whereas 15 introduces poetry as a new weapon in the arsenal against time. Everywhere else the family unit emerges as the icon of procreation, suggesting that if time cannot be vanquished it can still be domesticated.

On the other hand, sonnet 8 attempts something like a complete family portrait. It is also unique in turning to music as a source of imagery:

> Mark how one string, sweet husband to another,
> Strikes each in each by mutual ordering;
> Resembling sire, and child, and happy mother,
> Who all in one, one pleasing note do sing.

The unison referred to in "sweet husband to another" is that of sympathetic vibration between the double strings of instruments like the lute. Somewhat less precisely, the child's voice is joined to that of its parents as a further reverberation of other strings on the instrument. What the imaginary family sings is a warning to the single one: "thou single wilt prove none." The youth's supposed dislike of music ("why hear'st thou music sadly") thus becomes an emblem of solitude. His ear rejects "the true concord of well-tuned sounds, / By unions married," and his preferred music, if any, must be the plain chant of solipsism. Sonnet 8 is therefore more than a rhetorical conceit; by employing associational psychology, it provides the youth with an explanation of his own behavior. There is surely nothing modern about such conjectures. At the beginning of *The Merchant of Venice*, we find two of Antonio's followers making a similar attempt to second-guess his melancholy. Their highly rhetorical analysis seeks to uncover some unconscious associations in his troubled mind. Thus cooling his soup reminds him of "a wind too great at sea," while a church's stony walls evoke "dangerous rocks" and shipwreck.

Many of these sonnets continue to explain the youth to himself by constantly citing images of the family. They prompt him to play a double role, being in fact his parent's child and in potentiality his children's father. When he declines to do so, he is accused of violating the natural order. Significantly, of the three basic family roles, fatherhood receives the least development. Sonnet 1 mentions the "riper" being succeeded by "his tender heir" without providing any description of a living father. None of the following sonnets fills in that gap; in fact, these sonnets imply that the youth's father is deceased. The past tense in sonnet 13 seems unequivocal: "You had a father, let your son say so." In any case, most of the references to paternity are ethereal; they point to "husbandry" and what the youth ought to become, not to an existent person or function. In contrast, we do obtain a sense of actual presence when a maternal image appears in sonnet 3:

> Thou art thy mother's glass, and she in thee
> Calls back the lovely April of her prime.

The corollary is that when the young man becomes a father he, too, will be able to recall his "golden time." But sonnet 9 goes on to reestablish the previous link between the act of remembrance and a widow's loss:

> every private widow well may keep,
> By children's eyes, her husband's shape in mind.

Although there may be biographical import to this description, it is inherently psychological. The speaker is supplying a possible motive for the youth's reluctance to marry:

> Is it for fear to wet a widow's eye
> That thou consums't thyself in single life?

The question ascribes to the young man an unusually sensitive, possibly morbid temperament. Perhaps that characterization is unfair or inaccurate, but at least it does allow him a measure of humanity and avoids branding him a monster of self-love.

The young man's supposed attitude closely prefigures the speaker's own melancholy in sonnet 64:

> This thought is as a death, which cannot choose
> But weep to have that which it fears to lose.

The slightly morbid reasoning that is attributed to the youth in sonnet 9 may therefore be a projection of something that only the poetic speaker was capable of feeling. Not having a wife, presumably, will preclude loss and suffering on her part; consequently, the youth denies himself the joys of marriage for fear of causing later suffering to others. The speaker must correct that fallacy by defining solitude as itself a form of suffering, one that (unlike the widow's) lacks all consolation. The single man's metaphorical widow is the world that "will wail thee like a makeless wife." The poem. thus offers its auditor a choice of widows, real and figurative, arguing that the former is preferable. What is more, the speaker claims to know the youth's self-interest better than he:

> No love toward others in that bosom sits
> That on himself such murd'rous shame commits.

These lines suggest that the seemingly vacant role of the father is quickly being filled. If the speaker's attitude had initially been detached or avuncular, it is now nothing short of paternal, an unforeseen result of stressing patterns of family relation. Having attempted to invent a mythic family, with the reluctant youth at its head, the speaker increasingly addresses him as a child. Reserving the paternal role to himself, he is in effect blocking the youth from identifying with fatherhood. When we consider his images of childhood, which are far more numerous than those of the parental roles, we find further evidence that the speaker is beginning to dissociate himself from his argument.

The primary metaphors for procreation, in fact, tend to be quite artificial, even though they describe the most natural of processes. Distillation in sonnet 5 is a rather uninviting analogy with a disturbingly lifeless end product, "a liquid prisoner pent in walls of glass." Sonnet 6 changes that metaphor into one whose connotations are even more repellent:

> That use is not forbidden usury
> Which happies those that pay the willing loan.

Although the "usury of love" was conventional in Elizabethan poetry, Shakespeare's treatment of it does not escape the negative implications of ordinary usury. In fact, he seems to enjoy belaboring the mercantile aspect of this analogy:

> That's for thyself to breed another thee,
> Or ten times happier be it ten for one.

No less ingenious and mechanical is the couplet of sonnet 11:

> She [Nature] carved thee for her seal, and meant thereby
> Thou shouldst print more, not let that copy die.

There is no denying that an appeal to the youth's vanity is being made. He himself, as his father's child, is not represented as the copy of any one else but as nature's seal. However, his children will be replicas of their great original.

Other references to these imagined children are similarly subordinated to their father's own egotism. Two of the sonnets employ the epithets "thy blood warm" and "that fresh blood," suggesting that what is desired besides individual survival is an aristocratic lineage. Sonnet 16 also hints at that idea through the phrase "lines of life," while at least three other sonnets explicitly define the future heir as his father's image, using the epithets "another thee," "another self," and "your sweet form." The circularity of this argument and its continued appeal to the very self-love that the speaker opposes, are all too evident. In this respect, references to the family resemble the imagery of flowers and the earth. They do not themselves escape the irony that they direct at others; the speaker's awareness of time and change has the unintended effect of eroding all his defiant statements about withstanding them. Precisely this tension between the assertion and the denial of time's power underlies sonnets 12 and 15, making them the most complex and rewarding poems in the Procreation group.

Sonnet 12 is one of the few Procreation sonnets that has received a fair measure of critical attention. Its formal brilliance has been recognized by several critics, most notably by Stephen Booth, for whom the poem demonstrates "numerous coexistent schemes of organization."[5] Booth's analysis offers a number of insights that can be applied to the sonnets as a whole. His technique of explication resembles the plastic overlays found in an atlas or anatomy book. One transparent sheet can be superimposed on the other, forming a full picture of separate yet interdependent levels of structure. Sonnet 12 makes an excellent specimen for that mode of analysis. An unusual clarity of texture results from the way its imagery, argument, and sound patterns all reinforce each other. Yet the poem also contains important features that do not figure at all in Booth's skillful dissection of its parts. These are the interplay of its ideas, as related to the procreation argument as a whole, and the dramatic method by which they are presented. The sonnet actually culminates a long line of development; only three later poems—13, 14, and 16—carry on the procreation argument, and they do so with far less effectiveness. Sonnet 12 stands out so conspicuously because, for the first time in the 1609 sequence, prominence is given to the speaker's "I" as the

5. *An Essay on Shakespeare's Sonnets*, p. 83.

focal point of meaning. After the public "we" of sonnet 1 had disappeared, the following sonnets scrupulously excluded all first-person pronouns. They addressed their auditor in a self-effacing manner, as if a disembodied voice could alternately threaten, cajole, and humor him. Only at the *volta* of sonnet 10, the breaking point between the octet and the sestet, and between their respective modes of thought, does the speaker's individuality finally assert itself: "O change thy thought, that I may change my mind," and again in the couplet:

> Make thee another self for love of me,
> That beauty still may live in thine or thee.

Never before had the speaker entered directly into the argument he was expounding. Nature and received opinion had been authorities too powerful to require his personal endorsement. But now a dramatic change has taken place. If the speaker is addressing a patron, he can gradually permit himself some familiarity only after making a discreetly formal opening. On the other hand, the shift in tone may be simply a new rhetorical tack. Unimpressed by the pressures of convention, the youth might have been better approached through the expostulations of a growingly intimate counselor.

After the breakthrough in sonnet 10, the speaker reverts temporarily to his previous reticence, avoiding a personal perspective and keeping up for the last time his weakened myth of a consensus in nature. We are completely unprepared, therefore, for the self-portrait achieved by sonnet 12. Its structure is entirely personal, from the opening line that records the speaker's observation to the gradual unfolding of his thought. But that pattern reflects an underlying separation between the functions of perception and judgment. The "when" section, lines 1–8, reveals the speaker performing the action that will typify him throughout the sonnets:

> When I do count the clock that tells the time,
> And see the brave day sunk in hideous night,
> When I behold the violet past prime,
> And sable curls all silvered o'er with white.

He is a seer, one whose acuity of vision leads on inductively from observed details to the articulation of general ideas. The images of reversal compiled here, of sunset and flowers, silver curls and barren trees, are in themselves no different from those that previous sonnets had assembled. Yet now they are subsumed by an organizing sensibility. The ironic dimension of time and change, this sonnet explains, does not inhere so much in external things as in the human context of perception.

The speaker actively pursues time's vanishing present, rather than merely stating its power. Unable to perceive a living creature immune to time, he returns belatedly to "breed" as its sole antidote. The sonnet's cumulative effect becomes that of imbalance. Its simple lack of symmetry, with twelve lines that affirm time and two that defy it, could easily have been outweighed by an impassioned conclusion. But the problem again is one of quality; the success of offspring is merely stated as a given, whereas the effects of time are fully realized in imagery that grows immediately out of the speaker's sustained and accurate perception. Such imagery tends to be metonymic, creating less noticeable interconnections than do metaphors. Sonnet 12 embodies in its structure all the uncertainties of the procreation theme, an argument that does not always involve the poet's deepest emotions. Because of the speaker's discovery of his own perceiving and comprehending self, the sonnet marks a turning point. No longer will he be able to feign objectivity by assuming a nonexistent consensus. Having begun to speak for himself and not for the world, he continues to explore the nature of that self as he studies his relations with nature and society. In contrast, sonnet 10 had only introduced the poet's mind as a means of influencing the young man's. The phrase "for love of me" may have been added for the couplet's rhyme; however, it seems to allude politely to a newly formed friendship. Sonnet 12 is therefore the first sonnet that can truly be called personal; in other words, it enacts a process of tangible experience. At this point, the 1609 sequence makes a basic transition. The speaker is not writing about time and change as abstract ideas but primarily about his own response to those ideas. He has begun to acquire what the philosopher of science Michael Polanyi tellingly describes as "personal knowledge . . . an active comprehension of things known . . . a responsible act claiming universal validity." Such knowledge, he adds, "is indeed objective in the sense of establishing contact with a hidden reality."[6]

We can better understand the effects created by Shakespeare's ironic awareness if we compare them to a simple dramatic technique. When a character onstage fails to adjust to a changed set of circumstances known to the audience, he becomes a victim of "dramatic irony." For example, Hastings in *Richard III* boasts of his intimacy with the new Protector:

6. *Personal Knowledge: Towards a Post-Critical Philosophy,* p. vii.

> O monstrous, monstrous! and so falls it out
> With Rivers, Vaughan, Grey; and so 'twill do
> With some men else, who think themselves as safe
> As thou and I, who (as thou know'st) are dear
> To princely Richard and to Buckingham.[7] (3.2.64–68)

These predictions are absurdly ominous to an audience that knows so much more about the situation than Hastings does. Similarly, in *Part Two of Henry IV*, Falstaff's expectations of favor from Henry V ring hollow because we have already heard the new king's plans. In the sonnets, then, the irony of process is equivalent to a dramatic plot. Nature itself is the playwright that maps out a constantly changing set of circumstances. Those who do not perceive nature's changing course or act accordingly become its victims. The sonnets' speaker, however, attains the special perspective of "cosmic irony." Traditionally, this attitude requires an elevated vantage point from which men seem tiny and their actions trivial. But Shakespeare achieves cosmic irony in his sonnets by moving beyond time rather than space. His outlook is not one of superior height but on a level with other men. Rather than belittling the significance of life, he enhances present appearances through his knowledge of their origins and destinations. The speaker of the sonnets, being conversant with the brief limits of existence, must look beyond the physical realm for values that give life meaning.

It should be added that Shakespeare's distinction here lies not in his theme, as the commonplace *tempus fugit* was popular in Elizabethan poetry, but in his treatment of it. He cannot reconcile mutability into a philosophical framework, as Spenser does. Neither does he quite achieve an autonomous, sharply defined character like Sidney's Astrophel. The Shakespearean response to this theme remains focused on sense experience and avoids transcending it. The sonnets center on what occurs in the speaker's mind. He has neither a local habitation nor a name and thus becomes an Everyman confronting the most primary sorts of human experience.

This poetic Everyman serves no preconceived morality but is content to demonstrate certain qualities of thought and feeling. For an anticipation of his method, we can turn to some early Elizabethan lyrics. Surrey's "How No Age is Content with his own Estate" begins with an imaginative vision that looks ahead to sonnet 12:

---

7. G. Blakemore Evans, ed., *The Riverside Shakespeare*, p. 732. All references to Shakespeare's plays are from this edition.

> Layd in my quiet bed, in study as I were,
> I saw within my troubled head, a heape of thoughtes appere.[8]

What this poetic speaker sees is manhood in its three phases of boyhood, youth, and old age, each wishing to be other than itself. His response, however, lacks dramatic urgency: "now I sighed, & then I smilde, as cause of thought doth ryse." After recounting the discomforts of all three ages, the poem formulates a slightly more precise position:

> Wherat full oft I smilde, to se, how all these three,
> From boy to man, from man to boy, would chop & change degree.

The speaker no longer sighs, choosing to stress the humorous side of human inconstancy. He has not applied the lesson to himself or to any particular person. Neither has he in any way changed his mind, since the vision merely illustrated what he had known before.

A longer and more elaborate forerunner of sonnet 12 is found in *Tottel's Miscellany* (1557) and entitled "Of the mutabilitie of the world." Two variants of this lyric were published elsewhere under the more revealing titles "Fantasmes" and "The Fantises of a Trubbled mans hed." Here, as in the Surrey poem, we begin with insomnia:

> By fortune as I lay in bed, my fortune was to fynde
> Such fansies, as my carefull thought had brought into my minde.[9]

What follows is a succession of allegorical visions beginning with the introductory line "And sodeinly I saw a sea of wofull sorowes prest." The speaker of this poem is a perfectly conventional seer. He beholds a host of moralized abstractions, claiming, "I saw the world: and how it went, eche state in his degree." But he does not literally see the world; he is simply leading up to a rhetorical point: "that from wealth ygraunted is, both lyfe, and libertee." He envisions many more abstractions, such as envy, disdain, and desire, commenting bitterly on all. No less than twelve lines begin with the verb *I saw,* creating two-line units that link each vision with its commentary:

> I saw, how pleasant times did passe, as flowers doe in the mede:
> To day that ryseth red as rose; to morrow falleth ded.
> I saw, my tyme how it did runne, as sand out of the glasse.
> Euen as eche hower appointed is from tyme, and tyde to passe.

8. Hyder E. Rollins, ed., *Tottel's Miscellany,* 1:29.
9. Ibid., 1:131–32.

I saw the yeares, that I had spent, alosse of all my gayn:
And how the sport of youthful playes my foly dyd retayn.

Compared to the Procreation sonnets, which employ many of the same images, these lines are devoid of detailed observation. They hurry on to their moralizations and are not sufficiently concerned with the images themselves. Yet in contrast to the Surrey poem this speaker does gain from what he sees. His conclusion explains,

And when all these I thus beheld with many mo pardy:
In me, me thought, eche one had wrought a parfite proparty.
And then I said vnto my self; a lesson this shalbe
For other: that shall after come, for to beware by me.
Thus, all the night I did deuise, which way I might constrayn.
To fourme a plot, that wit might work these branches in my brain.

He has decided, it seems, to take up arms against this "sea of wofull sorowes," and his decision utilizes the same "when/then" construction employed in sonnet 12. However, it is confined to the concluding section of the poem, which contains a much more restricted progression: from "I thus beheld" to "me thought" and finally "I said vnto my self." That series of verbs informs us that the speaker has resolved to serve as a didactic model to all mankind "that shall come after." He also becomes an Everyman, devising a "plot" that will somehow further his traditional morality. How different from Shakespeare's sonnet-speaker, who might be called an ironic and, in a sense, transparent Everyman. Beginning in sonnet 12 he, too, becomes an example for those who follow, but his message seems to consist in a peculiarly mimetic act: he simply represents human experience, rather than trying to improve it. The formulation of personal insight, once subordinate to other themes, now becomes the speaker's primary goal.

The fifteenth sonnet best concentrates the ironic vision shared by the entire Procreation group. The speaker now displays his mode of seeing in order to confer on the youth an awareness of natural process. He uses two parallel verb phrases for this purpose: "when I consider" and "when I perceive." Both relate to an act of comprehension rather than physical seeing. They condense earlier observations and anticipate the purely imaginary "sight" of lines 10–11, in which the speaker envisions time debating with decay. The images that the speaker ponders are arranged in a significant progression. The phrase "everything that grows" in the opening line is vast enough to epitomize all the phenomena of organic process. But an even wider scope is achieved by lines 3–4, as the speaker notes,

> That this huge stage presenteth nought but shows
> Whereon the stars in secret influence comment.

These "shows" are appearances that include far more than external nature. Humanity performing on the world stage perennially regales the heavenly spheres with its vanity and folly. The allusion here, as in corresponding passages in Shakespeare's plays, is to our experience of history and society. However, the thematic dominance of natural process is soon reaffirmed by the second quatrain:

> When I perceive that men as plants increase,
> Cheer'd and check'd ev'n by the selfsame sky,
> Vaunt in their youthful sap, at height decrease,
> And wear their brave state out of memory.

The speaker of these lines appears as remote and detached from mankind as the stars themselves. The duality of the sky, which both encourages growth and ends it, may be a reflection of his own ambivalence. It accords with other sonnets in stressing that the same natural forces can preserve and destroy. For example, in sonnet 5 the "hours" that created beauty become "tyrants to the very same." Because of this strictly objective attitude, *increase* in line 5 lacks the biblical resonance that it enjoyed in the opening line of sonnet 1; what is described here remains a purely physical event.

The analogy between men and plants, so often implied by flower imagery, has now been rendered explicit. It is not a flattering thought, and quite contrary to the Renaissance notion of human dignity. Rather than placing man at the top of a hierarchy of animate creatures, the speaker reduces him by comparison with the mindless vegetable kingdom. If any human quality exists in this description of growth and decline, it resides in the allusion to pride and folly. Unlike the plants, man can both "vaunt" in his youth and, in his age, pretend to all that he has lost. The phrase "out of memory" in line 8 is usually glossed as "till it is forgotten that it ever was 'brave.' "[10] But since

---

10. Tucker's gloss cited in *Variorum*, 1:42. A similar reading is given by W. G. Ingram and Theodore Redpath, *Shakespeare's Sonnets*, p. 34: " 'when other people have forgotten what important people they once were.' " Stephen Booth's paraphrase in his edition is related but unaccountably confines "brave state" to its narrowest sense: "and wear their splendid finery (brave state) beyond the time when anyone remembers them or the outdated fashions they wear" (p. 157).

the decline from height has already taken place, the meaning of "their brave state" must be ironic: old men fondly pride themselves on the memory of what they were.

The vision presented in these eight lines, destroying the illusion of a static present, reflects the primary source of irony in the sonnets. Given this acute awareness of time, it follows that all things will be viewed diachronically. Their present state marks an intermediate phase that is constantly in transition. The speaker's diachronic vision is by no means confined to the Procreation group but serves as the point of departure from which he will launch his search for constancy. Thus in sonnet 64 he muses on the mutability suggested by the erosion of monuments and the physical interchange of land and sea. Disconsolate, he applies the lessons of his observation to himself: "Time will come and take my love away." The same image of the "dial's shady stealth" recurs in sonnet 77 as a sign of "time's thievish progress to eternity."

All these examples show that an urgent sense of time as the primary fact of existence pervades the sonnets. The first seventeen sonnets have given abundant sensory evidence of this fact, so that it can subsequently be taken as an axiom. They have also pointed out that the speaker's response to his discovery of the universal process will be one of resistance. Thus in sonnet 15 the cosmic perspective of the octet yields to the sestet's personal application:

> Then the conceit of this inconstant stay
> Sets you most rich in youth before my sight,
> Where wasteful time debateth with decay
> To change your day of youth to sullied night.

The qualities of youth and beauty are now embodied in a single person whom the speaker both visualizes and addresses. His imagination depicts the youth, since "my sight" here is equivalent to what sonnet 27 terms "my soul's imaginary sight." Moreover, the youth's symbolic role has been implied by his placement between personified time and decay.

Since the rule of time admits no exceptions, the speaker acknowledges that his beloved must succumb. Certain nuances of tone in these four lines actually testify to his acquiescence. The compliment "most rich in youth" carries ironic overtones because it echoes the derisive view of men who "vaunt in their youthful sap." The emblem of the beloved's "day of youth" changing to "sullied night" also leaves no doubt that time's conspiracy will succeed. This image of certain doom is synonymous in the sonnets with the

progression of life to death. Finally, since the two personifications are themselves not truly opposites, it is difficult to see what debate is taking place
between them. Only the rate of decline could come into question, with time
wishing to accelerate decay.

Against these signs of acceptance, the couplet in sonnet 15 abruptly asserts
its delayed defiance:

> And all in war with time for love of you,
> As he takes from you, I engraft you new.

The metaphor of engrafting would be obscure were it not for the link
between it and the opening of sonnet 16. Here, procreation will be urged as
the best way to "make war upon this bloody tyrant time." The speaker's
subsequent references to "my barren rhyme" and "my pupil pen" exalt
physical generation as they question the efficacy of art. Yet, even without
this self-deprecating continuation, we would still conclude that his response
to time lacks the force of his earlier description. The gesture of engrafting
follows closely from the plant imagery of the second quatrain. Its purpose is
to restore perfection to the ideal image of the youth. But there is no reference
to the writing of poetry or to any aspect of ordinary reality, as the engrafting
takes place within the speaker's mind. Just as "this huge stage" was influenced by the stars and the growing plants were "cheer'd and check'd" by
heaven, so the youth is placed between destructive forces and the productive
function of the speaker. In this third image, however, the prior balance of
power has clearly shifted. Even if engrafting means the writing of poetry, its
context remains the world of the imagination.

Perhaps it is appropriate that sonnet 15, the first to refer to poetry as a
weapon against time, should do so in such an oblique, diffident manner. Yet
the sonnet is typical, I believe, in that the speaker's negative vision outweighs his subsequent affirmation. Such an imbalance has already been
noted in sonnet 12 and will continue in later efforts to withstand time.
Nevertheless, if sonnet 12 introduces a distinctly personal voice, sonnet 15
lends that voice far greater resonance. It, too, presents the speaker as primarily a seer but grants him a more philosophical vision. Instead of detailed
natural imagery, it begins with the more abstract concept "everything that
grows." Where sonnet 12 moves on to invoking "breed," the later sonnet
ascribes a new role to its speaker. The "conceit" or concept of "this inconstant stay" triggers the workings of his imagination rather than his previously used faculties of memory and reason. Portraying himself as one who

engrafts new life to old by means of his verse, the speaker represents himself more fully and accurately. In this way, sonnet 15 extends the personal vision of sonnet 12, just as the latter had evolved from the cosmic irony of earlier Procreation sonnets.

II. The Dry Mock

There is, as we have seen, a close connection between Shakespeare's habit of seeing through time in the sonnets and the ironic techniques of his plays. His vivid sense of impermanence creates an ironic dimension in which he situates all processes of life. Rhetorical irony is an important device resulting from that awareness. It is what Renaissance theorists called the "dry mock," and it castigates the youth's refusal to give of himself for the sake of posterity.[11] Once the idea of cosmic change has yielded its harvest of perception, rhetorical irony introduces certain values and imposes them on the auditor. Its mocking is not confined to the egocentric youth but takes on man's universal inconstancy and false confidence.

The speaker's characteristic fusion of past and future undermines all those who fail to heed time's warnings. Their lack of awareness, in turn, creates a perennial conflict between what man is and ought to be. Using rhetorical irony as a critical tool, the speaker does not attack inconstancy itself; that blemish is as basic to mankind as time is to physical nature. Instead, he rebukes man's failure to admit his own inconstancy and to gain thereby an awareness of life's ingrained uncertainties. For example, sonnet 11 puts the distinction between procreation and self-love in the most general terms:

> Herein lives wisdom, beauty, and increase;
> Without this, folly, age, and cold decay.

Caught between those alternatives, the youth finds himself on the side of folly. The same sonnet ridicules his conduct by enlarging it:

> If all were minded so, the times should cease,
> And threescore year would make the world away.

This hypothesis is effective in reducing self-love to absurdity. The imagined situation is so contrary to reality that it turns singleness into an aberration. What is necessary for the world must presumably benefit every person. The youth's indifference to his own extinction becomes delusive because it

---

11. See Alan R. Thompson, *The Dry Mock: A Study of Irony in Drama.*

ignores the rule of correspondence between the microcosm and the natural world. Self-love thus marks him as the victim of two related ironies; one will result from natural process, the other has occurred in the speaker's rhetoric.

Throughout the sonnets, Shakespeare strengthens his arguments by presenting the contrary view as impossible or absurd. Using the grammatical forms "but if" and "or else," he makes untenable assumptions or unlikely courses of action the only alternatives to his own. In the Procreation sonnets, the vanity of self-love is therefore represented as a thoroughly inferior course of action. Most frequently, this rhetorical technique is applied as a reinforcement in the sonnets' closing lines. Sonnet 3 concludes this way:

> But if thou live rememb'red not to be,
> Die single and thine image dies with thee.

Since no one lives for oblivion's sake, dying single becomes a fate worse than death. Sonnet 6 simplifies the matter further by ruling out the existence of a choice:

> Be not self-willed, for thou art much too fair,
> To be death's conquest and make worms thine heir.

Just how procreation can forestall "death's conquest" is not explained. It should be recalled that the speaker had to contend with the traditional ideal of a rational abstinence that is superior to passion. He transforms abstinence into self-love, somewhat arbitrarily, in order to champion the cause of procreation. The first semantic reversal of this kind took place at the conclusion of sonnet 1:

> Pity the world, or else this glutton be—
> To eat the world's due, by the grave and thee.

What might have been extolled as chastity has been developed into a sin of appetite. The resultant paradox of celibacy is defined in this sonnet as "waste in niggarding." Conversely, the giving of life is both a spending and a saving. Sonnet 4 mockingly terms the youth "unthrifty loveliness" and "profitless usurer," since self-love is known to impoverish. These paradoxes achieve more than a display of wit. They correct the youth's mistaken notions and establish the speaker's more complex world view. A similar purpose is served by his use of puns, although these are perhaps less prominent here than in the sonnets generally. In addition to the puns already mentioned on "content" and "weed," there is a Latin double meaning in "tender heir" (sonnet 1)[12] and a sexual pun implied by the pen and drawing metaphor of sonnet 16:

> To give away yourself keeps yourself still,
> And you must live, drawn by your own sweet skill.

This equivocation becomes part of the recurrent spending-as-saving paradox.

In contrast to the cosmic perspective that creates what can be called pure or intellectual irony, the rhetorical mode is an applied form. Rather than surveying the entire process of life, it chooses specific, human targets and demonstrates their failings. Beginning with inconstancy rather than impermanence, such irony thrives on the immediate disparity between ideals and reality. It assumes definite values, often leaving them unstated, and attacks all swervings from them. The basic assumption, however, remains the speaker's vision of a dynamic universe. Society and the individual person, he realizes, change less predictably than do the days and seasons. Even after sonnet 17, when procreation as a central value is replaced by ideal love, rhetorical irony still serves as a critical tool. It demolishes the various falsifications of constant love, ranging between narcissism and promiscuity. Two related sources of value—beauty and poetry—will likewise be defended against their counterfeits.

In the operation of rhetorical irony, three verbal techniques help the speaker achieve his aims. First, the use of rhetorical questions places him in a position equal if not superior to that of his auditor. By answering themselves, such questions have the effect of directly manipulating the person spoken to. The first example, lines 5–8 in sonnet 3, has already been cited. Those two questions insist on the answers "nowhere" and "no one"; they take for granted that no "she" would reject so fair a youth and no "he" would willingly deny posterity. Both questions use the same structure— "For where is she . . . or who is he?"—in order to create a misleading resemblance between their very different propositions. The first pays the youth a compliment, whereas the second implies a criticism of his "fond" behavior. By using parallel syntax, the speaker masks the criticism and makes it appear to be an echo of the preceding compliment. Symmetry also distracts us from noticing that the second rhetorical question is questionable

12. See M. M. Mahood, *Shakespeare's Wordplay*, p. 92, where a comparison is made with *Cymbeline* 5.5.447–50.

indeed; in other words, one need hardly agree with the speaker that "no one" is necessarily the answer. In sonnet 4 the rhetorical onslaught continues by means of three perfectly balanced questions:

> . . . why dost thou spend
> Upon thyself thy beauty's legacy?
>   . . . why dost thou abuse
> The bounteous largess given thee to give?
>   . . . why dost thou use
> So great a sum of sums yet canst not live?

These remonstrations build upon line endings to separate the verbs from their predicates, interjecting a pause between the youth's actions and their consequences. They are not questions that can be fairly answered because they do not presuppose a dialogue so much as an indictment. What is more, the speaker goes on to state the answer that he has been implying all along:

> For having traffic with thyself alone,
> Thou of thyself thy sweet self dost deceive.

Here the sound of repeated reflexive pronouns acts as an echo to the sense, mimicking the youth's self-centeredness. At least seven of the remaining Procreation sonnets similarly submit their auditor to a barrage of rhetorical questions. Whatever reception they may have had originally, they show the speaker constructing an ethical superiority for himself. From that vantage point, he insists on convincing the youth to accept an argument that he may not fully believe himself.

The second, less obvious tactic of rhetorical irony supports the speaker's dominance further. Despite his deferential tone, he very frequently speaks in the imperative mood. Some sonnets have only a single command, which often serves to focus attention on a leading image. Sonnet 7 begins with "lo," much as 8 employs "mark," while 9 and 11 have the imperative "look." Many other commands are functional, intending to control some aspect of the youth's behavior:

> Pity the world, or else this glutton be (1)
> Look in thy glass . . . tell the face . . . die single (3)
> Make sweet some vial; treasure thou some place. (6)

Sonnet 10, because it constitutes a turning point, has no less than six imperative verbs. It is here that the speaker begins to assert himself more openly, although succeeding sonnets contain a more diffident proportion of commands.

The third rhetorical technique is also the most fully dominating. It can best be termed insinuation, since it makes specific suggestions on the use of language. Throughout these sonnets we note a persistent concern with speech and the very act of saying. The youth's introversion is noted and subtly mocked in sonnet 3 when he is requested to "tell" his own face of the need for renewal. But the speaker's presumption of authority in dictating to the youth what he is to tell himself has wider meaning. In the next sonnet, he envisions nature expecting an utterance that the youth cannot formulate:

> Then how when nature calls thee to be gone,
> What acceptable audit canst thou leave?

Again, the implied answer is "none, if you have failed to procreate." The only remedy must be to instruct the inarticulate young man in what to do and say. Sonnet 2 had accomplished just that by positing an imaginary dialogue between him and a future interrogator: "Then being asked where all thy beauty lies." Whoever asks that question, whether nature or another person, is being no less rhetorical than the sonnet's speaker. Overwhelmed by "forty winters" and by his persistent questioner, the youth fails to reply, a failure that corresponds to his physical decline. Rhetorical irony, coming to his aid, can imagine only two opposed alternatives, one of them unthinkable:

> To say within thine own deep-sunken eyes
> Were an all-eating shame and thriftless praise.

The second imaginary speech, we are told, would deserve "much more praise" because it builds on procreation. In that case,

> thou couldst answer, "This fair child of mine
> Shall sum my count and make my old excuse"—
> Proving his beauty by succession thine.

The strategy used here is theatrical prompting, literally putting words into another's mouth. In terms of manipulation, the speaker now goes beyond rhetorical questions and commands, since he is declaring what the youth should think, do, and ultimately say. Quotations are embedded in two other Procreation sonnets, although those statements are not attributed to the youth. One, the musical speech against singleness in sonnet 8, has already been quoted. It does not exactly prompt the youth, but it plants the speaker's favorite tune in the youth's subconscious. Sonnet 17 then ends the series by anticipating a future response to the poetry:

> The age to come would say, "This poet lies—
> Such heav'nly touches ne'er touched earthly faces."

The punctuated quotation suggests that a transfer of roles has occurred, for the speaker is now acknowledging his own inability to express himself effectively. Previously he had projected that fear into the youth, imagining him unable to account for himself before questioning nature. Other allusions to such a challenge are made in sonnet 11, which speaks of having children that "thou mayst call thine, when thou from youth convertest," and in sonnet 13: "you had a father, let your son say so." The notion of a speech chain linking the generations is clearly evident. Procreation itself seems to be unfulfilled unless it leads to a symbolic act of telling, saying, or calling. Such acts reflect the speaker's own concern, as yet undisclosed, about his poetic performance. His personal involvement with the continuity of speech, masked under the banner of procreation, will soon emerge in sonnet 18. But there is an anticipation of that in 14, which defines in detail what the speaker himself can and cannot say. He disclaims "astronomy" and is unable to predict "fortune to brief minutes." He therefore concludes with the familiar message: "this I prognosticate, / Thy end is truth's and beauty's doom and date." Despite the final reversion to "store" as the only means of preserving truth and beauty, the speaker's description of his own powers and limitations is unprecedented. It results from the same concept of language as an unbroken continuity that had led him to urge the youth toward making a summary statement about his role in the natural world. Thus rhetorical irony, manipulating its auditor with questions, commands, and insinuations, betrays the speaker's underlying faith in the efficacy of language.

Shakespeare's plays, of course, are filled with rhetorical irony. The celebrated funeral oration by Mark Antony in *Julius Caesar*, with its ironic innuendoes, exclamations and rhetorical questions, is an example. An even more appropriate selection comes from *All's Well That Ends Well*, when Parolles lectures Helena on the follies of virginity. His rhetorical techniques and the very idea he puts forward create some unmistakable echoes of the Procreation sonnets:

Loss of virginity is rational increase, and there was never virgin [got] till virginity was first lost. . . . Virginity, by being once lost, may be ten times found; by being ever kept, it is ever lost. 'Tis too cold a companion; away with't! . . . There's little can be said in't, 'tis against the rule of nature. . . . He that hangs himself is a virgin; virginity murthers itself. . . . Besides, virginity is peevish, proud, idle, made of self-love, which is the most inhibited sin in the canon. Keep it not, you cannot choose but lose by't. Out with't! Within [t'one] year it will make itself two, which is a goodly increase, and the principal itself not much the worse. Away with 't! (1.1.127–49)

Sonnet 1 is echoed in the allusion to "increase," just as sonnet 3 is by "self-love," while the reference to multiplication reminds us of sonnet 6. Moreover, the allusions to extenuating "nature" bring sonnets 4 and 11 to mind, while virginity as suicide is mentioned in sonnets 9 and 10. Despite these parallels, the sonnet-speaker is no Parolles. His rhetorical attack is not weakened by solecisms like "the most inhibited sin in the canon." Neither do the sonnets offer a refutation that would correspond to Helena's exultant reply, praising her own virginity as the symbol of her love for Bertram: "a thousand loves, / A mother and a mistress and a friend."

The sonnet-speaker's argument must be taken seriously because of the emotive power with which he presents the question of time and change. He may be aware that the procreation argument is in some ways inadequate, yet his hortatory tone remains unqualified. It is therefore impossible to agree with Katharine M. Wilson's reading of these sonnets as purely parodic: "All seventeen sonnets are structured to climb wittily to their inevitable end in an identical laughable climax which parodies equally Erasmus and the sonneteers. Although they give us a sophisticated pleasure with their flawless progress to absurdity and their 'honey-tongued' and 'fine-filed' phrase, the type of joke is quite common."[13] Such a view is not unfounded; at points the rhetoric does border on the incongruous. But this is a minor undertone, not to be confused with the *memento mori* intention of the procreation argument.

The emotional core of all the sonnets lies just here, in confronting cosmic irony with awareness and a series of mortal but enduring gestures: childbearing, idealized love, and even the art of poetry. Matthew Arnold's notion of "high seriousness" would apply equally well to all these resistant attitudes, including the initial faith in procreation. The fact that the speaker

13. *Shakespeare's Sugared Sonnets*, pp. 149–50.

abandons this argument after sonnet 17 strengthens the suspicion of a prior uncertainty, an impression also gained from our study of his less than fully controlled cosmic irony. But the idea of regeneration is never parodied. Katharine Wilson's comments take it for granted that procreation cannot possibly be a serious argument. She observes that sonnet 4 "culminates in the fatuous old man showing his child, and claiming that it has the beauty of his own youth." She finds "a mocking tone" in sonnet 9 and adds, "Fearing to 'wet a widow's eye' can hardly be an argument against marriage." It is assumed here that the widow is the youth's mother rather than his future wife. Again, in sonnet 13 this approach uncovers "the exaggerated cadence of parody," so that "all it prepares for is the fatuity 'dear my love you know, / You had a father, let your son say so.'" Shakespeare's use of Erasmus as a source for many of these arguments, first noticed by Sidney Lee, does not make them parodies.[14] One wonders if seventeen acerbic parodies could have so impressed Francis Meres into writing about "Shakespeare's sugared sonnets."[15] Indeed, it is the clearly expressed and unambiguous pattern of rhetorical irony that preserves their seriousness. Such irony has the effect of curbing the speaker's thoughts on mutability; it is designed to prevent the double-edged knife of irony from cutting into the procreation argument. In this it generally succeeds, although there is conflict between rhetorical irony, which assumes an utter certainty, and the cosmic irony that gravitates inevitably toward doubt. The tension will be better seen if we analyze two sonnets in detail, one from the Procreation group and the other closely following it.

Sonnet 7 offers an interesting example of some differences between these two types of irony. Its source is an anecdote reported in Plutarch's *Life of Pompey*, one that Bacon also made use of in his essay "Of Friendship" (1625). Bacon explains that when Pompey had begun to outstrip his former patron Sulla he "turned upon him again and in effect bade him be quiet; *for that more men adored the sun rising than the sun setting.*"[16] This is an accurate rendition of Plutarch's history, unlike Shakespeare's revision. Nevertheless, on returning

14. See *Variorum*, 1:7 and 2:192.

15. Wilson admits some uncertainty on this point: "This is not a good term for such poetry. Perhaps Meres had bad taste?" She suggests that Meres "referred to the sonnets as 'Shakespeare's sugared sonnets', meaning those in which he parodied the sugared verse of sonneteers. . . . It is in this sense that I have used the phrase in my title, although we cannot really know why Meres did" (*Shakespeare's Sugared Sonnets,* p. 155).

16. *Essays, Advancement of Learning, New Atlantis,* ed. R. F Jones, p. 77.

to sonnet 7 we recognize that its entire structure stems from the assimilation of the anecdote that it thoroughly transforms. The youth has replaced Sulla, being warned of his decline, while the speaker takes on something of Pompey's superior strength. Admittedly, the controlling context has been changed from a power struggle to the universal passage of youth to age. Only in the last line does the speaker provide an escape clause by positing procreation as the one alternative to oblivion.

Despite its central symbolism of the sun, this sonnet lacks the detailed natural imagery associated with cosmic irony. The diurnal course remains a fable rather than a personal perception. It has no visual appeal, unlike the imagery of sonnet 12 or the more analogous description to be given in sonnet 33:

> Full many a glorious morning have I seen
> Flatter the mountain tops with sovereign eye.

Instead there is an undercurrent of political satire reminiscent of plays like *Coriolanus* or *Timon of Athens*. It centers on the infidelity of "each under eye" turning from "homage" and adoration to being "converted" or looking "another way." Human inconstancy rather than natural process thus acts as the generating source of the speaker's irony. Moreover, sonnet 7 is so regularly, perhaps monotonously, developed that it allows for no shifts of thought or tone. What might ordinarily have served as one image among many others becomes the sole, slowly articulated conceit that sustains the entire sonnet. Such a structure, traditionally Petrarchan, is typical of Spenser's sonnets, whereas Shakespeare's tend to be more abrupt and varied. Having grasped that the first quatrain depicts the sunrise while the second shows noon "resembling strong youth in his middle age," we cannot help anticipating both the sun's setting and the man's decline. No discrepancy arises between the time scheme and the logical structure, nor is there surprise at the great man's desertion by his followers. That too is announced in advance as the octet ends:

> Yet mortal looks adore his beauty still,
> Attending on his golden pilgrimage.

For these reasons, sonnet 7 is an atypical and relatively unimpressive sonnet. Its consistency has a rhetorical, if not poetic, advantage. No one can misconstrue its argument for procreation, and its simpler irony has no hint of ambiguity. Its language, accordingly, can be termed precious rather than truly rich; for example, it persistently uses epithets for the sun: "the gracious light," "his sacred majesty," and "his golden pilgrimage." That artificial diction is redeemed only by the way in which it enhances the final wordplay:

> So thou, thyself outgoing in thy noon,
> Unlooked on diest unless thou get a son.

Just as the fable receives its belated application, the sun is finally named. In fact, the homophony of "sun" and "son" strengthens the underlying analogy between the solar orbit and the human lifespan. What might be considered too sharp a transition in purely poetic terms becomes an efficient rhetorical technique. Once again, the youth is forced to make an artificial choice between two extremes: either nothingness or offspring and remembrance. Even when we allow for the adjacent Procreation sonnets as a mediating context, the five small words "unless thou get a son" may be insufficient as a poetic alternative. The rest of the sonnet, with its high-flown diction, resists being so quickly overpowered. Yet the effect is rhetorically sound; it imparts a certainty of attitude that cosmic irony could not allow. Rhetorical irony, dryly mocking what it takes to be absurd, avoids the risk of undermining itself. It is the only kind of irony that Settembrini, Thomas Mann's latter-day humanist, would have approved of: "where irony is not a direct and classic device of oratory, not for a moment equivocal to a healthy mind, it makes for depravity, it becomes a drawback to civilization, an unclean traffic with the forces of reaction, vice and materialism."[17]

In sonnet 19 we note what seems to be a culmination of rhetorical rather than cosmic irony. The speaker is addressing "devouring time," Ovid's *Tempus edax,* who throughout the Procreation group had personified ruthless natural process. Sonnet 16 spoke of "this bloody tyrant time" after 15 had identified "wasteful time" as the speaker's warlike adversary and 12 had pointed to "time's scythe" as being invincible. A new note of confidence was then established in sonnet 18, defying death and predicting that the youth's beauty would grow "in eternal lines to time." A transfer of that confidence is effected here, as the speaker turns away from praising the young man and begins to disparage the force that will make him old. Indeed, the same techniques of rhetorical irony that had taunted the youth's self-love are now applied to castigating the previously all-powerful figure of time. The use of commands clearly signals this shift in attitude in sonnet 19.

---

17. *The Magic Mountain,* trans. H. T. Lowe-Porter, 1:281.

No less than ten are issued to time, half of these clustered in the first five lines. Given the sheer absurdity (according to these Procreation sonnets) of any attempt to control time, the speaker's directives must be seen as deliberately creating an unreal situation. Some of the imperatives become redundant by recalling the familiar imagery of reversal; they tell time to do what is already being done, to "make glad and sorry seasons as thou fleets." Rather than commanding time, the speaker is assenting to its commands, as he comes to realize:

> And do whate'er thou wilt, swift-footed time,
> To the wide world and all her fading sweets.

The more striking imperatives, such as blunting the lion's paws and extracting the tiger's teeth, are merely accelerated versions of ordinary change. We also find a condensed statement of the earth's duality as life's source and final resting place: "make the earth devour her own sweet brood." Only line 4, with its injunction to burn "the long-lived phoenix in her blood," crosses the border between fact and fancy. Yet that departure does not change our impression of the first seven lines as a single rhetorical gesture, commanding time to do what it inevitably will.

The speaker's stance as an orator giving redundant orders provides him with the illusion of controlling the uncontrollable. He proceeds to convert his supposed power into one great thou-shalt-not:

> But I forbid thee one most heinous crime,
> O carve not with thy hours my love's fair brow,
> Nor draw no lines there with thy antique pen.

Again, the impossibility of his wish is betrayed by the echoed imagery of previous sonnets like the second:

> When forty winters shall besiege thy brow
> And dig deep trenches in thy beauty's field.

In sonnet 19, the rhetorical stance and grandiloquent diction cannot hide the pathos of the speaker's hopeless request. Knowing that his wish cannot be granted, he puts it in the more palatable form of a command. But his language suggests an awareness of the futility involved, so we are not surprised when he yields:

> Yet do they worst, old time; despite thy wrong,
> My love shall in my verse ever live young.

By a change of epithets, from "devouring" and "swift-footed" to merely "old," the speaker attempts to assert his final triumph. Having at last granted time the power that he pretended to deny, he insists on claiming a greater power himself. Laying down the law to time, dictating what it can and cannot do, thus proves to be a compensatory act. By boldly applying the "dry mock" to time itself, then abandoning it, he betrays an inner tension between the two modes of irony discussed so far. Cosmic irony resists being channeled into narrow routes and never yields completely to a didactic aim, while rhetorical irony struggles to maintain a coherent value system based on clear-cut ethical structures.

The extended conflict between the two ironies, the pure and the applied, has much to do with the formation of the speaker's dramatic personality. Later sonnets, particularly those that apostrophize love or the speaker's eyes and soul, should be seen as more advanced exercises in rhetorical irony. There, too, a similar tension will be observed, for example in sonnet 146 where the speaker's instructions to his soul are so shrewd as to be nearly self-defeating. But before entering into such complexities, it is necessary to become acquainted with the third and most revealing form of irony that these poems contain.

III. *Dramatic Irony*

Dramatic irony in the sonnets differs fundamentally from cosmic and rhetorical irony in its object, its techniques, and its location in the 1609 sequence. Extending the ironic dimension from nature to mankind, the speaker gradually turns his vision inward and becomes the object of his own irony. With dramatic spontaneity, he discovers inner tensions and attempts either to justify or to resolve them. That technique cannot be found in the Procreation group, whose argument is never put to question. The speaker begins there as a hidden observer, discovering ironic change in the external world: "Then of thy beauty do I question make." As the sequence unfolds, however, he loses his initial certainty. His qualifications and revisions recall the dramatic ironies produced by the gap between a character's expectation and his fulfillment. One might be tempted to recall the example of Hastings in *Richard III,* yet a crucial difference must be recognized, for Hastings completely misunderstands his own position, whereas the sonnet-speaker's awareness of others and himself is accurate. A passage that more closely resembles such awareness is Hastings's subsequent recognition, when his arrest by Richard's agents has disabused him of false confidence:

> O momentary grace of mortal men,
> Which we more hunt for than the grace of God!
> Who builds his hopes in air of your good looks
> Lives like a drunken sailor on a mast,
> Ready with every nod to tumble down
> Into the fatal bowels of the deep. (3.4.96–101)

Even here, the enlightened Hastings has gained his wisdom too late to dispel the enormous gap between it and his earlier folly. He remains a victim.

In contrast, the sonnet-speaker serves as a conscious agent of the dramatic irony that he formulates by and against himself. Perhaps the subject/object distinction becomes impossible here, unless we say paradoxically that the same dramatic character can be both. That, however, is the meaning of dramatic irony, and Falstaff is the character who best embodies it. Unlike Hastings, who is defeated by the "irony of events," Falstaff triumphs in immediate dramatic irony. The distinction, as D. C. Muecke points out, is that the latter can be instantly understood, and does not require a series of events that gradually create a gap between intentions and results.[18] Although Falstaff, too, has expectations that will be dashed to pieces, his wit excels (especially in *Part One of Henry IV*) because he can laugh at himself. For example, his account of the Gad's Hill robbery is so specious as to beg the refutation that Prince Hal willingly provides: "Seven? why, there were but four even now." To this, the jovial thief replies with further, outrageous exaggeration. When his falsehoods are exposed, Falstaff devises an about-face that might have appeared at the *volta* of a sonnet. He claims, "I am as valiant as Hercules: but beware instinct; the lion will not touch the true Prince." Such an unexpected evasion gets Falstaff the laughter he desires, but it has also left critics (since Maurice Morgann in 1777) wondering if his character might not be far more complex than it appears.

Like Falstaff, the speaker of the sonnets becomes a dramatic character by means of the expressive qualities of his language. Lacking an external sequence of events, he does not resort to cosmic process as a substitute for plot. Instead, he invents an original scenario of successive thoughts and

18. *The Compass of Irony,* p. 102.

emotions. Even if he is not one *dramatis persona* among others, he is high-lighted by definite patterns of address to various auditors and himself. What underlies his dramatic characterization is the structure of the Renaissance love sonnet, whose *volta* pits octet against sestet to effect a reversal of thought. Many poets model their sonnet-speakers after Petrarch's lover, who experiences conflicting, if not contradictory, feelings. The Petrarchan formulas or "conceits" grow out of the knowledge that this mode of experience contains much that is intractable and strange. Thus Sidney's Astrophel exclaims "I willing run, yet while I run repent" and Spenser in the *Amoretti* bewails the force that "makes men love theyr bane, / and thinck they dy with pleasure, liue with payne." Throughout the sixteenth century, such poetic speakers traveled through realms Petrarch had mapped out, rarely making discoveries of their own. But these formal and psychological conventions gave Shakespeare an opportunity for dramatic irony within a lyric context; he exploited it far beyond the precedent of other sonneteers. In his sonnets, dramatic irony is executed with a precision equal to its analogues in the plays. It is more compressed, as its reversal occurs within the brief lyric form. It is intimate, as the poetic speaker does not address a public audience. Finally, the reversal that causes dramatic irony does not require an actual downfall but allows for the correction of erroneous ideas.

So long as the speaker absents himself from the poetry, he cannot partake of dramatic irony. When he does appear in the Procreation group, his own views are too consistent to establish any ironic contrasts: "change thy thought that I may change my mind." But from that pivotal line in sonnet 10 through the couplet of sonnet 17, his mind scarcely veers from the guide-line of procreation. Only sonnet 15, which introduced a poetic speaker who sees, thinks, and imagines, can be said to anticipate the unpredictable workings of dramatic irony. Yet that poem, which drops the procreation theme and gives the speaker a new freedom of expression, does not show the process by which he questions, analyzes, and changes his mind. Fully developed examples of dramatic irony must therefore be sought at least slightly beyond the sonnets' opening section.

Sonnet 29, "When in disgrace with fortune and men's eyes," aptly illustrates the techniques of dramatic irony typical of these poems. It lacks the obvious signpost of ironic intent that some critics have come to require. Yet irony pervades this sonnet, deriving from its basic contrast between love and self-love. As in the Procreation sonnets, the latter will be rebuked, but there is no direct criticism akin to that aimed at the youth. The speaker's reproach of his own egoism is, as we would expect, more subtle. It is implied when he turns away from his sorrows and transcends them by recalling his love. At the sonnet's end, his initial mood has been so completely forgotten that no self-deprecating statement is required. The sonnet's two main parts reflect the contrast between self-love and self-transcendence. The conjunction *yet* in the ninth line marks the *volta,* being the exact point of transition from octet to sestet and from one mode of thought to the other. Together, these two sections compose a single sentence: "When in disgrace" introduces the octet as the subordinate clause, while the sestet contains the main clause, "I think on thee." Looking closely at the octet, we find that its language contains evidence of the reversal that will follow. For if the speaker is despondent, he also basks in his grief. Abandoned by fortune and society, he condemns himself to utter isolation. His conclusion should strike us as erroneous, but understandably so. Since it comes in the opening line, as the premise from which the argument follows, we are not likely to notice the error at all. Fortune, it must be recalled, is notoriously unreliable. In Renaissance terms, she is blind, fickle, and incompetent in questions of value. For an illustration, we need not look further than Hamlet's reminder: "she is a strumpet." The sonnets themselves are consistently faithful to the Renaissance conception of a *Fortuna* whose judgments are irrelevant if not misleading. Thus sonnet 124 begins by contrasting love, as a constant quality, against fortune:

> If my dear love were but the child of state,
> It might for fortune's bastard be unfathered.

Sonnet 25 portrays the speaker as one whom "fortune of such triumph bars." Yet all that is denied him is "public honour and proud titles," gifts as dubious as the goddess who bestows them. What here is called the triumph of "great princes' favorites" must be viewed ironically, for the latter are soon likened to the fading "marigold at the sun's eye."

The disgrace dealt by fortune in sonnet 29 is no less illusory, although the qualifying irony is at first less conspicuous. Fortune must be recognized, according to Shakespeare's usage, as powerless to confer genuine triumph or disgrace. As for "men's eyes," they merely reflect fortune's false designs. The speaker's initial response, therefore, is impassioned and uninformed. It launches a consciously futile appeal to "deaf heav'n" using "bootless cries." The repeated first-person forms in lines 2 and 4 accentuate the speaker's self-indulgence:

I all alone beweep my outcast state . . .
And look upon myself and curse my fate.

Of the four verbs employed here, three are reflexive. By beweeping his state, looking upon himself and cursing his fate, he divides himself as both subject and object of the actions. This reflexivity points out the speaker's extravagant self-concern. The accumulative arrangement of the verbs, all of them simply linked by "and," also suggests a loss of articulate control. The speaker's list of emotive actions, we infer, could have been extended indefinitely. At the end of line 4 we find an almost arbitrary transition to the second quatrain. Here the speaker's dissatisfaction with himself yields to his desire to resemble other men. Again, his ostensible meaning is ironically qualified by an overly elaborate pattern of repetition. In lines 5–7 the speaker refers to no less than five different persons as objects for emulation. What he desires is not a personality but the specific features for which each of the five is known.

By presenting this gallery of enviable traits, the speaker moves away from reality toward an ideal, unattainable synthesis. Not content to be himself or anyone else, he reverts to wishful thinking. The implication that he lacks hope, good features, friends, art, and scope is melodramatic in its breadth. It virtually denies the speaker any human qualities. However, line 8 shows that some personal source of pleasure still marks the speaker's identity: "With what I most enjoy contented least." This paradox culminates the octet's movement. Complaint and envy, the dominant moods in quatrains 1 and 2, lead to the speaker's acknowledgment that his response to misfortune has been inadequate. Immersed in self-pity, he has lost whatever values gave his life meaning. This last line provides a truer account of his isolation than the previous seven did. It prepares us for the sestet's movement from self to other, from bathos to exaltation. Once that movement is completed, the self-concern with which the sonnet began will have been ironically discarded.

In keeping with the sonnet's careful design, its two parts are precisely counterpoised. The transition from self-love to love is not made immediately but begins with the introductory line: "Yet in these thoughts myself almost despising." The key words are "almost" and "thoughts," both of them serving to modify the speaker's attitude toward himself. The drastic understatement of "almost despising," after the weeping and cursing of quatrain 1, retracts most of what was so sweepingly uttered before. The admission that these powerful feelings were but "thoughts," tentative associations rather than finalities, signals that a major change has occurred. From such a modified position, the introduction of the beloved person in sonnet 29 follows more easily: "Haply I think on thee." At this point the dramatic turning from self to other can take place and bring results:

> and then my state,
> Like to the lark at break of day arising
> From sullen earth, sings hymns at heaven's gate.

The lark, as an image of ascent, is balanced against the previous descent into self-pity. Shakespeare often uses this image with its conventional connotation of awakening, for example in the song "Hark, hark, the lark" (*Cymbeline,* 2.2). In both the song and the sonnet, the lark sings at dawn and arrives "at heaven's gate." In the sonnet, his hymns mark a precise contrast to the "bootless cries" with which the speaker had troubled "deaf heav'n." Being self-descriptive, the image also contrasts sharply with his previous simile: "like to one more rich in hope." His search for an acceptable self has been completed symbolically by the lark's flight upward from "sullen earth." Overwhelmed by fortune and society, he had begun as the prisoner of "earth" in both Shakespearean senses: life in this world and the flesh itself. By rising to heaven from earth, he moves from the material to the spiritual realm. Such a transition underlies the change of mood in many sonnets that begin in melancholy or despair, for example sonnet 74.

What has occurred in sonnet 29 is not a detached study in introspection but a direct, seemingly spontaneous projection of the speaker's state of mind. Indeed, "state" appears in octet, sestet, and couplet, providing another sign of total coherence. In line 2, "my outcast state" has the connotation of political exile, whereas "my state" in line 10 is strictly personal. The same phrase is found in the closing line:

> For thy sweet love rememb'red such wealth brings,
> That then I scorn to change my state with kings.

Here "state" is both political and personal. It has gained its meaning of high social rank (as in sonnet 124's "child of state") rising to the opposite of an outcast. Another link between the couplet and the octet is made by the phrase "such wealth," which cancels the speaker's earlier envy of "one more rich in hope." As the couplet shows, he still defines himself by juxtaposition with others, but the comparison "with kings" is now to the speaker's advantage. By scorning them, he demonstrates a newfound confidence that contrasts with his original melancholy.

Although the techniques of repetition, balance, and qualification are not in themselves ironic, their interrelations are basic to the dramatic irony of sonnet 29. They enable the speaking voice to reverse its argument and tone. This voice, rather than its words or their supposed ambiguities, furnishes a focal point for the analysis of irony. Words themselves are usually polyvalent and the determined critic, aided by historical dictionaries, can invest them with countless niceties of meaning. However, a study of irony in the speaker's conscious voice need not unearth hidden significance that runs counter to what he thinks he is saying. Intricate structural patterns are seen to follow directly from the basic lines established by the speaker. In sonnet 29, a flawlessly designed change of mood conveys a dramatic discovery. The speaker discovers what he already knew—the value of love—but his belated recognition still comes to him, and to us, as a pleasant surprise. As with Falstaff in the tavern scene, Shakespeare has deliberately constructed an inconsistency whose essential purpose is to please. With a subtlety far greater than Falstaff's, the speaker's intellect or rational soul mocks his imagination and its fantasies. The sonnet is thus an exercise in retrospect that corresponds to everyday mental life. Moreover, at this relatively early point in the sequence, the idea of process, previously relegated to things of the earth and to shallower minds, becomes a structural factor in the poetry. The sonnets begin to reflect the adventures of an everchanging mind paradoxically seeking to put an end to change.

In sonnet 104, the inward movement of the speaker's mind is more extended than that of sonnet 29. At the risk of sounding grossly unhistorical, a comparison could be made between that movement and what Gerard Manley Hopkins called "inscape." But if Shakespeare's speaker has sought "species or individually-distinctive beauty,"[19] he now becomes conscious of his own mind as co-maker of that beauty. The opening line of this sonnet shows how effortlessly he differentiates between his own perceptions and reality. It is a distinction that the Procreation sonnets never made: "To me, fair friend, you never can be old." The dilemma raised here follows from setting off what appears "to me" against that which is seen by the rest of the world. Since there is a new disparity between personal knowledge and public opinion, the sonnet must juxtapose both perspectives in order to reconcile them. Its opening has the ring of uncertainty because the speaker fears that his eye may be unreliable.

19. *The Letters of Gerard Manley Hopkins,* ed. C. C. Abbott, p. 66.

Besides emphasizing "to me" by its initial position in sonnet 104, he also chooses the auxiliary "can" rather than "will" or "shall": "you never can be old." This distinction is a valid one, since "can" connotes active ability, going beyond the simple prediction of future events. The implication is that by his very nature the youth must be incapable of aging; it cannot happen. There is a stronger reference to ability since "can" in Shakespeare's usage often has an absolute construction in sentences like "they can well on horseback."[20] A more obvious sign of the speaker's uncertainty comes in line 3, where "seems" adds its usual contrast with "is." That antithesis is sharpened by the additional shading of past versus present: "For as you were . . . such seems your beauty still." Yet the two sides of this tentative equation are far from equal. Quite certain as to what his beloved really was, the speaker can indicate only what he now appears to be. We may also note that "you" and "your beauty" are not equivalent either, though they are probably intended to be. The unadorned pronoun points to the friend as a complete being, whereas "your beauty" selects a single attribute. Finally, the clause that intervenes between both references to the youth also registers an uncertain tone: "when first your eye I eyed." To most commentators, this is a regrettable piece of cleverness; one claims, "The modern reader wonders how Shakespeare brought himself to do it."[21] Perhaps so, but the sustained vowel sound and the strained wit are a fitting reflection of the speaker's awkward mood. One could also defend the clause by calling attention to the way it balances lover and beloved through visual patterning, with both parties linked to a variant of the same word.

What follows the opening sentence is an unmistakable recapitulation of the theme and imagery of time, very much as first presented in the Procreation group. In this section of sonnet 104, lines 3–8, the speaker attempts to reestablish his prior stance as an accurate, unbiased observer of nature:

> Three winters cold
> Have from the forests shook three summers' pride,
> Three beauteous springs to yellow autumn turned
> In process of the seasons have I seen,
> Three April perfumes in three hot Junes burned,
> Since first I saw you fresh, which yet are green.

The unstopped third line suggests a heightening of the argument because of

20. See Alexander Schmidt, *Shakespeare-Lexicon*, 1:166.
21. Edward Hubler, *The Sense of Shakespeare's Sonnets*, p. 14.

its stylized inversion, "three winters cold," while the rhyme with "old" brings back definite echoes of procreation, such as the couplet of sonnet 2:

> This were to be new made when thou art old,
> And see thy blood warm when thou feel'st it cold.

If the octet of sonnet 104 sounds repetitious, it is deliberately and effectively so. We are told repeatedly that three years have passed; in fact, "three" recurs five times in these six lines. And three different images of seasonal change are, most appropriately, provided. The tonal effect is that of utter certainty, as only quantitative measurement can give. Undoubtedly the speaker is fully aware of the years that have elapsed, each with its recurrent cycle of change. We can also recognize that he is using a pattern of natural reversal quite similar to that of sonnet 2 or 5:

three winters cold	three summers' pride
three beauteous springs	yellow autumn
three April perfumes	three hot Junes

Such is the inexorable "process of the seasons" with which sonnets 1–17 had launched the entire sequence. The pattern in sonnet 104 sounds more flexible than its forerunners, though, because of its less than perfect symmetry. In the first reversal, winter destroys summer's "pride" in the natural, not moral sense. However, the second and third images use passive constructions, and the transition is from spring to summer instead of the usual lapse of warmth to cold. When these powerful descriptions conclude, our initial doubts about the speaker's reliability have been allayed. He shows his usual sensitivity to change, recording all that has occurred "since first I saw you fresh, which yet are green." We would readily grant that the youth might be an exception to the rule being formulated were it not for the speaker's own disclaimer:

> Ah yet doth beauty, like a dial hand,
> Steal from his figure, and no pace perceived;
> So your sweet hue, which methinks still doth stand,
> Hath motion, and mine eye may be deceived.

These lines illustrate the kind of self-revelation produced by dramatic irony. They correspond to the shift away from self-love in sonnet 29 but contain a far more radical change. The speaker now admits what the opening lines suggested—his fallibility as a seer. He cannot proceed inductively from perception to inference in the confident manner of sonnet 12 because he has begun to doubt whether what he sees is true. The dial-hand simile shows that sense evidence can be misleading, an idea that makes the youth's unchanging appearance nothing more than an optical illusion. The use of "methinks" and the confession that "mine eye may be deceived" acknowledge the possibility of error. But the main statement goes further: "So your sweet hue . . . hath motion." It implies that the speaker's thought no longer follows his perception but doubles back to overrule it.

Sonnet 104 thus makes a discovery that the Procreation sonnets could not anticipate. Those sonnets had gradually endowed the speaker with a coherent identity, whereas this one begins to dissolve it. The dramatic irony here outdoes that of sonnet 29, with its single, well-modulated change of emotion, by giving different moods to four separate sections. As we have seen, the initial doubt of the first sentence is dispelled by the studied confidence of lines 3–8. The *volta* returns to a more profound uncertainty, doubting not only the youth's enduring beauty but also the speaker's ability to distinguish change from constancy. The couplet finally endeavors to make another swing of the pendulum:

> For fear of which, hear this, thou age unbred,
> Ere you were born was beauty's summer dead.

Whether that closing gesture really succeeds depends on our view of the speaker. One critic who analyzes this sonnet in detail, Gerald Hammond, differentiates between what he calls "the poet's affection for the young man and his own basic rationality: affection leads him to disbelieve in time . . . but reason tells him that even so short a period of time as three years must be called ageing."[22] That account of the basic tension seems unexceptionable, and the problem it raises is whether any reconciliation of these two forces is possible. Hammond believes it is not: "The incompatibility of emotional and rational responses to present time governs the couplet: while 'for fear of which' maintains the fiction that the eye may, after all, not be deceived, the sonnet closes on the certainty of the death of beauty."[23] But Shakespeare's speaker would never have attempted to deny the fact of mortality. He began the entire sonnet sequence by meditating on it, and sonnet 104 reconstructs that meditation. Since the procreation argument is no longer valid, this

22. *The Reader and Shakespeare's Young Man Sonnets*, p. 201.
23. Ibid.

sonnet must respond differently to the fair youth's impending decline. It does not adopt the eternalizing strategy of sonnets 15 and 18, for its last words ("beauty's summer dead") directly exclude the notion that "thy eternal beauty shall not fade."

What then, if anything, is achieved by the couplet's proud announcement to posterity? Rather than dismiss it as a "fiction," we should consider its function in dramatic terms. A similar transition from natural process to a declaration of faith can be found in *Hamlet*'s "mousetrap scene." The player king begins by observing periphrastically that thirty years have passed:

> Full thirty times hath Phoebus' cart gone round . . .
> Since love our hearts and Hymen did our hands
> Unite comutal in most sacred bands. (3.2.165–70)

To this his spouse adds an impossible wish for longevity if not eternity:

> So many journeys may the sun and moon
> Make us again count o'er ere love be done! (3.2.154–62)

The facts of the king's age and illness are not to be denied. Therefore, the queen at great length vows loyalty to his memory, concluding:

> Both here and hence pursue me lasting strife,
> If once I be a widow, ever I be wife! (3.2.222–23)

As the player king observes, " 'tis deeply sworn," and Hamlet, highly sensitive to the issue, immediately interjects: "If she should break it now!" Sonnet 104 resembles this dramatic sequence; it too progresses from an ornate statement about the duration of love to the establishment of personal and enduring value. For its speaker, the youth's beauty is never an illusion, even though its seeming permanence must be. The couplet thus palliates his fear of what he knows too well. By turning to posterity, denying that it can ever rival his beloved's beauty, he creates a uniqueness that implies immortality. His boast, like his commanding of time in sonnet 19, is another act of compensation; if that beauty must disappear, some solace still derives from the privilege of having seen and described it.

Another dramatic feature of the couplet is that it marks a sudden change of direction corresponding to the turn from self to other in sonnet 29. The sonnet began with intimately personal address, "to me, fair friend." That intimacy recedes somewhat when the youth is placed in the universal context of cosmic irony. The basic relation is no longer that of the speaker and his love but an inner debate in which he tries to square his changing thoughts about that love. The dilemma can be resolved only with the apostrophe to the future in line 13. Now the speaker is no longer isolated but maintains contact with the same continuity of language that rhetorical irony had assumed in sonnets 4 and 17. In fact, when the final line scornfully derides future beauty as inferior to this present, it marks a return to the carefully imperious tone of rhetorical irony, beginning with the command "hear this." The line is actually a statement of faith rather than perception, since neither the speaker nor posterity can see each other's ideal of beauty. It resembles the boasts that lovers traditionally made about the mistress's beauty, denying that any unknown lady could be her equal.

This rhetorical gesture pushes the speaker back into an attitude of self-confidence. It may not convince us, as the "age unbred," if what we are looking for is logical consistency. If the criterion, however, is psychological effectiveness (a far more appropriate one for the study of poetry), then the couplet succeeds in giving a dramatic representation. It tells us that the speaker may doubt the youth's exemption from time, his power to "hold time's fickle glass" that sonnet 126 alludes to, but he cannot question what is essential, his unmatched beauty. That is the speaker's personal knowledge, the ultimate stage in his comprehension of the world. As Michael Polanyi puts it, "personal knowledge is an intellectual commitment, and as such inherently hazardous. Only affirmations that could be false can be said to convey objective knowledge of any kind."[24] We can scarcely respond to sonnet 104 as Gertrude does to the player queen ("methinks the lady doth protest too much"), because the speaker's poetic performance validates his words. Later sonnets make similar vows when they reach a point at which logical proof for a vitally held opinion becomes impossible. Sonnet 116 attempts to define love through various statements, contrasts, and images, but the final proof must be a declaration of faith:

> If this be error and upon me proved,
> I never writ, nor no man ever loved.

And when the speaker's perplexity gets the better of him, in the Dark Lady sequence, he escapes by proclaiming that his swearing was untrue:

> For I have sworn thee fair, and thought thee bright,
> Who art as black as hell, as dark as night.

24. *Personal Knowledge,* p. viii.

In sonnet 104, therefore, we have seen cosmic irony, the "process of the seasons," and rhetorical irony, the couplet's "dry mock" of posterity, subsumed in a dramatic self-portrait. The sonnet has two pivotal points, lines 9 and 13, and presents a seemingly spontaneous set of reversals quite unlike the premeditated design of sonnet 29.

Sonnet 104 brings us to the third and final stage of awareness in dramatic irony. The 1609 sequence of the sonnets begins with the speaker's realization of a primary fact in our existence, that time passes. Where an ordinary mind would dismiss so elementary an idea as trivial, the poet imbues it with a host of vivid implications. Granting that time is invincible, he nonetheless forms a strategy of containment through regeneration. As sonnets 12 and 15 show, he becomes aware of his own selfhood as the entity that perceives and responds to external change. When he repeatedly demonstrates that self-love is a deadly sin, he begins to notice man's innate aversion to constancy. Sonnets 7 and 19 illustrate that second stage of awareness, employing a host of rhetorical devices to criticize those who, like the young man being addressed, resist or ignore natural process. Finally, the speaker descends from the orator's rostrum to acknowledge his own array of failings and contradictions. He recognizes that the cosmic irony of impermanence and the rhetorical irony of man's inconstancy exists not only in the external world but also in his inmost being. Sonnets 29 and 104 demonstrate how natural process and human fickleness have their equivalents in the speaker's no less unpredictable inner dynamic. Having discovered his own selfhood, he begins a conscious search for value. The sonnets that most single-mindedly continue that search may be called soliloquies; those poems, which first appear immediately after the Procreation group, together compose a sustained unit that now requires an extensive, separate discussion.

2 Soliloquy
Sonnets

The erotic is in no way, as might be supposed,
purely a compressing and unfolding of dialogue. . . .
Many celebrated extasies of love are nothing but the
lover's delight in the possibilities of his own person
which are actualized in unexpected fulness.

—Martin Buber,
Between Man and Man

That the speaker of Shakespeare's sonnets should have a coherent identity traceable through the 1609 sequence is hardly a new idea. The more the sonnets are analyzed, the more identities their speaker receives. For example, J. W. Lever states, "What distinguishes Shakespeare's *persona* . . . is his completely extroverted approach to life,"[1] whereas C. S. Lewis concludes, "The whole sequence becomes an expanded version of Blake's 'The Clod and the Pebble' . . . . Shakespeare, celebrating the 'Clod' as no man has celebrated it before and since, ends by expressing simple love, the quintessence of all loves."[2] Such contradictory generalizations can never be logically proved, and the annoying possibility that the sonnets are not uttered by a single voice remains. Nevertheless, Renaissance tradition beginning with Dante and Petrarch is on the side of unity. Sidney's Astrophel, for example, is one personality; like other sonnet-speakers named or anonymous, he follows the principle of a unifying persona who responds to various occasions. It seems correct to apply that principle to Shakespeare's sonnets, especially since number 144 with its contrast of "two loves . . . of comfort and despair" sets out the speaker's situation between the youth and the lady to whom he writes. Those who insist on seeing a plurality of friends, ladies, and even poets may have logical rigor on their side, but the sequence itself does not encourage such constructions.

The difficulty about Shakespeare's poetic speaker, assuming there is one only, is his many-sidedness; his vast range of moods, attitudes, and opinions precludes a consistent definition. For that reason James Winny posits a radical split; he hears two voices, "one proudly grandiloquent though never boastful, the other claiming little for himself."[3] But if we return to the concept of irony, as outlined in the previous chapter, we obtain a defin-

---

1. *The Elizabethan Love Sonnet*, p. 186.
2. *English Literature in the Sixteenth Century Excluding Drama*, p. 507.
3. *The Master-Mistress: A Study of Shakespeare's Sonnets*, p. 64.

ing feature that accommodates the speaker's range while preserving his unity. In both his extremes of mood, whether assertive or retiring, irony is present. Directed inward, it qualifies his confidence and prevents self-indulgence. Directed toward others, it reaffirms his dignity in spite of obligations imposed by his decision to serve his beloved loyally. Although a number of sonnets support Lewis's claim that the speaker's personality is clod-like or passive in its love, they are fewer than he assumes, and all are tinged with irony. What is much more typical of the speaker throughout the sequence is not self-disparagement but an ironic posture through which he subtly questions other poets, his beloved, and himself. Such a consistently ironic attitude marks the poetic speaker as a distinct psychological entity, even in the very first sonnets, which are devoted to an exposition of his selfhood. The Procreation sonnets, illustrating a cosmic irony with reference to natural process, laid a foundation for the speaker's personality. After sonnets 18 and 19 confer poetic immortality, and while 20, 22, and 24 portray the immortalized youth, sonnets 21, 23, and 25 constitute a triad introducing the ironic speaker. A close reading of these three sonnets, which together form a single essay in self-discovery, will isolate the speaker's strategies for defining himself through ironic comparison with others.

I. Self-Discovery

On the surface, sonnet 21 offers no more than a straightforward apology for a plain style in poetry: "So is it not with me as with that muse." Yet a number of troublesome complexities have been dealt with by commentators. T. G. Tucker observed that the sonnet "comes in strangely *after* those which have been so unsparing in laudation."[4] In their edition, W. G. Ingram and Theodore Redpath agree that 21 "differs appreciably in tone from its predecessors," although its language and structure are not exceptional.[5] An explanation is made by J. E. M. Latham, who detects echoes of Sidney's *Astrophel and Stella* and concludes, "The awkwardness of much of sonnet 21 is perhaps due to the need to approach close to the earlier poet without a clearly defined aim, like parody; under this unfocused external pressure it is hardly surprising that Shakespeare fails to find his own

4. Cited in *Variorum*, 1:60–61.
5. *Shakespeare's Sonnets*, p. 52.

voice."[6] However, the very features that make the poem awkward for Latham are analyzed at length and with enthusiasm by Stephen Booth, who finds that, "among the dizzying multitude of different kinds of couplement this poem exemplifies, it manages to include demonstrations of both true poetic wit and grotesque caricatures of the empty gestures it scorns." Booth's closely argued analysis attests to an appreciation of what he calls "this sonnet about comparisons."[7] Nevertheless, sonnet 21 marks a turning point in the 1609 sequence in both its form and, as the first sonnet to develop a genuine subjectivity, its content. It is a self-portrait in pronounced contrast to the self-effacing picture of the youth that was drawn in sonnet 20: "A woman's face, with nature's own hand painted." Although Shakespeare's speaker had entered the sequence in sonnet 10, his references to himself remained superficial and extroverted. Now, for the first time, his poetic personality becomes important enough to serve as the theme of an entire sonnet from its opening line, "so is it not with me," to its end: "I will not praise that purpose not to sell." Sonnet 21 should be recognized, then, as the first "soliloquy" in the sequence; the speaker addresses himself rather than an external auditor, never using "thou" or "you" because he is speaking both to and about himself. Such extended self-reliance is without precedent in the first twenty sonnets. The poem is not "about comparisons" in an abstract, impersonal manner but rather about the speaker who chooses to make certain comparisons and to ridicule some others. His choices in sonnet 21 are so much in harmony with later sonnets that I believe Shakespeare's sonnet-speaker can be said to find here, if not his "own voice," then at least a characteristic set of techniques for self-description.

The sonnet develops by expanding on its initial comparison. It defines the speaker primarily by what he is not. But the contrast, we soon realize, is entirely to his advantage. If the opening line appears neutral in its tone, placing "me" in an exact balance with "that muse," we find an immediate qualification in line 2: "Stirred by a painted beauty to his verse." The speaker's tone is thus charged with a confident irony from the very beginning of the sonnet. By deriding the beauty that inspires his rivals, he belittles the quality of their verse. Indeed, cosmetics and rhetoric are kindred evils throughout the sonnets in that both falsify reality. The poet who

6. "Shakespeare's Sonnet 21," p. 112.
7. *Shakespeare's Sonnets: Edited with an Analytical Commentary*, p. 168.

celebrates "painted beauty" must paint his language with the false colors of rhetoric. He is an impostor, like the Alazon figure in comedy, because he makes pretenses that must be exposed. Shakespeare's speaker reduces these boastful poets to their true proportion and in himself embodies the opposing figure of comic tradition, the Eiron. His self-disparagement is purely tactical, for by pretending to be less than he is he uncovers the exaggerations of others.

The actual effect of sonnet 21 differs markedly from its ostensible argument. While dismissing the grandiose style of "that muse," the speaker skillfully exploits its possibilities. He temporarily removes all references to himself after the opening line, allowing the pretentious muse to dominate the scene. The speaker's "I" will reappear only in the pivotal ninth line of the sonnet and in the last. The octet thus evokes a false poetry that nevertheless stirs the imagination:

> Who heav'n itself for ornament doth use
> And every fair with his fair doth rehearse—
> Making a couplement of proud compare
> With sun and moon, with earth and sea's rich gems,
> With April's first-born flow'rs, and all things rare
> That heaven's air in this huge rondure hems.

These lines compose an effective parody. Using cosmic imagery and a rich interplay of sound patterns, they do not ridicule the style that they criticize; instead, they imitate its best qualities. The passage begins and ends with references to heaven, reminding us of the unlimited height to which "that muse" aspires. The speaker shows a definite admiration for those minds that ransack "heav'n itself for ornament" and range freely over all that "this huge rondure hems." Heaven is thus the source and boundary of their invention. Within that framework, the other lines unfold an impressive breadth of vision. The imaginative sequence moves from the remoteness of "sun and moon" to the rarity of "earth and sea's rich gems." It concludes with an image of familiar but remarkable beauty, "April's first-born flow'rs," whose adjective gives a human quality to nature. The sequence is built on the rhetorical techniques of amplification, since all three images are located in parallel prepositional phrases. Finally, the generality of "all things rare" subsumes the images under the rubric of an abstract term. Although "rare" refers to any unusual beauty, it also echoes the earlier idea of extravagance.

Corresponding with the speaker's exercise of his imagination, we note his creation of a suitable auditory background. A rich texture of sound results from intricate alliteration, as in line 5: "Making a couplement of proud compare," in which three different sounds—m, k, and p—are all repeated three times. Repeated sounds, especially â, also serve to interweave the lines. After "fair" is repeated within line 4, its vowel sound carries over into the next lines and furnishes the basis for the rhyme link between lines 4 and 7, "compare" and "rare." From this line, the â moves to a medial position in line 8, "heaven's air." The words "fair" and "heaven's air" then reappear to rhyme lines 10 and 12. This repetition of the â sound limits the sonnet to six rhyme sounds instead of the usual seven.

What reveals the speaker's professedly ironic purpose in these lines is not any conspicuous flaw in thought or diction. He is explicitly critical of "proud compare" that leads to the formation of a misleading analogy between human and inanimate beauty. A lack of discrimination is also suggested by "every fair" and "all things rare" as objects for comparison. But the main irony is implied by his use of an extremely loose and monotonous syntax. The entire octet consists of a protracted sentence that could have ended, in terms of grammatical completeness, with the first line. Lines 2–8 continue to describe "that muse," giving progressively less information as each line contains a shorter section of the syntactic whole. The movement is from a one-line opening sentence to a series of four clauses that compose lines 2–5, then to a series of four phrases that make up lines 6–7. Line 8 adds a relative clause that shows a shift in the speaker's attention because it modifies "all things" rather than "that muse." The original contrast between the speaker and other poets has yielded to an extended description of the latter. Yet the sentence that extends throughout the octet is not periodic in structure. There is no suspension of meaning from one line to the next. Instead, we find a simple division between lines 2–4, which modify the noun phrase "that muse," and lines 5–8, which modify the verb "making." The speaker thus extends his thought, rather than qualifying it, through a series of parallels linked by "and." He begins by using a double verb, "doth use . . . doth rehearse." This is followed by the facile symmetry of three "with" phrases leading to "all things rare." It is in the leisurely padding of this outmoded Euphuistic syntax that the speaker subtly mocks the artificially elegant style of his more ostentatious counterparts.

Despite its critical function, the octet remains strikingly effective. Shakespeare assimilates the grandiloquent style to his own purposes while deploring the ways other poets have used it. The presence of cosmic imagery and elevated diction in many of the sonnets does not, however, contradict the argument of sonnet 21. The speaker modifies his argument and his style in the sestet, transcending eloquence without abandoning it. A sharp transition takes place when line 9 introduces a simpler, more colloquial style: "O let me true in love but truly write." The *polyptoton* present in the linking of "true" and "truly" works against the previous tendency toward richness of diction with its simple repetition. The speaker returns here to reiterate his initial statement, in which beauty and poetry are corresponding truths in contrast to the falsity of "painted beauty" and its rhetoric. He makes a modest "couplement" of his own for the sake of furthering that contrast:

> my love is as fair
> As any mother's child, though not so bright
> As those gold candles fixed in heaven's air.

True and credible comparisons, we gather, should be confined to members of the same group. But the poetic imagination cannot function within such logical restrictions. The speaker's use of "any mother's child" as an appropriate image opposed to the artifice of "gold candles" is successful only as a debater's point. For imaginative power we should prefer his earlier descriptions, despite their ironic purpose.

The couplet makes another stylistic shift, this time from plain speaking to pointed wit:

> Let them say more that like of hearsay well;
> I will not praise that purpose not to sell.

In spite of his denial, the speaker has been praising himself, in his own way, throughout the sonnet. His self-description as a dutifully simple lover is after all a pose. It is belied by the skill with which he parodies other poets. Moreover, his mastery is conveyed by the combination of three distinct levels of style arranged in a casuistic progression. If he does not sustain the first and most elaborate style, the cause cannot be his supposed lack of ability. On the contrary, he demonstrates a greater range and a wider awareness than he attributes to his rivals. By referring to other poets in such an ironic manner, he creates a foil against which he defines himself at first apologetically but at the end with unabashed confidence. Sonnet 21 thus introduces a pattern of psychological disguise that enables the speaker to conceal himself while revealing a central character trait, his inclination to play the Eiron. This technique becomes his basic method of self-presentation as the sequence continues.

In sonnet 23 the speaker uses what seems to be a simpler, more straightforward technique. Again, he makes himself the central subject, continuing not only from his soliloquy in 21 but from the intervening dialogue of 22: "my glass shall not persuade me I am old." That opening line led to a reciprocal relation based on the conceited interchange of hearts, "which in thy breast doth live, as thine in me." Sonnet 23 returns to soliloquy and differs from both preceding poems in that the speaker portrays himself directly, making no contrast with others: "As an unperfect actor on the stage." Although the sonnet's style is still elaborate, it lacks ironic variation and, except for one brief reference, refrains from parody. Thus the only question debated by commentators on this sonnet since the eighteenth century is whether "books" in line 9 should be emended to "looks." The speaker's ironic strategy throughout 21, 23, and 25 justifies the emendation. As Hyder Rollins explains, "the whole point of 23 is the poet's failure to write or speak his love's (perhaps his friend's) praises. He forgets to say over love's rite, he hopes that his looks will speak for him, he urges that his eyes, his looks, be read. Exactly the same idea is stressed in 85."[8] The speaker's failure is feigned rather than real; it is belied by the poem itself. Just as 21 illustrated that the speaker could write in the very style he protested against, 23 performs the act of communication that he claims to be incapable of.

The octet consists of a single sentence, as in 21, whose structure is more

8. *Variorum*, 1:67. This view is challenged in the edition of W. G. Ingram and Theodore Redpath, who contend, "Mere citations of parallels for 'looks' are no argument" (*Shakespeare's Sonnets*, p. 57). Their case for "books" thus ignores the contexts both of poetic convention and of the Q sentence: 21, 22, 23, and 24 are all indebted to specific "conceits," perhaps reflecting an initial uncertainty in the speaker's newfound relation with the youth. The theme of "looks" and eyes is present, moreover, in 20, 22, 24, and 25. Judged on its own terms, the argument of Ingram and Redpath does not convince because it depends on two subsidiary meanings: "books" becomes "other poems" or "a paper with writing on it," while "read" must mean "comprehend," since the youth was not illiterate. In his edition, Stephen Booth prints "books" but notes that, "although 'books' is the Q reading, and makes sense, most editors have emended it to 'looks'" (*Shakespeare's Sonnets: Edited with an Analytical Commentary*, p. 172).

convincingly ornate. The speaker devises two similes to represent himself: "as an unperfect actor . . . or some fierce thing." Both images illustrate an excessive emotion that interferes with action. The two emotions are not identical, so that Shakespeare's linking of them deserves attention. The actor suffers from a specific fear, stage fright. He is "unperfect" in the sense that he lacks control and, as a result of nervousness, forgets his lines. Instead of concealing his own identity behind a dramatic role, the actor is "put besides" his part. The precision with which this image depicts a definite emotional state can be appreciated even before it is applied. In contrast, an imprecise image follows. Here the excessive emotion is "too much rage," but the cause is not known. Such feeling may be endemic to the kind of animal called "some fierce thing," but again the speaker seems reluctant to be exact. He does not name the beast and only refers obliquely to its nature. Moreover, the logic that relates emotion to performance is less than clear. Why should his "strength's abundance" weaken the animal's courage, "his own heart"? The absence of an internal explanation could lead to a search for a historical one. Yet even to the Elizabethans, with their love for Pliny and other "unnatural natural histories," the idea would be farfetched. It would certainly be less convincing than the image of a frightened actor. The stage image may have came so easily to Shakespeare because it was drawn directly from his own experience. For that reason, he begins with it. Then, in need of a second, parallel simile, he devises an image that is less effective because it derives from learning, or hearsay, rather than observation. The important thing, however, is not that the second image is less exact; precision of imagery is a modern rather than an Elizabethan criterion. Instead, the structure of the quatrain proves significant, revealing that the poet achieves an exact symmetry in the arrangement of both images.

Lines 2 and 4 have a close parallelism: "Who with his fear is put besides his part" and "whose strength's abundance weakens his own heart." Both relative clauses describe the results of uncontrolled emotion. They imply an inner division in which the first part of each clause relates to a disruptive inner force. Each line ends with the function that has been impaired, "his part" and "his own heart." The close link between these functions is reinforced by their rhyme, which is grammatical, sharply auditory, and twice introduced by the genitive "his." This symmetry of structure and sound brings us back to the basic connection between the images. They share the assumption that control over the emotions is required in order to channel them toward action. The frightened actor and the fierce animal are opposite to the ideal of self-control defined in sonnet 20: "A man in hue, all hues in his controlling."

Since such self-discipline is a virtue, though perhaps not an ingratiating one, the speaker of sonnet 23 regrets his lack of it. He overlooks the difference between the opening images, and between the emotions they express, because he is concerned with their illustration of this central theme. In quatrain 2 he applies both images to himself. Line 5–6 recall the actor by referring to a memory-lapse:

> So I for fear of trust forget to say
> The perfect ceremony of love's rite.

The speaker's "fear of trust" is not stage fright but lack of confidence. He expects that his words will not be believed. What he forgets is presumably the formal praise that ideal love requires. Its "rite" and "perfect ceremony" cannot be performed by such an "unperfect actor" as himself. In this way, the underlying conception of life as a practiced art, rather than a spontaneous emotion, gains credibility. Strong feelings that are not controlled threaten their own articulation.

Lines 7–8 take up the more problematic image of "some fierce thing":

> And in mine own love's strength seem to decay,
> O'ercharged with burthen of mine own love's might.

By inserting the verb "seem," the speaker evades the logical complexities of cause and effect. Since his decline is merely apparent, it is impossible to say whether "love's strength," echoing "strength's abundance" in quatrain 1, actually causes it. The man is "o'ercharged" with love just as the beast was "replete" with rage. Again the disturbance is from within, shown by the genitive phrase "mine own love's might." This phrase corresponds exactly with "his own heart" in line 4, serving to conclude both the line and the quatrain.

As in sonnet 21, a transition is achieved in the *volta* of line 9, which implies a request of the beloved. In both poems, the hortative verbs "let me . . . write" and "let my looks . . . be" serve to locate the speaker at the exact structural center. In sonnet 23, however, his request does not conclude a comparison between himself and others but rather introduces one. There is no sharp break in style between lines 8 and 9, between octet and sestet. Moreover, the use of "then" as "therefore" reminds us that the speaker's request derives logically from the inarticulateness he has described. Having employed two similes for self-description, he now turns to metaphor: "Let my looks be then the eloquence / And dumb presagers of my speaking breast." Despite the supplicating mood that envelopes this metaphor, it creates an identity between the speaker's looks and his power of speech whereas his professed silence had only been suggested by simile. The progression toward greater certitude coincides with the emphasis placed on the speaker's newfound powers, "who plead for love and look for recompense." This line, with its double verb and symmetrical phrasing, invites comparison with the relative clauses in lines 2 and 4. It differs from them by stressing actions that are directed outward, whereas the earlier lines reflected inner conflict. The line forms part of a condensed comparison between the speaker and other men, corresponding to that of sonnet 21, and is completed by line 12: "More than that tongue that more hath more expressed." The rhetorical repetition of "more" three times within the line should be seen as a touch of deliberate parody. It ridicules "that tongue" whose facility in saying more and saying it more elaborately is as unconvincing as the hyperbole of "that muse" in sonnet 21. The speaker's new confidence is marked when he outdoes his poetic foil by placing "more than" at the beginning of the line. His silent expressions thus say more than others' bombast.

Having established so strong a self-defense, the speaker is able to make another plea to his beloved. In sonnet 21 he had returned to his rivals in the couplet, "let them say more." But now his attention stays with his auditor:

> O learn to read what silent love hath writ.
> To hear with eyes belongs to love's fine wit.

Underlying this couplet is the familiar conceit of the lover's soul as a book. Samuel Daniel, whom Shakespeare probably read, speaks of "the booke of my charg'd soule."⁹ In another sonnet, he implores the beloved to "read in my face, a volume of despayres."¹⁰ An even more substantial parallel to Shakespeare, and possibly a source, is sonnet 43 of Spenser's *Amoretti.*¹¹ The sestet of this sonnet develops a similar argument to that of Shakespeare's sonnet 23:

9. *Poems and A Defence of Rhyme,* ed. A. C. Sprague p. 11.
10. Ibid. p.30.
11. First noted by Conrad (1882); cited in *Variorum,* 1:66.

Yet I my hart with silence secretly
Will teach to speak, and my iust cause to plead:
And eke mine eies with meeke humility,
Love learned letters to her eyes to read.
Which her deep wit, that true harts thought can spel
Will soon conceive, and learn to construe well.[12]

Both passages contain the words *plead, eyes, to read, learn, wit.* Spenser also mentions *silence* and *to speak,* whereas Shakespeare uses *silent* and *speak.* Both poets employ the conceit of a speaking breast, or heart, whose message is conveyed by looks or eyes. In Spenser's poem the eyes read out "love learned letters," while Shakespeare more simply refers to "what silent love hath writ." The main difference, however, is that Spenser never presumes to address his lady. His sonnet is introverted in its discussion of "her wrath." It does not invoke an understanding of body language and takes "her deep wit" for granted. But Shakespeare's beloved still must "learn to read" the poet's looks. The speaker unhesitatingly instructs his auditor "to hear with eyes" and explains almost condescendingly that this is part of "love's fine wit."

Reviewing the structure of sonnet 23, we notice that the speaker has again dissimulated. His likening of himself to "an imperfect actor" and to "some fierce thing" cannot be taken at face value given the sonnet's ending. In sonnet 21, the speaker feigned plainness of style even while he outdid the eloquence of other poets. His pretense in sonnet 23 is more extreme, for he now professes to be incapable of any discourse. Setting aside the fact that the poem's mere existence inevitably belies that claim, we can also point to the rich artifice of its construction as contrary to its argument.

Any utterance such as "I cannot speak" is contradictory, but a poem that describes a speechless person must use language—even if that person is its speaker. In this sonnet the discrepancy between what the speaker says about himself and what he achieves in the poem is so great that it can only be understood as deliberate ploy. He takes pleasure in belittling himself, as in sonnet 21, while giving us sufficient evidence to see the opposing truth.

12. *The Poetical Works of Edmund Spenser,* ed. J. C. Smith and E. de Selincourt, p. 569. Although Katharine M. Wilson (*Shakespeare's Sugared Sonnets,* p. 179), speaks of parody in sonnet 23, she does not cite this source. She claims that "Shakespeare substitutes for communication by eyes . . . communication by the written word" and that this "joke" justifies the Q reading of "books."

Such is the characteristic strategy of the Eiron, who, for whatever reason, is always unwilling to display his real self. If sonnet 23 is less openly ironic than 21, that is because its speaker takes fewer opportunities to compare the pretenses of others with his own achievement. He comments briefly on "that tongue" that, unlike his own, finds no difficulty in expressing what it does not feel. He thus maintains Shakespeare's habitual distrust of verbosity and reminds us especially of Cordelia, who in the opening scene of *King Lear* confesses, "I cannot heave / My heart into my mouth" (1.1.93–94), realizing that she must "love, and be silent." The speaker in sonnet 23, however, deals with the qualities of courtly rather than filial love. He uses parallel possessive phrases to denote the conflict between "love's rite" and "mine own love's strength . . . mine own love's might." By devising an intricate work of art paradoxically based on the protestation that he cannot express himself, he demonstrates that the "love's fine wit" for which he pleads is very much his own. The essence of that wit lies in the deceptive yet characteristic irony with which he presents himself.

The final sonnet in this triad of soliloquies that introduce the speaker's newfound subjectivity is the twenty-fifth. It culminates two tendencies that continue from sonnets 21 and 23, being at once the most fully ironic poem and the most interiorized soliloquy. Its basic structure consists of two comparisons between the speaker and his counterparts. The first occurs within quatrain 1, which is evenly divided between "them" and "I." The second comparison is not similarly balanced, for the next two quatrains are entirely devoted to describing others rather than the speaker himself. Only in the couplet does the "I" return, briefly noting his advantage over those he has described. The sonnet begins with another hortative verb construction:

> Let those who are in favor with their stars
> Of public honour and proud titles boast.

Even if we have forgotten the corresponding line in sonnet 21, "let them say more that like of hearsay well," we cannot miss the controlled irony that is now directed against those who are considered fortunate. They are marked as Alazon characters by their boasting, which the speaker urges them to continue. What they boast of is patently unworthy, as we infer from the adjectives in "public honour" and "proud titles." In contrast, the speaker presents himself with seeming humility as one "whom fortune of such triumphs bars." Yet their triumph, with all its connotations of

Renaissance pageantry, is recognizably hollow. And line 4 suggests that the speaker's misfortune may be a blessing: "unlooked for . . . [I] joy in that I honour most." This obscurity, being "unlooked for," does not impress us as a disaster when we recall the sharp attacks that many sonnets make against "the world."[13] There is also an undeniable advantage in "joy," which is the speaker's single, representative action. Unlike those who search outside themselves for things to boast of, he cherishes an ideal that is part of his own self to "joy in." A clear-cut distinction separates the two types of value, "public honour" and "that . . . [which] I honour most." The second reflects personal knowledge that has been acquired through experience, whereas the first is merely based on what sonnet 29 dismisses as "fortune and men's eyes."

In quatrain 2 the speaker's unnamed counterparts acquire a more specific reality. They are identified as courtiers, "great princes' favorites," giving a more earthly explanation to the previous phrase, "in favor with their stars." These courtiers are transfigured by the natural imagery that represents them. First the image of a flourishing tree is created through the phrase "their fair leaves spread." It is an image that implies growth but also eventual decline, as in "lofty trees barren of leaves" in sonnet 12 and the "yellow leaves" and shaking boughs in 73. But this sonnet adds a second image that puts immediate stress on the courtiers' vanity and doom: "But as the marigold at the sun's eye." The striking disparity between great and small, or strong and weak, speaks for itself. Since the image of the sun also denotes royalty, the possibility of a political allusion arises here. Indeed, "marigold" has some interesting connotations in Elizabethan poetry.[14] But like Shakespeare's other allusions to his own times, this one moves toward a general level of meaning. His scorn for the courtiers' fickle state becomes more apparent as the quatrain continues to describe them through flower imagery that is reminiscent of the procreation sonnets. Line 7 uses "pride," echoing the "proud titles" of line 2, in the sense of splendor. But the critical tone is unmistakable: "And in themselves their pride lies buried." This recalls the fair youth who in the opening sonnet is accused of self-love: "Within thine own bud . . . [thou] buriest thy content." The courtier's doom, however, is not the gradual decay that flower

13. See sonnets 71, 72, 75, 90, 112, 121, 138, 140, 148.
14. Michael Drayton in *Ideas Mirrour* mentions "Marygold" in an apparent allusion to the Countess of Pembroke. See *The Works of Michael Drayton,* ed. J. W. Hebel, 1:124, and the commentary by Kathleen Tillotson, 5:17–18.

images suggest. What the speaker foresees is an abrupt, highly ironic over-throw: "for at a frown they in their glory die." The word *glory* is charged with irony, being so easily overwhelmed by a mere frown. The physical imbalance between the flower and the sun, and the utter dependency of the former, have been transformed into social terms. Conversely, we could say that the "public honour" of quatrain 1 has been recognized for what it is by means of an analogy with nature.

Although quatrain 3 appears simply to give an additional illustration, it actually modifies the poem's argument by replacing the courtier with a very different example of "those who are in favor." No suggestion of irony is found that might reduce our esteem for "the painful warrior famoused for fight." He is not represented figuratively, and his downfall is not fore-shadowed in his description. What finally happens to the warrior is not justified by the speaker, although he seems to accept the world's injustice easily enough. For a single defeat "after a thousand victories," the warrior "is from the book of honour razed quite." Thus "public honour," now symbolized as a book, again bears the brunt of ironic criticism. Being its victim, the warrior himself cannot be seen as an Alazon type. He simply loses his reputation "and all the rest forgot for which he toiled." The speaker dwells on this point in a way that appears to question the purpose of any effort in an inconstant world. He stresses the futility of all that had been accomplished only to be lost, as if to echo the *vanitas vanitorum* of an explicitly ironic world view. Indeed, the same attitude can be found in the speeches of some of Shakespeare's shrewdest and most deceptive charac-ters. For example, Mark Antony states categorically,

> The evil that men do lives after them,
> The good is oft interred with their bones.
> (*Julius Caesar*, 3.2.75–76)

And Ulysses is even more emphatic;

> For beauty, wit,
> High birth, vigor of bone, desert in service,
> Love, friendship, charity, are subjects all
> To envious and calumniating Time.
> (*Troilus and Cressida*, 3.3.171–74)

These quotations are very much in the spirit of sonnet 25. But the sonnet returns to an affirmation in the couplet that completes the "I-they" comparison. The speaker had hinted at his own superiority in lines 3–4. Now he proclaims it:

> Then happy I that love and am beloved
> Where I may not remove nor be removed.

As in sonnets 21 and 23, "then" is the sign of a logical transition. It announces the speaker's realization that he is "happy" as opposed to "fortunate." The choice of this homespun, native word is appropriate, for *favor, honour, triumph,* and *famoused* are all of Latin derivation. The resulting contrast is one of plainness against formality, corresponding to the speaker's basic distinction between private and public pleasures. He recapitulates his theme through the use of two verb pairs that indicate reciprocal interaction: "Love and am beloved" and "not remove nor be removed."

In these three sonnet-soliloquies, a recurrent movement from self-deprecation to self-assertion can readily be discerned. The speaker begins by a comparison with others that is superficially biased against himself. He gradually confirms our suspicion that this self-deprecation may be an ironic pose. The pretensions of flattering poets and the false confidence of public figures are easily deflated by the Eiron. Moreover, a growth of confidence and a refining of ironic technique are evident in sonnet 25, as compared to the other poems. The speaker makes no veiled address to his beloved and seems more firmly in control of the possibilities offered by a soliloquy situation. Yet the artistry he has attained clearly derives from the model developed in sonnets 21 and 23. These three sonnets compose a close-knit progression of thought and imagery. They consistently bear out the superiority of the speaker's set of values over those of his foils. Truthfulness outweighs the "proud compare" that is imitated in 21, while 23 establishes "love's fine wit" as preferable to the formalities of "love's rite." Finally, simple happiness based on personal values is seen to triumph over ambition in 25. In this way, for the first time in the 1609 sequence the speaker comes to define his character through a series of comparisons with others. His irony enables him to distinguish true values from false and to defend them polemically. The impression of a passive, clod-like speaker is therefore misleading. The surface simplicity achieved by Shakespeare's speaker would be lacking in substance were it not the end product in a complex process of ironic comparisons.

II. Introspection

Two questions will probably arise from the above discussion; the first challenges "soliloquy" as a meaningful category for lyric poems, which are almost always monologues and in a sense soliloquies as well. However, the term is used here in a very specific sense referring only to poems from which all second-person forms are excluded, so that the speaker is addressing himself rather than an external auditor. These poems can be easily identified in that they have no "thou" or "you." They describe a relationship between the speaking "I" and others referred to only as "he," "she," and "they." The distinction is not merely formal; these soliloquies engage in "speaking of," a mode of address that is opposed to "speaking to." Their subject matter is presented directly to the reader, who also serves as their only auditor. As a result, we hear the speaker's thoughts directly rather than overhearing what he says to the youth, to the lady, or even to a personification like Time. Soliloquy allows no form of address except perhaps "to whom it may concern" or, more likely, "to myself."

By recognizing certain poems as soliloquies, we gain a valuable contrast with all the others that do use "thou" or "you" to imply a definite relation between speaker and auditor. Those poems that engage in "speaking to" may be termed "dialogues." For example, while sonnets 21, 23, and 25 introduce "speaking of" through soliloquy, the intervening 22 and 24 are dialogues speaking to the youth and praising him. Both sets of poems rely on wit to ingratiate their auditor, but the element of direct address in the dialogues makes the speaker's efforts much more overt. In the soliloquies, as we have begun to see, self-address tends to correspond with self-concern. Thus the distinction between soliloquy and dialogue can be useful to criticism in several ways. A poet's preference for either of the two modes, throughout his work or in a given selection, is in itself revealing. Such preference should be compared with the practice of his contemporaries and correlated with the main themes of his work. In reading a particular text we can apply the distinction to determine whether the work employs "speaking of" or "speaking to" and to describe the way in which the mode of address is linked to other stylistic features.

An additional question arising from the discussion of the first three soliloquies centers on the word *first*. Since the arrangement of the sonnets in the 1609 quarto is uncertain, possibly not Shakespeare's own, what basis is there for speaking of earlier or later poems? Here, too, the soliloquies offer some useful information. As we have seen, not even one is found among sonnets 1–17, where the speaker has not yet defined his selfhood. The Procreation group therefore functions as an introductory section. When sonnet 18 announces a new theme, and a new personal relationship, it also requires more self-disclosure. Thereafter, in the Fair Youth section (sonnets 18–126) we find thirteen of the twenty soliloquies contained in the entire collection. These can be divided into three groups: (1) 21, 23, 25; (2) 63, 64, 65, 66; (3) 116, 119, 121, 124. These three groups account for all but two of the thirteen soliloquies, 33 and 105. Such patterning may be relegated to chance, but it seems rather to reveal a definite process of psychological growth. The first three soliloquies began what the procreation sonnets had carefully avoided, a definition of the speaker's identity. The second group, sonnets 63–66, comprises a single soliloquy that is located precisely at the midpoint of the Fair Youth section. This extended soliloquy displays a speaker who is no longer concerned with self-definition; his introspection now explores the consequences of being what he is. Finally, the last four soliloquies (anticipated by 105) form a cluster that is unified by repeated verbal links and by continued focus on love and selfhood. It is difficult not to read these sonnets as cumulative statements that epitomize the speaker's crisis of personal knowledge.

Situated between the first two groups of soliloquies, sonnet 33 marks the speaker's first attempt at introspection. Its contrast to sonnet 7 has already been noted; that poem used the sun to build a fable about human decline, whereas this one visualizes nature in the direct manner of sonnets 12 and 15:

> Full many a glorious morning have I seen
> Flatter the mountaintops with sovereign eye,
> Kissing with golden face the meadows green,
> Gilding pale streams with heav'nly alchemy.

The brilliance of this description lies in its combination of precision with imaginative heightening by means of personification ("with sovereign eye . . . with golden face") and metaphor ("with heav'nly alchemy"). Imagination does not supplant the representation of nature but enhances it within the confined space of three parallel prepositional phrases, two of which also rhyme. This quatrain leads us to expect a shift in imagery, as in sonnets 12 and 15, so that "morning" would launch a new series of images related to the governing idea. Instead, line 5 simply extends the personification, keeping the sun as subject of the long, suspended sentence that composes lines 1–8: "Anon permit the basest clouds to ride / With ugly rack on his celestial face."

Inevitably a hiatus is formed as we turn back to ascertain that "morning" is the subject of "permit," even though it is also the object of "have I seen."[15] Until this point, we could not know whether the sonnet would hinge on the seer or on what he sees. The method of sonnets 12 and 15 would have put the speaking "I" immediately at the poem's center, with "morning" and subsequent images being assimilated into the process of reflection. So, too, the earliest soliloquies had resolved precisely around the speaker. But now the verbs *permit, hide,* and *stealing* are actions performed by "glorious morning," continuing from *flatter, kissing,* and *gliding* in quatrain 1. The unanticipated lengthening creates an accumulation of action and lends increased momentum to the series. Similarly, when quatrain 3 reveals via "even so" that what we are reading is an epic simile, the poem gains additional continuity. In this section the speaker who had withdrawn behind the landscape he evokes, much like his cloud-covered sun, reappears at the focal point of the poem. His experience, we now realize, had inspired all the elaborate symbolism:

> Ev'n so my sun one early morn did shine
> With all triumphant splendor on my brow;
> But out alack, he was but one hour mine,
> The region cloud hath masked him from me now.

Nevertheless, the sonnet does not become a parable. Its descriptive opening is too vivid to be obscured by the subsequent analogy, while the "message" is in any case too vague to be allegorical. We do not know who the sun is, whether patron, friend, or lover, and in what sense he has concealed himself. Whatever speculation we may supply, the vagueness as to the speaker's identity remains. Unlike the first three soliloquies, this one does not attempt self-description through comparison with others. The speaker reverts to his earlier role of seer, subordinating himself in the octet to the task of natural description; in the sestet he then identifies the scene as his own invention, as if to acknowledge that detached observation has become impossible. The external world and its overcast beauty become a vehicle for expressing those personal events that Robert Frost called "inner

15. Booth, ed., *Shakespeare's Sonnets*, p. 186.

weather." Yet the relation between both spheres of experience is never clarified because the phrase "my sun" is so evasive. It may entail a position of inferior gazing from below as in sonnet 7, or it may suggest the paternal relation that earlier sonnets prefigured. That parallel is activated by the closing pun, "suns of the world may stain when heav'n's sun staineth."

A comparison is often made between this imagery and that of Prince Hal's soliloquy in the first act of *Part One of Henry IV.* But Hal speaks as the sun itself, explaining the motives for his masking; in the sonnet we have the opposite perspective, similar to Falstaff's chagrin at being denied the light and warmth he had once enjoyed. Line 14 finally offers an explanation, one that need not be dismissed as simple rationalizing:

> Yet him for this my love no whit disdaineth;
> Suns of the world may stain when heav'n's sun staineth.

By likening the earthly and heavenly "suns," the couplet recalls sonnet 18's transformation of summer into a symbol that transcends ordinary nature: "sometime too hot the eye of heaven shines, / And often is his gold complexion dimmed." Against that background stood the idealized youth whose "eternal summer shall not fade." In marked contrast, sonnet 33 reduces the youth and all men to the inconstant level of the cloud-stained sun. It combines the two sources of irony set forth in the Procreation sonnets: physical impermanence and human inconstancy. Sonnets 18 and 33 thus resemble "couplements" of the kind that sonnet 21 ascribes to the inferior poet "who heaven itself for ornament doth use." What we now find is scarcely a "couplement of proud compare" because it registers for the first time a sharp disparity between the idealized youth and his actual performance. The speaker finds himself no different from the courtier mocked in sonnet 25 as "the marigold in the sun's eye"; he, too, lacks the mutuality of love supposed by the couplet: "I may not remove nor be removed." He has therefore linked the sun image to his beloved because of the latter's disappointing behavior.

Seeking a more detailed account of what has occurred, we need to turn to sonnets 34 and 35. These are dialogues and better suited to an exposition of the relations between speaker and auditor. We learn in 34 that the clouds symbolize a "strong offence" for which the youth subsequently apologized: "though thou repent, yet have I still the loss." The offense must involve sensuality, since 35 speaks openly of a "sensual fault" that the speaker is willing to forgive. He repeats the explanation that just as "clouds and eclipses stain both moon and sun . . . [so] all men make faults." Moreover, he is moved by the youth's repentance, by tears that "ransom all ill deeds." It appears from these two dialogues that the offensive deed must have been seducing the speaker's mistress. Sonnet 35 shows how the speaker, somewhat reluctantly, foregoes his indignation:

> I an accessary needs must be
> To that sweet thief which sourly robs from me.

Except for the mistress, the speaker can be robbed of nothing by his younger, more powerful friend. Sonnets 40–42 take up that occurrence and frequently echo sonnets 33–35. The language of the speaker's self-accusation in sonnet 35 is repeated in the pardon he grants in line 9 of sonnet 40: "I do forgive thy *robb'ry,* gentle *thief*." Likewise, lines 7 and 8 in sonnet 41 reiterate not only the adjective *sourly* from 35 but also the homonymous *son,* from the "suns of the world," found in sonnet 33: "And when a woman woos, what woman's *son* / Will *sourly* leave her till he have prevailed?" The parallels in the language between lines 11–12 of sonnet 34 ("Th'offender's sorrow lends but weak relief / To him that bears the strong offence's cross") and lines 4–5 of sonnet 42 provide a clear insinuation about what has happened: "A *loss* in love that touches me more nearly. / Loving *offenders,* thus I will *excuse* ye."

Readers who insist on precise biographical data will not be satisfied by these parallels, but they do indicate what sonnet 33's veiled complaint refers to. By its very nature, soliloquy need not provide explicit information; "speaking of" often omits items that would aid our understanding. As in sonnet 33, this type of discourse enables the speaker to take a first step toward self-expression. The dialogues that follow, 34, 35, and 40–42, then modify his attitude so that it can be conveyed directly to the auditor. One function of soliloquy, then, is to allow a tentative exploration of thoughts and images for further development. We can even point to a stylistic feature of 33 illustrating that it seeks less to interpret ideas than to arrange and categorize them. The sonnet contains no less than six adverbial phrases using "with." Three of them have already been quoted:

> with sovereign eye
> with golden face
> with heav'nly alchemy
> with this disgrace

> with all triumphant splendor
> with ugly rack.

Each of these phrases shows the manner in which an action is performed; together, they betray a concern with *how* things occur rather than why. At this initial stage, the speaker is concerned with accurate description; analysis and response will follow. We infer that his experience is a surprising one and not yet fully understood. Unlike phenomena with which he is familiar, "*full many* a glorious morning," the youth's favor and disappearance are unique: "My sun *one* early morn did shine . . . he was but *one* hour mine." For these reasons sonnet 33 cannot achieve much depth of introspection. It moves beyond the first three soliloquies by avoiding a predetermined strategy for self-presentation. Its irony is more cosmic than rhetorical, allowing for a measure of dramatic spontaneity, yet it does not achieve self-knowledge.

The second group of soliloquies, sonnets 63–66, records a striking growth of poetic insight. Having dropped his ironic mask, the speaker discovers his own real features. He does not contrast himself with rivals through an "I/they" pattern but begins to probe the more involved relationship between himself and his beloved. The youth around whom his thoughts revolve is no longer an inaccessible, superior figure. Equality of stature is granted by the "I/he" orientation, which in fact tends to elevate the speaker as the acting subject while the beloved is merely the object acted upon. The function of soliloquy here is that it lends distance, creating a perspective through which the speaker can better see himself. Surprisingly, except for Benson's edition of 1640, these four sonnets have never been considered as a single unit. One editor refers to the last three as a single "poem of marvellous power, insight, and beauty."[16] But sonnet 63, having obvious links with the opening of 64 and the couplet of 65, introduces the themes of the entire quartet. The main interconnections of all four poems are presented in Table 1.

The first four of these nine links shown in the table are based on the simple repetition of key words. References to "time" appear at least twice in 63, 64, and 65, but never in 66, where the emphasis shifts from nature to society. Time's "injurious hand" and "fell hand" are cognate in 63 and 64, but a reversal takes place in 65, which represents time as a runner: "what strong hand can hold his swift foot back?" Similarly, "brass eternal" in 64

16. Palgrave (1865) cited in *Variorum*, 1:169.

Table 1. Interconnections among Sonnets 63–66.

	63	64	65	66
1.	time's injurious hand such a time	time's fell hand time will come	time decays time's best jewel time's chest	—
2.	injurious hand	fell hand	what strong hand	—
3.	—	brass eternal	brass, nor stone	—
4.	against my love	and take my love	my love may still	I leave my love
5.	confounding age's	confounded to decay	time decays	—
6.	crushed and o'erworn	outworn buried age	o'ersways their power	by limping sway
7.	I now fortify	towers I see down razed	siege of batt'ring days	captive good
8.	shall in these black lines be seen	when I have seen	in black ink my love may still shine bright	as to behold
9.	my lover's life . . . they shall live	this thought is as a death	sad mortality	restful death

anticipates the opening line of 65: "Since brass, nor stone, nor earth, nor boundless sea. . . ." The latter poem, beginning with "since," concludes the former's observations. So much verbal repetition seems to reflect the speaker's central concerns; the only phrase borne throughout all four sonnets is "my love," an expression that entered the sequence in sonnet 19 where it denotes the beloved youth: "my love's fair brow." In sonnet 33, it gains the additional sense of referring to the speaker's own feelings: "Yet him for this my love no whit disdaineth." Subsequently, sonnet 40 deliberately confuses the two senses: "Take all my loves, my love, yea, take them all. . . ." As a result, the way in which the phrase is being used here is no longer certain. Its position is significant; it appears in the first line of 63, "against my love shall be as I am now," and then concludes the thought process by appearing in the couplets of 64, 65, and 66. Thus the image of the beloved and the idea of love itself, both implied by "my love," underlie the speaker's speculations about himself.

These four soliloquies are further bound, in items 5 and 6 of Table 1, by the rhetorical figure of *antimetabole* that blends repetition and substitution. For example, the central phrase "confounded to decay" in 64 looks back to "confounding age's cruel knife" in 63 and ahead to "time decays" in 65.

Antimetabole also unites the phrases listed as item 6, but in a more complex way, including all four of the sonnets and splitting words rather than phrases. Thus "o'erworn" in 63 sends its root to "outworn" in 64 and its prefix to "o'ersways" in 65 whose root, in turn, appears independently in 66 as "limping sway." The effect of such subtle linkage is to deepen our sense of the four sonnets' underlying coherence while allowing a distinctive tonal quality for each poem. The coherence is further strengthened by the third type of correspondence, whose examples (items 7, 8, and 9) are distributed through all four parts of the compound soliloquy. This repetition is not verbal but based on kindred images and ideas. Warfare, introduced by the speaker's "fortify" in sonnet 63 and continued through time's "towers" and "siege" in 64 and 65, ends with the capture of good by "captain ill" in 66, so that a single metaphorical battle has been planned, fought, and lost. Another extended metaphor is that of sight and seeing. Sonnets 63 and 65 prophesy that the youth's beauty will be seen by posterity, whereas 64 and 66 center on what the speaker himself observes. Finally, all four poems deal with the concept that 65 terms "sad mortality." The speaker's awareness of impermanence, his sense of the possible futility of life itself, is manifest in all four soliloquies.

Each sonnet in the quartet forms part of a cyclical progression moving from confidence to doubt, then returning to a more cautious reaffirmation. In sonnet 63 the speaker begins to demonstrate the inner tension that is necessary before he can gain a better understanding of himself. Abandoning his mask of wit, he solemnly predicts the defeat of time through poetry. Several sonnets have already entertained that argument, but a new dimension now arises because "speaking of" has eliminated the pressures of confronting an external auditor, someone with a mind of his own. The tone of this sonnet is rather tentative; it has no line that rivals the strength of earlier boasts, such as the couplet of sonnet 18:

> So long as men can breathe or eyes can see,
> So long lives this, and this gives life to thee.

Or that of 55:

> So, till the judgement that yourself arise,
> You live in this, and dwell in lovers' eyes.

Besides sheer strength, such statements have a touch of bravado that is absent here. Since the beloved is not being addressed, there is no need to convince him. The speaker can content himself with an unretouched account of what he is doing and why. As the maker of eternal verse, he takes a prominent role rather than presenting his creation as an autonomous entity. Indeed, the poem reconstructs the creative process from which it emerges. In the beginning (once again) is the recognition of time's effects, but they are located within the speaker himself and transferred imaginatively to the youth:

> Against my love shall be as I am now,
> With time's injurious hand crush'd and o'erworn . . . .

This equivalence is more modest than the full interchange of identity that had been claimed before, as in 62: " 'Tis thee, myself, that for myself I praise." What is shared in 63 is merely the common fate of mortality; the idea appears to be a deeply felt belief, not a poetic convention. Concerned with rescuing his beloved from time and oblivion, the speaker does not realize that the measures he takes are his own salvation from despair:

> For such a time do I now fortify
> Against confounding age's cruel knife.

The verb *fortify* is ambiguous; does it mean strengthening the beloved for survival, or is it reflexive, so that the speaker is arming himself? Probably "now" points to the act of writing; the poem itself is a fortification against time that will outlast all other monuments. In sonnet 16 the youth had been urged to "fortify yourself in your decay / With means more blessed than my barren rhyme." Now it is the poet who builds a strong defense while the benefit, at least psychologically, is also his own:

> His beauty shall in these black lines be seen,
> And they shall live, and he in them still green.

This closing presents a solution for the speaker, not his love. Its repeated "shall" shows his desire to determine the future rather than fear it, as he had earlier in the sonnet. In order to "prove" the case to his own satisfaction, the speaker reasons syllogistically:

1. My beloved's beauty will appear in these lines.
2. They will live.
3. He, too, will live in them.

He equivocates by substituting "he" for "his beauty," the whole person in place of a single attribute. Nevertheless, he ends the sonnet in a resolute tone that we might consider final were it not shattered by the next section of this four-part soliloquy.

From the relatively facile achievement of 63 the speaker advances to authentic insight in 64. The perspective of this poem is broader, not being limited to one personal relationship but comprehending a wide range of natural elements and the "lofty towers" of the social world as well. The speaker thus resumes his role of seer but in doing so drops the dramatic "now." He employs the present perfect "when I have seen," which places his vision at a point anterior to the moment of utterance. Inevitably, that introductory clause invites a transition from the observed data to an inference, from "when" to "then." The previous sonnet had linked that structural transition to a change of mood from weariness to strength. But neither of these predictable changes occurs here, making 64 a significant departure from the norm. There is no *volta* at the usual turning point; line 9 is merely another time clause: "When I have seen such interchange of state." In lines 12–13 we come upon a change, but scarcely what was expected:

> Ruin hath taught me thus to ruminate,
> That time will come and take my love away.

Poetry is not mentioned here, though it had always been credited with making the beloved youth an exception to the rule of time. We approach the couplet, assuming that it yet will manage to reverse the downward movement. But the rescue from melancholy never comes:

> This thought is as a death, which cannot choose
> But weep to have that which it fears to lose.

In those concluding lines something unprecedented takes place. They present us with an anticlimax; instead of refuting lines 1–12, they demolish all the previous claims about eternal poetry. With a new candor, the speaker admits that no compensation for time and death really exists. There is a refreshing honesty to that admission; it suggests that he is being faithful to his original vision of impermanence and refuses to argue it away. Perhaps the form of soliloquy makes this breakthrough possible, for the speaker enjoys a total privacy of discourse, freeing him of the need to consider anyone's feelings but his own. The same irony that recorded the "process of the seasons" and criticized "that other muse" now undermines its own master and his persistent attempt to build a time-proof monument. Such self-directed irony makes possible a greater depth of introspection. The deepening can be detected in the varied use of personifications, beginning with the standardized expression "time's fell hand" and continuing with the unexceptionably "hungry ocean." Toward the end of the sonnet, the personifications become less obvious because they derive from within. "Ruin" is not a conventional abstraction; it externalizes the speaker's own insight, lending it an independent existence. "Ruin" in itself can teach him nothing; his own observation of decline, reified as an external object, led him "thus to ruminate."

A similarly subjective personification occurs in the couplet. The telling phrase here is "this thought," which represents what might have been called "my mind" or "my state." The entire couplet is a remarkable example of objectification; it could very crudely be paraphrased as "I die to think of this [my beloved's inevitable death] and even regret having what must be taken from me." Rather than continue in the first person of "when I have seen," the speaker has shifted to an impersonal mask, detaching himself from his ideas. He had written about his own mental life before, in "conceits" like sonnet 46: "Mine eye and heart are at a mortal war." But never did he give his own thoughts such authentic existence. It is a sign of his growing insight that his own words and thoughts have become his subject matter, rather than the external world. Even the account of earth and sea in quatrain 2 is not based on actual observation but on a favorite passage in Ovid's *Metamorphoses*:

> When I have seen the hungry ocean gain
> Advantage on the kingdom of the shore,
> And the firm soil win of the watery main,
> Increasing store with loss, and loss with store.

Having stressed man's obliteration by natural forces, the speaker shows how those forces are themselves subject to decay and "interchange of state." The description of sea and land exchanging "store with loss and loss with store" is a paradox whose symmetrical structure echoes his own weary mood. Each element vies with the other in a process that is as futile as it is endless. Similarly, brass is "eternal slave to mortal rage" precisely because it is used for memorials; its durability thus defeats its purpose. But the final paradox, of a mind that must "weep to have," best reflects the speaker's ability to see the obverse side of human experience. The very passion of love, by involving potential loss, becomes the source of sorrow as well as of joy. Sonnet 64, the second section in this four-part soliloquy, is therefore the adagio in the quartet. Its last four lines, except for "ruminate," consist of slow-moving, monosyllabic words. These lines submit totally to time, making no supernatural distinction between body and soul and admitting no claim for poetic immortality.

Just as the thought and imagery of sonnet 63 were reversed in 64, the following sonnet also effects a continuation and a change. Sonnet 65 begins with a resonant summation of previous themes and imagery:

> Since brass, nor stone, nor earth, nor boundless sea,
> But sad mortality o'ersways their power,
> How with this rage shall beauty hold a plea,
> Whose action is no stronger than a flower?

Lines 1–2 concede the strength of mortality and reiterate the changing elements mentioned in 64, but this strength has been relegated to a subordinate clause that begins with "since." The speaker has regrouped his energies sufficiently to admit impermanence as an axiom and to ask again what can be done against it. Posed in lines 3–4, that question will be repeated four times throughout the varying imagery of lines 5–12. These parallel, if not quite synonymous, questions assume that there still must be an answer:

> Or what strong hand can hold his swift foot back?
> Or who his spoil or beauty can forbid?

The final question, which urgently adds a human context, raises concern that the entire series has been rhetorical, implying the answers "nothing" and "no one." The sonnet so far has not been a true soliloquy but an impersonal disquisition. The speaker has never referred to himself in lines 1–12. Again, the turning point at line 9 fails to provide a change of attitude as it simply introduces one more question:

> O fearful meditation; where, alack,
> Shall time's best jewel from time's chest lie hid?

The "fearful meditation," however, points to the mind that has been disclosing itself through these soliloquies, much as the "best jewel" represents the beloved youth. The symmetrical questions reflect the speaker's central theme and relationship, but if his response will be the acquiescence of 64 or the defiance of 63 is not known. Just how closely intertwined his doubts and his faith have become appears quite clearly in the opening words of the couplet:

> O none, unless this miracle have might
> That in black ink my love may still shine bright.

These two lines scarcely yield a definite claim. Nothing can resist time, they say, except perhaps this verse. The affirmation is considerably weaker than that of 63, where the speaker had simply assumed success. Poetic immortality, if it now occurs, will be no less than a "miracle." The beloved may "still shine bright," but that paradox is less striking than the earlier transformation of black into green. Nevertheless, there is a tangible sense in which the conclusion of this sonnet shows greater self-awareness. The dramatically delayed entry of personal value in the couplet suggests that belief in poetic immortality is an act of faith. The speaker has retained that faith despite the opposing evidence that his senses recorded so accurately in the first twelve lines.

Less certain than before, his affirmation is also more genuine; he has achieved it by working through doubts and reconsideration, rather than by maintaining an untried confidence. The sonnet makes an important contribution to the soliloquies in that its personal affirmation of value transcends the negation offered by its objective study of the world. In soliloquy there can be no turning from self to other, nothing that would correspond to sonnet 29's pivotal recollection: "haply I think on thee." But in sonnet 65 the analogous movement is from objective to subjective, form "it" to "I," even though the speaker's only reference to himself comes characteristically within the phrase "my love." The extent of his self-consciousness, meditating not on nature but on his thoughts about nature, underlies the phrase "O fearful meditation." That interjection objectifies his own emotion, as if it existed outside and independent of himself.

A further sign of introspection is the question-and-answer structure that runs through this sonnet; it assumes an inner colloquy in which one part of his being discourses with another. In Shakespearean terms, this is a dialogue of the eye, perceptive but skeptical, with the more credulous heart and mind. We may also call it a conflict between cosmic irony and the personal need for faith and for the "miracle." The speaker has reached the stage at which irony proves insufficient, being a test but not a source of value. That source he now discovers in himself as he writes more discerningly about his inner life and the art it produces. In this sonnet he does mention "summer's honey breath" and states that beauty's "action is no stronger than a flower." But very little sense experience is communicated. The "honey" of summer cannot be perceived, due to a mingling between the senses of taste and smell; "honey" merely substitutes for "sweet." As for the flower, it too serves as a shorthand symbol that cannot be compared with earlier images such as "violets past prime" (12) or "the darling buds of May" (18). Such descriptions may not be sensuously precise, but they do evoke associations of our experience in nature. In contrast, sonnet 65's flower grows in a field of legal imagery, after "plea" and "action." The mixed metaphor effectively expresses the speaker's state of mind, but it also implies that his imagination may be weakening because it has begun to work with secondary associations instead of physical sensation.

Because of its unusual design, sonnet 66 stands out from its context and marks a recognizable conclusion to the sustained, four-part soliloquy. Typographically, it resembles a pillar whose column is a catalog of the world's injustices. At the top of the pillar stretches a single line: "Tir'd with all these, for restful death I cry." At its base, the couplet incorporates that opening line, placing a personal framework around the seemingly universal diatribe against the world:

> Tir'd with all these, from these would I be gone,
> Save that to die, I leave my love alone.

The main part of this symmetrical design is the schematic list of grievances in lines 2–12. The effect of that extended complaint is to revive the melancholy that was overcome in 65. In a tone of dull resentment, the speaker begins to specify:

> As to behold desert a beggar born,
> And needy nothing trimmed in jollity.

How this abuse affects him, or why he has chosen to speak of it, is not told. He complains of the general dishonesty and inconstancy that traditionally serve as targets of satire. The moral qualities that he finds neglected are too familiar to require definition: faith, honor, virtue, truth, and good. Yet he also enumerates qualities of personal achievement rather than morality: perfection, strength, art, and skill. Since his concern is for active virtue, he is especially disturbed by the obstacles that the world puts in the way of merit. After the initial contrast between "desert" and "needy nothing," he lists the reversals of faith, honor, virtue, and perfection without specifying their opposites. Each of these abstractions is linked to a parallel past participle and an adverb of manner. The effect of this passive verb construction is to exclude the subject of each action. If we ask by whom these virtues are "unhappily forsworn" or "shamefully misplaced," we can only answer "mankind" or "the world." As the speaker's catalog continues, lines 8–12 present a series of contraries rather than simple negatives. We find strength, art, skill, truth, and good displaced by sway, authority, folly, simplicity, and ill.

Despite the symmetry of these parallels linked by the repetitive figure of anaphora, some subtle differences exist. It is significant that the speaker complains of "art made tongue-tied by authority," since the two nouns are not necessarily opposites in the manner of "good" and "ill." From this deviation can be inferred an acute resentment, not of censorship but of learned restrictions. The line thus corroborates the argument, often reiterated in the sonnets, that this poetry is truthful and not derivative. Another line that makes a revealing distinction is: "And simple truth miscalled simplicity." Here, too, the protest corresponds with a major characteristic of the speaker, who frequently insists that plain virtue underlies his love and his poetic style. It should also be noted that two of these eleven lines depart from the overall pattern by using an active verb. One of these is line 12, whose generality sums up the entire series: "And captive good attending captain ill." The other is line 10: "And folly, doctor-like, controlling skill." The stress on "folly" results from the unusual adjective "doctor-like," so that it stands out as the only abstract noun that is both modified and the subject of a verb.

The closest parallel to the thought and structure of sonnet 66 is not found in the sonnets but as a part of Hamlet's soliloquy, "to be or not to be." Hamlet, too, reflects on the world's basic injustice. Like the sonnet-speaker, he would willingly "be gone," but he also attributes that view to all men. He is deterred only by the fear of death, "the undiscovered country from whose bourne no traveller returns." The sonnet differs radically, therefore, in its response to a similar mood of world-weariness. Its couplet attains a triumph of understatement, stating that love (rather than the fear of death) sustains the speaker and suggesting that personal relation can compensate for all the world's dishonesty. Love survives the destruction of all other ideals because it is a personal rather than a conventional value. In this way, the final sonnet in the quartet follows from its predecessor by re-achieving affirmation in purely personal terms. Moreover, the couplet of 66 exactly inverts that of sonnet 64, showing how far the speaker has progressed from his previous melancholy. Instead of weeping to have what he "fears to lose," he transcends self-concern. He does not remain in the corrupt world to reap any benefit but to comfort his beloved. Sonnet 66 thus ends the longest soliloquy in the sonnets by introducing a theme that will become increasingly prominent in the latter half of the sequence. A widening gap begins to separate the speaker from what the first sonnet, among others, had uncritically referred to as "the world." Rejecting the dictates of public life, he has begun to probe deeper into the sphere of personal value, creating a striking discrepancy between this poem's polemical critique of falsehood and its subsequent affirmation: "Save that to die, I leave my love alone." Like "unless" at the end of 65, "save that" introduces an escape clause by which the speaker rescues himself from self-pity. He concludes the long soliloquy by recognizing the need to look beyond himself.

III. Final Statements

The sonnet-speaker's final soliloquies in the Fair Youth sequence include some of the best known poems in the sonnets. When these texts, which conclude this series of soliloquies, are studied as examples of "speaking of" rather than addressing to, their individual achievements integrate into a more revealing pattern of the speaker's development. The soliloquy serves once again as a technique of definition. In this group the speaker is not concerned with ironic self-portraiture or with delineating the figure of his beloved against a background of mutability. He now contemplates the essential idea of love as something quite distinct from his own experience; that idea transcends the boundaries of selfhood and furnishes a link with all humanity. Thus, the speaker extends his role as an Everyman, embodying not only the awareness of change but also the no less universal striving for constancy. In sonnets 105, 116, and 124, he presents the theory of ideal, constant love; in 119 and 121, he makes an apology for his real, inconstant practice. The disparity between these two positions evidences the growing difficulty experienced by the speaker as he delves further into the uncertainties of self-knowledge.

The first of these five sonnets is best regarded as an experiment that is only partly successful. Sonnet 105 appears to be a formal imitation cast in a repetitive, rather static framework reminiscent of Spenser's *Amoretti*. The opening sonnet in Spenser's sequence uses the adjective "happy" to modify three key words, "leaves, lines, and rymes," in its three quatrains before neatly recapitulating them in the couplet:

> Leaves, lines, and rymes, seek her to please alone,
> Whom if ye please, I care for other none.[17]

Such a gently harmonious form is congenial to Spenser's poetic style, not Shakespeare's. Accepting monotony as its very theme, 105 does not escape the consequences:

> Let not my love be called idolatry,
> Nor let my beloved as an idol show,
> Since all alike my songs and praises be
> To one, of one, still such, and ever so.

Given the central task of defining "my love," the speaker begins by distinguishing it from "idolatry"; however, both this quatrain and the entire sonnet strengthen the comparison that line 1 protests against. The use of "since" in line 3 establishes a similarity rather than a difference, as both the speaker and the idolator are totally absorbed by their service to an ideal. What these opening lines do accomplish, if nothing else, is the delimitation of "my love" to "my idea of love," while "my beloved" denotes the person in question. The former phrase will continue to carry that separate meaning in sonnet 124, where love becomes an entity quite independent of the person who is its object. Nevertheless, line 5 returns to the personal sense: "Kind is my love today, tomorrow kind," indicating that the distinction between these two meanings of "my love" has not yet crystallized. The sonnet shifts to a rather idolatrous praise centering on three key words that are repeated three times:

> Fair, kind, and true, is all my argument,
> Fair, kind, and true, varying to other words . . .
> Fair, kind, and true, have often lived alone,
> Which three, till now, never kept seat in one.

For some readers, that repeated claim is disturbing because it contradicts the powerful criticisms previously directed against the same person. Turning to other sonnets, we recall the many explicit censures of the

17. *The Poetical Works,* p. 562.

youth's misconduct in matters of love and sex. If now he remains "fair," that quality is often reduced to a misleading cover; sonnet 69 sympathizes with those who "to thy fair flow'r add the rank smell of weeds." If he is "true" seems to be an open question, as sonnet 92 acknowledges: "Thou mayst be false, and yet I know it not." As for his being "kind," sonnet 120 will express some reservation: "That you were once unkind befriends me now," adding only that the quality is mutual: "If you were by my unkindness shaken, / As I by yours." There is ample evidence, then, that the youth is not entirely "fair, kind, and true," even though 105 concludes by claiming that these "three, till now, never kept seat in one."

Sonnet 105 does have a religious, if not quite idolatrous, ring to it because of the triple repetition and because the sound of the highlighted words is reminiscent of a liturgical refrain. One should bear in mind that in Shakespeare's time "idolatry" was often used as a synonym for Roman Catholicism by its opponents. This sonnet denies that faithful, idealized love resembles the veneration of the saints, but its argument and design only strengthen the analogy. The speaker has chosen to write poetry that "one thing expressing, leaves out difference," and the sonnet displays the unhappy effects of that restriction. Several technical terms suggest that the poem's style is hampered by its single-minded devotion: "my verse . . . confined," "all my argument," and "my invention spent." Then, trying to redeem his case, the speaker claims to have found "three themes in one, which wondrous scope affords." Sonnet 105, however, does not make good that claim, any more than it succeeds in dissociating love from idolatry. It is a programmatic soliloquy, clearly setting forth intentions that it cannot fulfill. Its rhetoric is far more appropriate to the shallow-minded Lorenzo in *The Merchant of Venice,* who lauds Jessica in a strikingly similar passage while she is busily searching for more of her father's ducats:

> Beshrow me but I love her heartily,
> For she is wise, if I can judge of her,
> And fair she is, if that mine eyes be true,
> And true she is, as she hath prov'd herself;
> And therefore, like herself, wise, fair, and true,
> Shall she be placed in my constant soul. (2.6.53–57)

Sonnet 116 can now be approached as successfully accomplishing what 105 had attempted—a definition of perfect love. The similarity between these two poems begins with their opening lines: "Let not my love be called idolatry" and "Let me not to the marriage of true minds / Admit impediments." The greater complexity of the latter illustrates the basic difference of style. From the very beginning, sonnet 116 is charged with metaphor, which was totally absent from 105. The definition of love takes on an imaginative power quite unlike the pallid repetition of "fair, kind, and true." The speaker is more absolute and universal in referring to "love" rather than the ambiguous "my love." That concept, coupled with the verb "to be," recurs in a series of defining statements:

> Love is not love / Which alters . . .
> O no, it is an ever-fixed mark . . .
> It is the star . . . / Whose worth's unknown . . .
> Love's not time's fool . . . .

As that series moves gradually toward personification, love becomes capable of acting and not merely being:

> Love alters not . . .
> But bears it out ev'n to the edge of doom.

Interestingly, this line, which occurs just before the couplet, closely resembles the corresponding line in sonnet 55:

> your praise shall still find room,
> Ev'n in the eyes of all posterity
> That wear this world out to the ending doom.

In 116, love rather than poetry is the means of enduring till the judgment day. However, the effectiveness in both poems of "doom" as the last word before the couplet hints that the poet has symbolically exhausted all the time that is available to man. The end of time and the ending of the sonnet coincide.

From the vast wealth of definitions and denials in lines 2-12, the speaker has scrupulously excluded himself. He is present in the "let me not" and returns only in the couplet:

> If this be error and upon me proved,
> I never writ, nor no man ever loved.

Again, as in sonnet 66, the first and last lines form an encompassing framework of personal reference; "love" is given an autonomous existence, as if entirely displaced from the speaker's field of consciousness. The power of

love, which "is" one thing and not another, which "alters not" but "bears
it out," is reinforced in the couplet, which grants that this view is the
speaker's and, perhaps, erroneous. That is not the qualification it seems,
but an even more extreme assertion. It implies that if this idea of love is an
"error," then no other can possibly exist. The speaker claims exclusiveness
for the point of view that he so passionately feels. Some critics assert that
the couplet adds nothing to the poem; Yvor Winters calls it "a mere tag,
which has no dignity or purpose in relationship to the sonnet or within
itself."[18] But in view of the speaker's gradual discovery of himself through
the medium of soliloquy, the couplet adds a great deal. It reveals that he has
achieved a sense of purpose. He recognizes that "love" as a value surpasses
"my love" and sustains him as a writer and as a man. What is more, he
reaffirms his conscious choice; the premise cannot be logically proved, but
for him there is no alternative. The couplet, then, is a statement of the
faith on which the speaker is willing to stake his very being. He is scarcely
a minister officiating over the "marriage of true minds" but a participant
anxious to get on with the ceremony.

If the marriage metaphor seems obtrusive, an exact, situational meaning need not be ascribed to it. By explaining what love is and is not, the
speaker clarifies his own understanding and his readers'. That in itself is an
intellectual union, so that the marriage metaphor may well connote the act
of reading that these sonnets so often call attention to. For example, sonnet 23 has already been mentioned: "O learn to read what silent love hath
writ." In other sonnets, such as 18, 55, and 81, the couplets also stress the
act of being read by the "eyes not yet created" of posterity. It could be
objected that 116 begins as it does because the speaker wishes to reprimand
the inconstant friend. A case can also be made for reading these lines as self-
defense, since sonnet 110, among others, registers his own inconstancy:
"Alas, 'tis true I have gone here and there."[19] Both of these interpretations
suffer from being narrowly dramatic; they limit the poem's frame of reference to its own microcosm. Shakespeare's sonnets often transcend themselves, peering out toward those future readers on whom the promise of
eternity depends. It is reasonable, then, to take the "marriage of true
minds" as an understanding in a general sense, and perhaps as the reading

18. "Poetic Styles in Shakespeare's *Sonnets,*" in Barbara Herrnstein, ed., *Discussions of
Shakespeare's Sonnets,* p. 109.

19. For the latter position, see Hilton Landry, "The Marriage of True Minds: Truth
and Error in Sonnet 116."

process itself, especially since the sonnet concludes with yet another reference to writing. Whether one attributes inconstancy to the speaker or to his friend is immaterial; both are clearly capable of it.

Filled with striking aphorisms and images, this sonnet has become an anthology piece. Yet its meaning inheres in the context, not merely in relation to the adjacent, contradicting poems, but even more in the speaker's psychological growth as recorded in his soliloquizing. Sonnet 105 failed to solve the tension between what love really is and what the speaker wishes it to be, whereas 116 makes more convincing claims for ideal constancy. One reason for its success, besides the varied metaphors, is the use of negative definitions that constitute an experiential test by which to recognize false, changing love. The couplet, by allowing for the speaker's fallibility, also renders the argument more credible. The concession "if this be error," while undermining the certainty of his previous, uncompromising statements, leads to a fuller realization that this is the only truth about love that the speaker can imagine. The question raised here, in light of his ironic attitudes elsewhere, is why he now insists so forcefully on love as an absolute, unchanging value.

Perhaps it is inevitable that a mind so sensitive to the study of change in nature and in man should desire a respite from its dizzying sense of process. Despite its technical mastery, sonnet 116 does not differ fundamentally from 105; it, too, is focused on what the speaker against his better knowledge wants to believe. His abstract definition of love seems to be a projection of all that he is not and would like to be. That in turn may be another source for the sonnet's popularity. It reassures us by describing what we have heard and read about but probably never encountered, a perfectly ideal and constant love. In terms of the speaker's progression through soliloquy, this sonnet functions as a *credo,* reflecting only that part of his being that is compatible with a carefully rehearsed performance. There is something forced, almost shrill, in its repeated assertions, as if the speaker's real purpose in "speaking of" at this point were to convince himself.

Whether by chance or design, the final poem in this second triad of definitions is also the richest and most complex. After the sheer simplicity of 105 and the surface clarity of 116, sonnet 124 offers the most powerful restatement of the speaker's faith in ideal love. The sonnet does not utter grandiose claims but maps out an argument for constancy that is graphically refigured in its language:

> If my dear love were but the child of state,
> It might for fortune's bastard be unfathered,
> As subject to time's love, or time's hate,
> Weeds among weeds, or flow'rs with flowers gathered.

As in sonnet 116, the opening and closing lines mark the speaker's presence in the poem, while the "enclosed" lines appear to be objective. Again, he begins with what love is not but, because he emphasizes that strategy of negation throughout, avoids overstating his case. He is defining "my love," not love as an abstract universal, so his statements carry a more modest tone.

In its reference to "state" quatrain 1 shows that this discourse on love is firmly enclosed in the social world. The word denotes greatness as well as pomp, so that, even if this love is not the "child of state," it still exists in the context of the speaker's connection with someone who is his social superior. (The next sonnet will continue to argue that his love differs from mere service and the hope of preferment: "Were't ought to me I bore the canopy . . . ?") The repeated use of possessive forms, in this quatrain and throughout the sonnet, subtly calls attention to the question of affiliation: who owns love and has control over it? The speaker tells us it is "*my* dear love," neither "the child *of* state" nor "*fortune's* bastard," nor "subject to *time's* love or to time's hate." Quatrain 1 is difficult, nonetheless, because its ideas are so condensed; each line retains something of its predecessor but simultaneously alters the thought. The bond between lines 3 and 4, in particular, is unclear for lack of a transitional word, but the sense can be pieced together by paraphrasing the quatrain as a whole: "my love owes nothing to social consideration. If it did, it would be a false love, attendant on opportunism and willing to temporize by allying itself with contrary forces." The implication of a father-child relationship between the speaker and his love follows from his rejection of the three other paternities: state, time, and fortune. All of these are aspects of impermanence, whereas his love is constant. Quatrains 2–3 explicitly make that claim through two positive verbs, *was builded* and *alone stands.* These are set against five negative verbs: *It suffers not, nor falls, It fears not, nor grows, nor drowns.*

This central section of the poem requires less explication than the beginning or end. It is worth noting, however, that two dissimilar areas of imagery have been merged. These are the architectural, evoked by "builded," and the organic implied by "heat" and "showers." The speaker defines his love as an artifact, strongly constructed against the elements. Neither weed nor flower, it is impervious to the sun and rain. There is also a continuation of terms related to "state," as this love "fears not policy" but "stands hugely politic." Since "policy . . . that heretic" means Machiavellian plotting, a love that stands aloof from courtly factions and intrigue is finally more expedient and "politic." If we compare that description to the relatively extravagant image of 116, "it is an ever-fixed mark," sonnet 124 seems more concrete, securely grounded in the speaker's experience of social reality. His tendency to idealize love does not lead him to invent too many superlatives. He simply argues that his love avoids the extremes of servitude and rebellion:

> It suffers not in smiling pomp, nor falls
> Under the blow of thralled discontent. . . .

The couplet introduces new perplexities into this sonnet. The speaker is in need of external support; rather than swearing by his own art and all men's love, as he did in 116, he remains in the social world and evokes a dramatic courtroom scene:

> To this I witness call the fools of time,
> Which die for goodness, who have lived for crime.

The traditional gloss calls attention to the "eleventh hour repenters," those convicted of sedition, for whatever cause, who would often confess their real or imagined crimes prior to their execution.[20] That view is challenged by Gerald Hammond, who doubts that "such specificity is possible at the end of a sonnet so vague and wide ranging in reference" and sees "'fools of time' as a description of all men."[21] The problem here is that the speaker would thereby be accusing all mankind of living for crime and dying for goodness, an extreme view unwarranted by the sonnet as a whole, although certain others (notably 66) might be capable of that cynicism. A less drastic reading can be made if we heed an echo from the previous soliloquy:

> Love's not Time's fool, though rosy lips and cheeks
> Within his bending sickle's compass come.

20. See Palgrave (1865) and Lee (1907) cited in *Variorum*, 1:313–14.
21. *The Reader and Shakespeare's Young Man Sonnets*, p. 221. See also Mizener (1940) cited in *Variorum*, 1:314: "In general in Shakespeare everyone is in one way or another made a fool by Time."

To this we should add Hotspur's dying words in *Part One of Henry IV*: "But thought's the slave of life, and life death's fool." The phrase "the fools of time" therefore refers to much more than the eleventh-hour repenters, but it certainly does not involve all mankind. In sonnet 116, "time's fool" means a soulless, sensual love, caught up entirely in the natural world and eventually its victim. In Hotspur's bitter humor, "slave" and "fool" are interchangeable terms for what he is himself, the victim of a greater force. By invoking "the fools of time" at the end of 124, the speaker calls on all those inconstant lovers who should recognize that his love is greater than theirs. The "crime" they have lived for is not treason against the state but simply the "policy" criticized earlier in the sonnet. They need not "die" at the gallows but will have to supplicate themselves to "goodness" and divine love in their final prayers. This couplet may also be read as an attack on the inconsistent division between two types of love, the profane and natural against the sacred and supernatural. The sonnet has given the speaker's best definition of "my dear love" as a reflection of his own integrity, something that is present in the real world yet points beyond it.

Even in sonnet 124, Shakespeare's most persuasive definition of love, there is no doubt that certain aspects of his sonnet-speaker have been deliberately suppressed. Other sonnets make it clear that his actions are often at odds with his claims for constant love. That discrepancy is acknowledged most openly in sonnets 119 and 121, which do not attempt to define love as an abstraction located outside the speaker but focus more closely on his structure of values. Sonnet 119 contends that love can be strengthened by infidelity, whereas 121 does not mention love at all. The relation between these two poems is again that of a crude preliminary and a polished continuation. The former proclaims the same complacency that earlier sonnets (especially 42 and 63) had only hinted at, converting it to a plea for sympathy:

> What potions have I drunk of siren tears,
> Distilled from limbecks foul as hell within—
> Applying fears to hopes, and hopes to fears,
> Still losing when I saw myself to win!

The errors and fever to which the speaker willingly admits are a triumph of lust over love. Indeed, much of the poem's vocabulary foreshadows his impersonal indictment of lust in sonnet 129, "Th'expense of spirit in a waste of shame." He describes his prior self-deception as "losing when I saw myself to win." He also recognizes that his heart committed errors "whilst it hath thought itself so blessed never." Moreover, the balanced structure of "fears to hopes, and hopes to fears," like the interrelation of land and sea in 64, mirrors a process that is endlessly self-perpetuating. Yet all these faults are supposedly redeemed by the transition made in line 9:

> O benefit of ill, now I find true
> That better is by evil still made better.

A study of the poem's language will show that this paradox and its development are too facile to be convincing. The diction of the sestet is closely related to the "triangle" situation of poet, friend, and mistress, even though sonnet 119 is not explicitly part of that group. In particular, sonnet 144 is anticipated by "better," which suggests "the better spirit," while "ill" and "foul as hell" remind us of the mistress "coloured ill." The speaker's return "rebuked to my content" can be construed as a return to the youth, so that his love "grows fairer than at first." This paradox of a love that "is by evil still made better" is not simply an abstraction but alludes to the double plot that unites the sonnet sequence. The speaker insists that his encounter with evil, the "female evil" of 144, reinforces his original, ideal love. He therefore claims to "gain by ills thrice more than I have spent." The objection here is not to the immorality of his argument but to the sonnet's failure to make it valid in poetic terms. The confessional quality of lines 1–8 does not accord with the easy self-justification that follows. We come away from the sonnet unconvinced because its argument has been superficial. Any wrongdoing could likewise be excused as an incentive to virtue. In this instance, the speaker has not shown how evil leads to good or why the entire experience was necessary. He has given us no reason to take him at his word.

The critical problem raised by the speaker's ready wit, and his ironic perspective, is that on occasion it leads him to evade some of the complex issues that he deals with. In fact, the method of soliloquy may disappoint us whenever it lacks a sufficiently clear structure of ideas; it can become an ideal vehicle for rationalization. Whatever arguments cannot be used to influence others will suffice for the speaker to convince himself. Yet the final impression throughout the Fair Youth sequence is that the speaker consistently employs "speaking of" in order to pursue a set of values that will survive his profound awareness of inconstancy. Sonnet 121 exemplifies his fullest achievement of self-knowledge. It is a poem that has often been reduced to a single, prefabricated statement rather than recognized as an essay in self-discovery. Earlier critics read this sonnet as Shakespeare's self-defense, possibly responding to Puritan attacks on the theater.[22] Another view, advanced by G. Wilson Knight, adds that the defense is innovative in its morality and contains "some kind of beyond-good-and evil claim."[23] The centrality of sonnet 121, and its poetic effectiveness, was not challenged until Stephen Booth opined that the speaker sounds "smug, pretentious, and stupid."[24] Gerald Hammond extends that judgment further, describing the "speaker's state of mind as a combination of self-righteousness and self-pity." He adds, "As a possible final sonnet, it is both depressing and degrading . . . it smells of decay . . . a singularly barren poem."[25] It is not clear why these two commentators become so severely judgmental here—unless one shares their uncanny ability to see into "the reader's" mind. However, the critical issues surrounding this sonnet can be summarized by two simple questions: "What is the real subject matter of the poem?" and "What is the speaker's attitude toward his subject?" Any answer to the first question claiming that the sonnet "is about" a single theme—be it reputation, sexuality, or self-knowledge—can be dismissed as an oversimplification. All these themes do have a place in the sonnet, but none can rightly be called its comprehensive subject. But if we allow that the poem's subject may be defined as a process rather than as a product, then these thematic motifs can be collocated in a unifying framework. The intellectual substance of the sonnet should not be formulated in abstract, static terms but recognized as inseparable from the dynamic structure composed by the four sections. The mind of the speaker, manifesting itself in an intricate thought pattern, constitutes the irreducible subject matter of the poem. Such a statement could conceivably be applied to many of the soliloquies; here it is a required premise.

In most of the sonnets, there is little difficulty in isolating a central theme, such as destructive time or poetic immortality. When the speaker gives an extended contrast between his love and a summer's day, or when he constructs a series of images to illustrate his decline into death, we can readily apply the "theme and variations" method of analysis advocated by

22. See also Alden (1913) in *Variorum*, 1:314.
23. *The Mutual Flame: An Interpretation of Shakespeare's Sonnets*, p. 49.
24. *Shakespeare's Sonnets*, p. 410.
25. *Shakespeare's Young Man Sonnets*, pp. 193–94.

C. S. Lewis.[26] But in sonnet 121, no introduction of a main theme serves as the basis for variations. The opening line, " 'Tis better to be vile than vile esteemed," leads directly into the qualifying clause that completes the quatrain. For several reasons, this line cannot be read as the statement of a theme. The meaning of "vile" and the context in which it is to be understood have not yet been established. Nor do we know whether the speaker sincerely or ironically defends being vile. The opening line is a comparison between two unknowns, "to be vile" and "not to be," rather than an assertion whose meaning is self-evident. However, it launches a complex, unparaphrasable sequence of thought that cannot properly be compared to the rather trivial musical form of "theme and variations." A more appropriate analogy for the form of this sonnet in which several poetic themes are simultaneously developed, like voices in the Elizabethan "divided music," is the fugue. The sonnet is not "about" any single theme but derives its polyphonic effect from the continuous interplay of stated and implied ideas.

The second basic question about sonnet 121 follows logically from the first. If the speaker's state of mind provides the subject matter, his attitude toward that subject becomes synonymous with self-consciousness. The speaking "I" who draws forth his themes by introspection also shapes their meaning through his diction, imagery, and syntax. Thematic and tonal functions overlap so extensively that the evaluation of one will depend of the interpretation of the other. These interrelations of thought, structure, and tone can be illustrated by a comparative analysis of the four strophes. The three quatrains and the couplet are sharply demarcated not only by punctuation and pivot words but also by their contrasting textures. Since the sonnet places these discrete sections in a coordinating sequence, it is impossible to comprehend the first line fully until all the others, especially the couplet, have been considered.

The difficulty of the first quatrain derives from its being a complex sentence whose concluding clause precedes the conditional. This sequence reverses the when/then pattern that is used so successfully elsewhere in the sonnets, which usually leads to the conclusion by a series of conditionals: When/when/when/then. The inverted form that begins sonnet 121 is far more challenging. It surprises the reader, intensifying his response to the unconventional sentiment. When the opening line is shifted back to its

26. *English Literature in the Sixteenth Century,* pp. 506–8.

logical place, the entire stanza becomes more intelligible than any paraphrase:

> (2) When not to be receives reproach of being,
> (3) And the just pleasure lost, which is so deemed,
> (4) Not by our feeling but by others' seeing,
> (1) [Then] 'tis better to be vile than vile esteemed.

This rearrangement falls far short of the original because it makes the logical and syntactic patterns coincide. Its purpose is to show that the first line is neither a statement of fact nor a wished for ideal but a hypothetical conclusion. So long as innocence ("not to be") is groundlessly accused and "the just pleasure" (either of freedom or of reputation) has been destroyed, the reality of being vile is to be preferred over the false accusation. But if these conditions do not exist, and the poem never terms them permanent or universal, the conclusion will be groundless. The speaker never affirms the value or the attraction of being vile. He presents that mode of being as the unwanted result of evil circumstance. Thus the worst consequence of being misjudged is that it encourages living up to an undeserved reputation. The language of this argument is perfectly impersonal and unimpassioned. The speaker does not refer to himself in the entire quatrain; even the phrase "our feeling," as balanced against "others' seeing," is general rather than personal.

In the second quatrain the "I" discloses that this thought-process reflects his own situation. The process itself has accelerated; instead of a complex four-line sentence the speaker presents a pair of two-line questions parallel in form and nearly synonymous in their content:

> For why should others' false adulterate eyes
> Give salutation to my sportive blood?
> Or on my frailties why are frailer spies,
> Which in their wills count bad what I think good?

By these unambiguous questions one is guided to a better understanding of the opening quatrain. For example, the meaning of "vile" is clarified by the context of closely related adjectives: *false, adulterate, sportive, frailer.* Similarly, "vile esteemed" is glossed by "count bad what I think good." But the main function of this quatrain is to elaborate the conditions described in lines 2–4. The conditional clause of line 2, "When not to be receives reproach of being," was an objective description. It presented an evident injustice without explaining causes and effects. But the subjective, interrogative mood of the second quatrain allows the speaker to argue that the "reproach" comes from those who ascribe their own flaws to him. He withdraws from the perfect innocence of "not to be" by admitting his "frailties" and "sportive blood." This confession is counterpoised by his claim that the detractors are worse than he. Their "false adulterate eyes" exceed his merely "sportive" inclination; they are "frailer spies" whose own passions ("wills") lead them to condemn his normal frailty. The sense of the second line has now been qualified to "When not to be [excessively frail or vile] receives reproach of being."

A similar development is conferred by quatrain 2 upon lines 3–4 of the preceding quatrain. The neutral "others' seeing" yields to the highly charged "others' false adulterate eyes," while the impersonal "our feeling" is replaced by "my sportive blood." Finally, the ambiguous "just pleasure lost" receives an intensification, if not a resolution. If the "pleasure" is that of a good reputation, the two rhetorical questions of quatrain 2 must be read as protesting biased judgment but not the necessity of being evaluated by others. If "pleasure" refers to the gratification of allegedly "vile" behavior, a plausible case could still be made for its reinforcement here. The speaker's resentment would be directed against an inflexible system of values that condemns him without understanding.

What has been observed so far in the first eight lines is nothing like the embellishment of a theme through a set of variations. Instead, the continuity derives from the gradual crystallizing of the speaker's frame of reference. From an appraisal of social judgments he moves to a well-defined contrast between his own and others' moral qualities. This progression is completed in the third quatrain, where the gap between "I" and "they" is extended furthest:

> No, I am that I am, and they that level
> At my abuses reckon up their own;
> I may be straight though they themselves be bevel.
> By their rank thoughts my deeds must not be shown . . .

The mood is indicative, resolving the suspended state of mind that governed the previous conditionals and interrogatives. Having described a prevailing condition, having questioned its justice, the speaker now reveals his defiance. His "no" emphatically answers the two rhetorical questions and rejects corrupt jurisdiction. The interjection also prepares the way for the shortest complete statement in the poem: "I am that I am." This utterance brings the process of syntactic acceleration to its climax. Sentence length has been reduced from four lines to two lines to six words. Here, at the traditional *volta,* the speaker's rising self-confidence is marked by his most incisive statement. "I am that I am" is a sentence whose formal symmetry reflects its semantic obscurity. However, its location within the "I/they" contrast provides a clue to its meaning. In the next sentence, "they" becomes the subject of two transitive verbs rather than of "to be." Their actions are self-defeating since they "level at" one object only to "reckon up" another. Such confusion is antithetical to the speaker's self-sufficiency.

Two more antitheses are enclosed in lines 11–12. Both are complete statements, although the latter is joined to the couplet. The texture of quatrain 3 is therefore distinguished by the relative brevity of its statements and the absence of syntactic coordination. The then/when and for/or constructions that organize the first two quatrains have no equivalents, resulting in a disjointedness that corresponds to the speaker's increasingly emotional tone. The rhymes in this quatrain are not grammatical, further evidence of increasing tension; both "level/bevel" and "own/shown" combine a verb with a modifier. The former, being the only feminine rhyme in the sonnet, adds to the irregularity of the quatrain. A far greater degree of coherence had been imposed on the first quatrain by its perfectly grammatical rhymes, "esteemed/deemed" and "being/seeing," where the first rhyme presents a semantic equivalence as well as an identical part of speech. The second quatrain contains less uniformity than the first, since "eyes/spies" is a grammatical rhyme with semantic affinity while "blood/good" is a purely auditory rhyme. Above all, the synthetic parallelism of the two questions intensifies the speaker's feelings and anticipates his self-disclosure in line 9.

Despite its parataxis, the third quatrain remains highly coherent in its thought. The inner organization results from the repeated use of antithesis, a figure that pervades the entire sonnet. The antithetical pattern in sonnet 121 can be summarized as follows:

(1) to be vile	vile esteemed
(2) not to be	being
(4) by our feeling	by others' seeing
(5) others' false adulterate eyes	————
(6) ————	my sporting blood
(7) my frailties	frailer spies

(8) Which . . . count bad	I think good
(10) my abuses	their own
(11) I may be straight	they themselves be bevel
(12) their rank thoughts	my deeds

The antithesis becomes personal in the second and third quatrains. In the opening lines the contrast is between abstract states of mind, while the "our/others'" contrast in the fourth line anticipates the extended disjunction of "I" and "they" in lines 5–12. This disjunction gains intensity by reiteration while the contrasts themselves become more pointed. In line 7, "I" and "they" are distinguished in comparative terms only. The difference between "frailties" and "frailer spies" is of degree rather than kind, continuing the parallel between "false adulterate eyes" and "sportive blood." Comparison gives way to contrast in line 8, but the opposition is purely intellectual and contains no moral judgment. The speaker has not stated whether it is better to "count bad" or "think good," although the connotations make his preference clear. The decisive turn comes in the ninth line where, in place of an antithesis, he declares his integrity in terms of an inner consistency. In the next three lines, the "I/they" contrast is reiterated, each time conveying an explicitly moral judgment. Line 11, with its traditional contrast of the straight and the crooked, makes the speaker's most direct claim for moral superiority. Lines 10 and 12 imply that "my abuses" are fewer, or less flagrant, than "their own" and that "my deeds" differ qualitatively from "their rank thoughts." These three lines bring the disjunction of "I" and "they" to its climax.

At the core of sonnet 121 lies a series of carefully developed antitheses. They are personalized in the two inner strophes and come to their focus at the exact turning point of the sonnet—the question and answer of lines 8–9. Antithesis, as Renaissance rhetoricians defined it, is a figure "of thought" and "of words." To a degree unmatched by other figures, it unites *res* and *verba,* so that the sonnet's sustained use of antithesis must have a thematic significance. The key to that significance, I believe, lies in the fact that antithesis is a traditionally moral structure. In setting forth a sharp contrast, it usually effects an evaluation of the two opposing terms. Thus many of the most basic antitheses, such as light/dark and up/down, have acquired moral connotations. The antithetical structure, therefore, seems to work against Wilson Knight's interpretation, which finds direct expression of the poet's independent and somewhat ambiguous morality. The obvious objection is historical: his antinomian Shakespeare seems to be drawn from nineteenth-century thought. The best reflection of these claims is the logical structure of the sonnet. Ambiguity, however central to romantic morality and modern criticism, has no place there. Instead, the sonnet contains a series of statements linked to nonambiguous implications. The poetry is of suggestion no less than of statement, but enough statements are present to make the implications clear. The very language of sonnet 121 is so heavily saturated with disjunctive terms (and halves of antithetical pairs) that it must be regarded as unfit for expressing any morality "beyond good and evil." The old terminology is not used in a new way; the old categories are not transcended. The only statement in which moral judgment has not been absolutely fixed would seem to be line 11: "I may be straight though they themselves be bevel." Yet the meaning of "may be" should be recognized as "may still be" or "am allowed to be" rather than "can possibly be." It is improbable that a speaker who has denounced his enemies in unequivocal terms, who now represents them as undoubtedly crooked, would cast doubt on his own innocence. What he means by "I may be straight" is that his morality, in spite of allegations to the contrary, is unimpaired.

For rhetorical reasons, the speaker is reluctant to protest too much in his own behalf. He employs a technique by which his virtue seems to speak for itself. An analysis of the I/they contrast in lines 5–14 shows that the speaker's emphasis falls on the hated contraries by which he is defined. Perhaps the most telling contrast involves the verbs. The "I" predicates only two: "to be" in lines 9 and 11 and "think" in line 8. By twice using the verb of identity, the speaker stresses but does not describe his mode of being. This reluctance to evaluate himself also shows in the relative absence of modifiers for the "I." The adjectives used to describe him ("sportive" and "straight") do not agree in their meaning, whereas the five adjectives describing the "they" are virtually synonymous. The speaker's only action is to favorably construe his own deeds and those of other men. He gives this benefit of the doubt because of the precise antithesis between "think good" and the evil thinking that is attributed to the "they." The verbs "count bad" and "level at" are explicit signs of evil intention. In addition, "give salutation" with its implied equality in sin, "reckon up" [abuses] and "maintain" [evil] all represent the essential act of false imputation. If the speaker has gone beyond the narrow good, there is no sign that his enemies have transcended evil! The continuous use of familiar moral terms for the description of evil gives evidence that the traditional dichotomy has been retained. The speaker who is the antithesis of conventional evil must also be good in the conventional sense. A further and no less central implication lies in the connection between being and thinking. Those who are evil themselves find it necessary "in their wills" to accuse others. They illustrate Hamlet's dictum that "reason panders will." In contrast, although the speaker is unwilling to proclaim his own virtue, he implies it in unequivocal terms. For if those who think evil are evil, then the converse holds no less true: he who "thinks good" must *be* good.

In sonnet 121 an uncompromising series of contrasts between the explicitly bad and the implicitly good establishes a moral outlook that contains no innovation of values. The speaker admits that his "blood," "frailties," and "abuses" are sinful in the strictest sense. He argues that imperfection should not be equated with corruption and constructs the antithesis of "I" and "they" to make this distinction clear. The "frailer spies," whose "eyes," "wills," and "thoughts" tend toward the imputation of "general evil" or "badness," cannot rightly judge his "deeds." As the sonnets prior to 121 remind us, the speaker has sacrificed his good name for the approbation of his beloved. In 112 he is indifferent to "vulgar scandal . . . So you o'ergreen my bad, my good allow." But the only presiding judge in 121 is the reader himself. It is appropriate that a sonnet dealing with the question of reputation (or the image of the self in others) should depend so heavily on the reader's imputation of its meaning. Reconstructing the speaker's meaning on the basis of what is said and suggested, the reader is in a position comparable to that of the "spies." Since it is assumed that he will judge fairly, the reader finds himself placed on one side of an implied antithesis. Just as the speaker is contrasted to others as a moral agent, the reader is contrasted to others as an arbiter of moral actions.

The crucial appeal to the reader's judgment comes in the couplet and its opposition to the preceding lines. Enhancing the contrast between "I" and "they," the couplet is restricted to the latter and functions as a logical corollary:

> Unless this general evil they maintain—
> All men are bad and in their badness reign.

Hilton Landry points out that the last line gives a "preposterous antithesis of [the] traditional view of man's nature." He adds, "Since it is unthinkable that the poet's slanderers could actually maintain such a generalization, it serves to destroy the case against him by reducing their position to the absurd."[27] Somewhat similarly, Stephen Booth observes, "The couplets of 117 and 121 are general contradictions of the premises upon which the poems have progressed."[28] Neither critic notices that the "traditional view" (or the premise) contradicted by the couplet does not ever appear in the poem. The couplet implies its own contrary; it is the final and most revealing example of the speaker's technique of suggestion. The use of antithesis to stress this implication culminates in another process that has operated throughout sonnet 121. Moreover, the absence of the "I" establishes a definite correlation between this last strophe and the first. There, too, the consequences of an unwanted premise were explored in an impersonal manner. The *polyptoton* of "bad/badness" corresponds to the repetition of "vile" in the opening line. If bad men reign in a world of universal evil, then good men must become either vile or vile esteemed. The circularity of structure, created by the couplet as the coda or recapitulation of the fugue, imparts new meaning to the first four lines. The conditional clauses in lines 2–4 can be equated with the "general evil" that "all men are bad." Since this rule of universal corruption can admit no exceptions, it requires the vilification of all who are not vile. The "just pleasure lost" in line 3 must refer therefore to the loss of good name rather than to forbidden physical or psychological gratification. Presumably, a true epicure would be undeterred by public criticism. As sonnet 70 suggests, such criticism can serve to enhance one's pleasure: "For slander's mark was ever yet the fair, / The ornament of beauty is suspect." Since the speaker refrains from any explicit transvaluation of morality, there is no reason to assume that he here approves of forbidden pleasure and calls it "just."

Landry's objection to this reading is less than convincing: "How can slander deprive a man of the pleasure of a good conscience?"[29] Yet he gives a list of Renaissance authorities testifying to the importance of reputation to one's well-being. For that matter, C. Knox Pooler had made the meaning clear: "slander deprives a man of the second of the two natural rewards of virtue, viz., a good conscience and public approbation."[30] To this compare Landry's reading of quatrain 1: "It is better to be evil than to be judged evil when we receive this disgrace without deserving it and even lose, by

27. *Interpretations in Shakespeare's Sonnets,* p. 95.

28. *An Essay on Shakespeare's Sonnets,* p. 46.

29. *Interpretations,* p. 91.

30. C. Knox Pooler, ed., *The Works of Shakespeare: Sonnets,* p. 116. Cited by Landry, *Interpretations,* p. 90.

not experiencing or feeling it, what is considered to be the appropriate or rightful pleasure in the view of others who slander us."[31] Credulity is taxed here by the translation of "lost" into "lose, by not experiencing or feeling." Nor is it apparent what the lost pleasure really is: "what is considered to be the appropriate or rightful pleasure in the view of others who slander us." Again, the loss of pleasure that is only "just . . . in the view of others" can hardly explain the writing of a sonnet, but the antithesis of good and evil, and the attempt of slander to confuse them, is a weightier matter. Any paraphrase introducing moral relativism works against the sonnet's own movement, toward clarity of definition.

Rather than paraphrase, we can indicate the sonnet's range of meanings by outlining its development of the speaker's thought. The first quatrain contains a general, impersonal description of an evil-thinking environment. In violation of the logical order, this description starts with the speaker's hypothetical conclusion: in such an environment, evil fares better than innocence. The second quatrain effects a transition from the abstract to the personal. The two rhetorical questions ask whether such an environment, established by the speaker's inferiors, has any reason for being. The third quatrain is decisive in its personal and closely reasoned rejection of those who reveal their own sins by censuring others. As a corollary, the couplet adds that universal evil is an untenable assumption for the management of human affairs. It is strongly implied that the converse of this assumption should be accepted.

This rough outline substantiates the initial description of sonnet 121 as an unparaphrasable process of ideas and implications in which meaning cannot be dissociated from structure. The sonnet could also be described as a series of enigmatic variations on a hidden theme. However, as the comments of Landry and Booth indicate, any approach to a single summary statement of the theme must be based on the implied converse of the last line: "All men are good and in their virtue reign." The speaker has rested his self-defense and his counterattack on this unstated postulate. The much-debated "I am that I am" can best be understood as a particular application of this general rule. Any man who is truly himself will realize the potential virtue that all men share. If such a statement sounds like a modern plea for selfhood or authenticity, the orthodox formulation by Sir John Davies should be heard instead:

31. *Interpretations*, p. 89.

But whoso makes a mirror of his mind,
And doth with patience view himself therein,
His Soul's eternity shall clearly find,
Though the other beauties be defaced with sin.[32]

Through the carefully wrought structure of sonnet 121, the speaker mirrors at least one aspect of his mind. His statement of identity is central to his argument, since the "law of identity" is one of the three traditional laws of logic that are combined in the sonnet. It follows the "law of contraries" which is applied in the second quatrain and precedes the "law of the excluded middle" which stands between the couplet and its implied converse. Thus the first rule ("A is not B") dissociates the speaker from evildoers; the second ("A is A") stresses his own integrity, and the third ("B is either A or Not-A") underlies his closing statement that he and all men must be classed either as evil (a self-fulfilling judgment) or as good. There is no middle ground.

That "I am that I am" is a quotation of Exodus 3:14 is neither as revealing nor as irrelevant as various critics have thought. It is inconceivable, in the light of the subtle allusions contained in his plays, that Shakespeare could have written this sentence without being aware of its biblical counterpart. Hyder Rollins cites two earlier Elizabethan uses of this sentence, both of them direct quotations of Exodus.[33] In Lyly's *Eupheus,* the hero converts a remarkably agreeable atheist by reminding him, "When Moses desired of God to know what hee should name him to the children of Israell, hee aunswered, thou shalte saye, I am that I am. Agayne, hee that is hath sent mee vnto you." Brian Melbancke's *Philotimus* refers again to God "whose name is in Scripture, I am that I am." Even the poem by Wyatt that Landry cites as "a partial analogy" is by no means contradictory to Exodus: "I am as I am so wil I be."[34] This refrain establishes the speaker's personal integrity on the human level, corresponding to the unity of the divine being. There is nothing daring or blasphemous about such a correspondence. The speaker claims for himself only the qualities of honesty and temperance. However, a spirit of Stoic self-sufficiency underlies his attitude. Having stated his good intentions, he displays indifference to those that think otherwise. *Honi soit qui mal y pense* [Evil to him that evil

---

32. *Nosce Teipsum,* in *The Poems of Sir John Davies,* p. 167.
33. *Variorum,* 1:306.
34. *Interpretations,* pp. 92–93.

thinks] might well serve as the motto to this poem, especially in its awareness that slander is degrading to those who commit it:

> Yet some there be that take delight
> To judge folkes thought for envye and spight,
> But whyther theye judge me wrong or right,
> I am as I am and so do I wright.

Throughout the poem, Wyatt's speaker explicitly asserts his own virtue as opposed to the sins of other men:

> I lede my lif indifferentelye,
> I mean no thing but honestelie . . .
> Bothe mirthe and sadnes I doo refraine,
> and vse the meane sins folkes woll fayne.

Yet, as in sonnet 121, a strong declaration of constancy in the face of slander is sufficient evidence of virtue. The connection between righteousness and the repudiation of slander becomes even more obvious in William Teshe's "Verses on the Order of the Garter." Here Elizabeth I speaks to request divine aid against detractors:

> "Shame to the mynde that meanes" (Quod shee) "amisse,"
> whereby was seene her mynde did meane no ill:
> 'Lo! thus, my Lordes, our verdict geuen vp is,
> lett them do well that looke for our goodwill,
> A quj mal pense a luy tout honj Soit;
> and for myselfe, Mon Dieu *et* seul mon droit.
>
> "Highe God" (*quod* shee) "be alwayes our right hand,
> and thinck on me, semper eadem, still.
> He is the staye on which our harte shall stand,
> our stronge defence from those that thincke vs ill;
> where wronge makes warre, we must with patience arme:
> Tyme trieth truthe, good myndes can meane no harme."[35]

The principle plainly demonstrated by Wyatt and Teshe underlies Shakespeare's sonnet and lends it a precise moral sense. All three poems demonstrate that the denunciation of evil in absolute terms requires the existence of an absolute good. Sonnet 121 offers the most subtle expression of a set of ideas whose immediate origin is proverbial and whose ultimate

35. F. J. Furnivall and W. R. Morfill, eds., *Ballads from Manuscript,* 2:68.

source is the Bible. Teshe is, of course, the crudest of the three poets in expressing dependence on divine virtue. Wyatt refers to God only in passing:

> Who judgith well, well god him sende:
> Who judgith evil, god theim amende.

Yet his poem is no less pious than his two letters exhorting his son to take the path of virtue: "if you wil seme honist, be honist, or els seame as you are. Seke not the name without the thing . . . . get the thing and the othir must of necessite folow as the shadow foloweth the thing that it is of."[36] Here again good name is defined as the direct reward of virtue; it is better to be honest than honest esteemed. In the just world that this letter assumes, "seeming" follows "being" like a shadow. But in the unjust world, confronted in Wyatt's song and Shakespeare's sonnet, there must be an unbridgeable gap between "our feeling" and "others' seeing."

The just man wrongfully accused can appeal to divine protection, as Elizabeth does in the poem by Teshe. He can also be consoled by the inferior nature of his adversaries. After Elizabeth quotes the motto of the Order of the Garter, Teshe comments that this protestation is itself a proof of innocence: "whereby was seene her mynde did meane no ill." The motto itself—"Shame / evil to him who shame / evil thinks"—was proverbial by Shakespeare's time.[37] Closely related in significance, another proverb is embedded in the last line: "good myndes can mean no harm."[38] Both sayings illustrate the central assumption that as man is, so he sees. The evil man ascribes evil to others; the good man finds good. The same assumption is made in the poems of Wyatt and Shakespeare, though far more explicitly in the former.

The most likely biblical source for this attitude appears to be Titus 1:5, "Vnto the pure, are all things pure."[39] This indebtedness, combined with additional biblical parallels in sonnet 121, suggests that the echoing of Exodus 3:14 is scarcely accidental. The two examples of figurative lan-

36. *The Collected Poems of Thomas Wyatt*, ed., Kenneth Muir, pp. 154–55.

37. M. P. Tilley, *A Dictionary of the Proverbs in England in the Sixteenth and Seventeenth Centuries*, S 277.

38. Ibid., G 312, "Good finds good."

39. Compare Psalm 18:21, "With the pure thou wilt shewe thy self pure and with the frowarde thou wilt shewe thy self froward." All biblical quotations in the text are from the Geneva Bible.

guage in this sonnet both have strong biblical associations. The contrast between "straight" and "bevel" as well as the "false adulterate eyes" evoke two of the most recurrent images in the Bible.[40] In addition to its imagery, the sonnet's evaluative terms are of distinct biblical origin. The word *vile*, which in Latin means both "cheap" and "base," acquires much of its emotive force as the translation of several Hebrew words that describe extreme immortality. The illusory idea of universal evil, "All men are bad and in their badness reign," is mentioned and dismissed in Psalm 116:11, "I said in my feare, All men are lyers." The verb *reign*, which concludes the sonnet, brings unmistakable biblical connotations.[41] Furthermore, the situation described in the sonnet is remarkably similar to that of the so-called persecution psalms. The speaker, finding himself maligned, reaffirms his virtue and calls for effective justice.[42] Shakespeare's speaker is not far removed in spirit from the Psalmist in Psalm 15:4 "In whose eyes a vile persone is contemned."

The all-important difference is that sonnet 121 has no equivalent to the Psalm's direct appeal for divine assistance. Such an appeal, retained fully by Teshe and more casually by Wyatt, forms no distinct part of the sonnet but is strongly suggested by the whole. Its balanced, antithetical structure is itself a central feature of biblical style, especially prominent in the Psalms; its imagery, its diction, and its concern with moral judgment all show a marked biblical influence, indicating that Shakespeare's purpose was not to challenge traditional morality but to present his sonnet-speaker favorably in its light. He employs "speaking of" as the mode of address because sonnet 121 continues and fulfills the kind of introspection developed in sonnets 63–66. The argument that this sonnet is addressed specifically to the Puritans therefore has no structural, let alone historical, evidence; it imposes an unjustified restriction on the poem's meaning. However, to say that this sonnet replies to the evil-thinking "world" has all the disadvantages of generalization. The above analysis has stressed the importance of self-address and shown how soliloquy enables the speaker to move toward a dramatic discovery of his own virtue after an initially cautious response to evil. This movement, in the absence of an auditor and of any simply stated theme, constitutes the subject matter of the sonnet, while the speaker's

40. For "crooked," see Psalms 101:3–4 and 125:5. For eye-imagery related to moral quality, see Psalms 18:28 and 19:9.

41. Landry, *Interpretations*, p. 94, cites Romans 5:17, 21 and 6:12.

42. See Psalms 3, 4, 5, 7, 11, 12, 13, and 14.

increasingly confident tone and his use of biblical diction provide the reader with reliable guides to his meaning.

Of the many possible glosses to the sonnet that can be drawn from Shakespeare's plays, the most fitting would seem to be Albany's words to Goneril: "Wisdom and goodness to the vild seem vild; / Filths savor but themselves" (*King Lear*, 3.2.38–39). As in the opening line of sonnet 121, the repetition of "vild" as noun and adjective exposes the circularity by which evil justifies itself. Albany at this point makes a crucial realization of the gap between good and evil. By repudiating Goneril, he asserts himself as a man and reaffirms his moral nature. Both personae, the lyric and the dramatic, thus achieve self-discovery through the wider recognition of moral law.

3 Dialogue Sonnets

> At the height of being in love the boundary between ego and object threatens to melt away. Against all the evidence of his senses, a man who is in love declares that "I" and "you" are one, and is prepared to behave as if it were fact.
>
> —Sigmund Freud,
> *Civilization and Its Discontents*

The soliloquies discussed in the previous chapter represent only one of the four possible modes of address. Based on the interaction of speaker and auditor, these modes offer a means of classifying Shakespeare's sonnets, a method that avoids the random factor of thematic grouping and does not rely on the 1609 numbering. These four modes together compose a single progression from anonymity to intimacy. The first mode is entirely impersonal, inasmuch as it excludes both "I" and "thou" pronouns while permitting only those of the third person. It presents poetic themes and imagery in their most abstract form. The second mode admits "thou" but not "I," so that the central themes are closely linked to the person who is being addressed. Then soliloquy, as the third mode in this progression, allows the first person but not the second. As we have seen, it concentrates on the clearly defined figure of the "I" whose thoughts and feelings it articulates. Finally, dialogue dissolves the soliloquy situation by incorporating both "I" and "thou." This fourth mode gives the fullest and most dramatic expression of thematic material by providing a framework in which speaker and auditor can fully interact.

I. Four Modes of Address

When the sonnets are divided according to these four modes, we obtain four groups of poems that form a corresponding progression in order of increasing size and importance. Group one consists of only five poems—5, 67, 68, 94, and 129—in which an anonymous speaker addresses an unspecified audience. There is no inherently dramatic element in these poems and no sense of dialogue. They may be read as soliloquies only if a dramatic scene is artificially imposed, for the tonal quality of these poems is discursive, not dramatic. The speaker discourses in general terms on time, self-control, and lust in sonnets 5, 94, and 129. He ponders the character of a specific "he" in sonnets 67 and 68, which acquire a slightly more pointed quality. Yet the fact remains that explicitly dramatic elements are missing here, as in all five sonnets. A deliberately wide range is an important component of each poem's meaning. The ideas, unrestricted by any direct reference to the speaker and auditor, loom larger and less mediated than would otherwise be possible. Their relation to the surrounding context is one of detachment or withdrawal; the speaker who has been praising or complaining suddenly disappears. Sonnet 5, for example, presents a rather cryptic discussion of flowers whose sweet odor is preserved by distillation, so that they "leese but their show, their substance still lives sweet." The poem provides no clue by which its imagery can be decoded; were it not for the enveloping context of procreation, it might remain impenetrable. However, given the insistent refrain on "breed" in adjacent poems, its reticence comes as a welcome modulation.

A more intricate example of impersonal withdrawal occurs in sonnet 94. This sonnet, precisely because of its lack of a personal focus, has inspired great quantities of redundant controversy. Rather than revisit those heavily traveled roads, suffice it to say that the text contains a subtle blend of feelings that are not only mixed but also intertwined beyond all hope of separation. The speaker begins by setting forth a group or type of persons:

> They that have pow'r to hurt, and will do none,
> That do not do the thing they most do show.

He praises such persons for being "unmoved, cold, and to temptation slow," after apparently criticizing them for "moving others" while being "themselves as stone." Studying sonnets 90-96 in order to define a context does not clarify the ambiguity that is built into 94. Yet the sonnet is in many ways quite a representative one. It clearly reflects the capacity for reconciling contrarieties that is a basic component of the speaker's ironic attitude. When we consider that Shakespeare's sonnets were probably not intended for publication in their present form, that according to Francis Meres they circulated "among his private friends," another advantage of the impersonal mode appears. It avoids identifying and addressing people too powerful to be criticized, although it drops some tantalizing hints. An informed readership would enjoy being riddled, while the poet could not be accused of slandering anyone. That is the strategy writers have often used when confronted with possible reprisal.

Sonnets 67 and 68 are impersonal exercises that perform one of the speaker's favorite activities, excusing the inexcusable. They begin with the complaint, "Ah wherefore with infection should he live," yet each of them concludes with unqualified praise. The first sonnet finds that the person described is retained by nature "to show what wealth she had, / In days long since, before these last so bad." The second amplifies that point, calling him a "map . . . to show false art what beauty was of yore." Instead of mixing contrary judgments, these sonnets move through the entire gamut of evaluation, shifting from one polarized attitude to its opposite. Impersonality functions as a smokescreen; we are ignorant of "his" identity and we do not know whose strangely inconsistent opinions about him these are. Although some of the impersonal poems have been extolled as dramatic, it seems more reasonable to treat them as anomalies.[1] They lack the intrinsically dramatic element that is so central to these sonnets.

The second mode of address, by admitting "thou" or "you" while excluding "I," has taken the first small step away from impersonality. This mode can be termed "self-effacing" because the speaker seems oblivious of his own existence while lavishing all his attention on the auditor. Not surprisingly, we find much of the Procreation group written in this mode: nine of those first seventeen sonnets are self-effacing, while only eight more examples of this mode are distributed throughout the 1609 quarto. No less significant is the complete absence of the self-effacing mode from the Dark Lady sonnets, 127–54. The reason for such a pattern of distribution is clear; this mode of "thou" without "I" implies an unqualified respect for the auditor; it constitutes an act of deference. Throughout this group, the subject matter or "it" gains meaning by its connection with the "thou." For example, in sonnet 53 the "you" becomes the main subject. This sonnet begins with a direct question that might serve as motto to the entire group: "What is your substance, whereof are you made?" In the hyperbolic description that follows, the auditor is termed the source of all beauty. Elsewhere, however, he is praised by conjunction with other significant themes: poetry in sonnets 55 and 84; the social world in 69, 70, and 95; absence in 56; and the writing of a copybook in 77. These seven sonnets do not give full-length portraits of the "thou" but render particular aspects of him. The outer world of time, beauty, and death becomes embodied by the person addressed. At the same time, the speaker's absence precludes any chance of

1. See Giorgio Melchiori, *Shakespeare's Dramatic Meditations: An Experiment in Criticism,* for an extended study of the impersonal sonnets 94 and 129, as well as 121 and 146, which are not impersonal.

an inherently dramatic situation. If the impersonal sonnets of group one can be described as poems of unmediated subject matter, of "it/he/they" in isolation, the sonnets of the second group imply a "thou/it" relation. The speaker imposes a personal dimension on his themes by joining them to another person while excluding himself. That exclusion refers to more than the physical absence of "I" pronouns; the context of such poetry tends to reflect a social consensus rather than personal opinion.

Not only Shakespeare's sonnets but also those of his contemporaries show this use of the second mode. For example, in Samuel Daniel's *Delia,* sonnets 31 and 32 mark the only point at which this mode appears. The two poems, linked by a repeated line, address their auditor by name as Shakespeare's speaker never does: "Looke *Delia* how wee steeme the half-blowne Rose."[2] But the speaker's self-effacing stance is substantially the same since he refers to himself only once, within the community of "wee." His orientation toward the auditor is one that is often found in Shakespeare, as he tells her to observe the workings of time and to apply that lesson to herself. Perhaps it is the familiarity of this carpe diem theme that leads the poet to ignore himself completely, as if to acknowledge that the idea is not his own invention:

> No April can reuiue thy withred flowers,
> Whose blooming grace adornes thy glorie now:
> Swift speedy Time, feathred with flying howers,
> Dissolues the beautie of the fairest brow.

The poet's personality need not intervene in the virtually mythic encounter between his beloved and the forces of time. His presence lies behind the commands that are meant to guide her response in that encounter:

> O let not then such riches waste in vaine;
> But loue whilst that thou maist be lou'd againe.

Turning that last line into the first, he adds more imperatives in 32: "vse thy Summer smiles," "ioye thy Time," "thinke thy morning must haue night." Just as the first poem began with "wee," the second concludes with another appeal to consensus:

> Men doe not weigh the stalke for that it was,
> When once they finde her flowre, her glory passe.

2. *Poems and A Defence of Rhyme,* ed. A. C. Sprague, p. 26.

To this rule there can be no exceptions; the vanishing speaker has allied himself entirely with conventional wisdom, inducing his auditor to do the same.

Looking briefly beyond the Renaissance, we may cite Samuel Johnson's "A Short Song of Congratulation" as also illustrating the second mode of address. There is now a social disparity between the young heir being congratulated and his self-effacing adviser:

> Long-expected one and twenty
> Lingering year at last is flown,
> Pomp and Pleasure, Pride and Plenty,
> Great Sir John, are all your own.[3]

The ensuing set of instructions differs from Daniel's because it is unmistakably ironic. The speaker who urges Sir John to "bid the slaves of thrift farewell" is in effect warning him not to. He has the weight of moral authority and worldly experience on his side, so that these ironic counsels cannot be spurned as merely Johnson's or any man's:

> Wealth, Sir John, was made to wander,
> Let it wander as it will;
> See the jockey, see the pander,
> Bid them come, and take their fill.

The underlying received idea is that of the rake's progress, a convention that Sir John Lade went on to embody. Johnson does not introduce his own person or refer directly to himself; in that way, he keeps us from considering that the complex of ideas he outlines can be modified. The self-effacing mode of address thus implies a speaker who serves as the voice of disembodied wisdom and whose attention is focused entirely on that auditor.

Sonnet 77 is a poem in this mode, and one whose way of thinking is of considerable interest. In 1780, George Steevens made the observation that this was probably a dedicatory sonnet, inscribed in a new and empty copybook.[4] The references to "this book" and "these waste blanks" reinforce the notion that 77 is a sonnet uniquely centered on the writing process. In fact, its couplet invites us to approach the preceding twelve lines as a course of practical instruction:

3. *The Yale Edition of the Works of Samuel Johnson*, 6:307.
4. *Variorum*, 1:198.

> These offices, so oft as thou wilt look,
> Shall profit thee, and much enrich thy book.

If we ask what the "offices" are, we will at once recognize the very same method Shakespeare has been using in writing his sonnets. The empty notebook will be filled, we are told, if it is used together with two other implements, the mirror and the sundial. These are both devices that mark the passage of time, in personal and objective terms respectively:

> Thy glass will show thee how thy beauties wear,
> Thy dial how thy precious minutes waste.

Not surprisingly, in view of our reading of the sonnets, the disembodied voice of 77 assumes that the discovery of cosmic process (and of one's inclusion in it) marks the beginning of wisdom. That is the essential "learning" he seems to have made in his own writing of these poems, and he now passes it on through what seems to be a deliberate method. Quatrain 2 follows earlier sonnets in using the mirror to point out time's effects on a microcosmic level:

> The wrinkles which thy glass will truly show,
> Of mouthed graves will give thee memory.

In contrast, the sundial indicates a larger dimension of process in which personal concerns become insignificant:

> Thou by thy dial's shady stealth mayst know
> Time's thievish progress to eternity.

That he ignores the actual mechanics of writing reveals the speaker's confidence. Once time is perceived in all its finality, a series of appropriate ideas has somehow been produced and only awaits transcription to paper: "The vacant leaves thy mind's imprint will bear." A rather misleading analogy is thus established between the mirror and the dial, which cast simple patterns of light and shade, and the book, which contains so much more than a physical reflex. Printing had already served as a figure for procreation in sonnet 11, "thou shouldst print more, not let that copy die," and the link with that embedded idea becomes apparent when quatrain 3 in sonnet 77 envisions thought as progeny:

> Look what thy memory cannot contain,
> Commit to these waste blanks, and thou shalt find

> Those children nursed, delivered from thy brain,
> To take a new acquaintance of thy mind.

The act of writing corresponds to parturition, with the text as brainchild just as in the dedicatory letter to *Venus and Adonis*: "But if the first heir of my invention prove deformed, I shall be sorry it had so noble a godfather." An additional shade of meaning in the sonnet accords writing the function of a nurse weaning newborn ideas so that they can stand independently after being "delivered" from the writer's brain.

To extract a philosophy of composition from these lines would be rash, yet it seems that Shakespeare's speaker is advising the auditor to follow his own example by becoming aware of and reflecting on natural process. The progression of observation leading to commentary is the exact structure of sonnets 12 and 15, and in a looser sense also that of the 1609 quarto as it moves from scrutiny of time's effects in the Procreation group toward a series of dramatic responses. Since 77 is a self-effacing sonnet in which direct reference to the speaker is suppressed, the "I" pronouns can never appear. Nevertheless, the speaker presents himself indirectly by projecting his own attitudes and employing the ever-present "thou" as a vehicle for their expression. He supposes that the mind he addresses must operate like his, overflowing with more ideas than it can store and able to "commit" them instantly to paper. What marks this mode of address, therefore, is the imposition of one mind on another and the speaker's complete certainty of prediction. He is sure that writing can be generated by his method and that the exercise he prescribes can be repeated "so oft as thou wilt look." Any sense of dialogue is obviated by the underlying assumption of sameness, so that the "thou" has no existence except as a reflection of the speaker's experience. Instead of Samuel Johnson's worldly irony, we find an idiosyncratic set of instructions offered as if derived from a universal consensus.

Soliloquy, the third mode of address, inverts this self-effacing mode and serves (as we have seen) primarily as a vehicle of introspection. What needs to be recognized now is that this mode plays a relatively minor role in Shakespeare's sonnets, in distinct contrast to those of his contemporaries. Of the 1609 quarto's 154 sonnets, only 20 are soliloquies. That represents 14 percent of the total, whereas for Spenser and Daniel (following Petrarch's example) soliloquies had accounted for more than half. In the less Petrarchan sequences of Sidney and Drayton, this mode represents 36 and 22 percent respectively, a proportion that is still much higher than Shakespeare's. It is not soliloquy that characterizes the sonnets, though some of them are of great importance, but rather dialogue, which occurs in 112 of these poems. Shakespeare's preference for the "I/thou" mode, remarkable in itself, becomes even more so when compared to the practice of other Elizabethan sonneteers. The results of such a comparison are presented Table 2.

Table 2. A Comparison of Shakespeare's Use of Modes of Address with Those of Other Elizabethan Sonneteers

	I Impersonal	II Self- Effacing	III Soliloquy	IV Dialogue	Total
	("it")	("thou-it")	("I-it/he/she")	("I-thou")	
Spenser (*Amoretti*)	5	2	47	31	85
Sidney (*Astrophel and Stella*)	5	3	39	61	108
Daniel (*Delia*)	0	2	26	22	50
Drayton (*Idea*)	0	1	14	48	63
Shakespeare (sonnets)	5	17	20	112	154

These statistics would mean little if they did not reflect a major component in this reading of the sonnets. Each of the four modes of address sets up a quantitative scale by which different groups of poems can be sorted out and weighed against each other. But there are also qualitative features that characterize these modes because they assume different relationships between speaker and auditor, thus influencing the tone and the psychological perspective of each poem.

Sonnet 42 demonstrates the different qualities of dialogue and soliloquy because it moves, almost imperceptibly, from one mode to the other. The speaker begins by informing the youth that losing him will be a greater loss than losing the mistress: "That thou hast her, it is not all my grief. . . . That she hath thee is of my wailing chief." He then turns to both his loves in what seems to be an imaginary defense: "Loving offenders, thus I will excuse ye." Both have acted "for my sake," the friend loving the mistress "because thou know'st I love her" and the mistress "suff'ring my friend . . . to approve her." At this point, the speaker's explanation becomes entirely internalized;

he shifts from "speaking to" to "speaking of" after line 10; when he addresses his friend for the last time, he turns inward. Line 11 replaces "thee" with "my friend," so that lines 12–13 show us the speaker soliloquizing instead of continuing the dialogue:

> If I lose *thee,* my loss is my love's gain,
> And losing her, *my friend* hath found that loss;
> Both find each other, and I lose both twain,
> And both for my sake lay on me this cross. (Italics mine)

Rather than appealing to either party, he conveniently resolves his quandary through chop-logic. He continues quite appropriately in the mode of pure soliloquy because his train of thought could hardly be presented to either of his auditors:

> But here's the joy, my friend and I are one;
> Sweet flatt'ry, then she loves but me alone.

Thus a sonnet that began as an earnest appeal for understanding concludes with a private jest. The "sweet flatt'ry" of the last line is the speaker's own, since he knowingly deludes himself with the "joy" of spacious reasoning. The resolution stated in the couplet, he realizes, is inadequate. He has not fully expressed his grievances or attempted to correct their evil cause. Yet he is content to end his series of three "triangle" sonnets (40–42) by taking this evasive action.

We may expect the speaker to employ "speaking of" rather than "speaking to" when what he says is either too uncertain, too secret, or possibly too dangerous to be directly communicated to another. That tendency was exemplified by the soliloquies examined in the previous chapter. In contrast, dialogue follows from an active choice to involve his auditor as a co-partner in discourse. This does not mean that the person spoken to actually replies; there are no dialogues of the conventional sort. But a definite sense of presence is exerted by the "thou" within the poetic text. To use Martin Buber's terms, soliloquy reflects "the primal setting at a distance . . . the presupposition of the other." Dialogue, on the other hand, replaces distance through the movement of "entering into relation . . . the apperception of a being as a whole and as a unity." Whereas distance presents the world "only as an object . . . an aggregate of qualities that can be added to at will," relation offers man "the world in its full presence . . . truly as whole and one."[5] No

5. "Distance and Relation," in *The Knowledge of Man,* ed. M. Friedman, pp. 36, 60–62.

longer does a single person dominate the poem as soliloquy by dividing himself into speaker and auditor. He now shapes his speech according to his perception of the "thou" who is listening, so that the anticipated response becomes part of the speech act itself.

Just as the soliloquies provide us with a portrait of the speaker's mind gradually becoming more aware of itself, the dialogues are also a source of information regarding his emotions and values. We cannot point here to a progression, for the dialogues early in the 1609 quarto are as well developed as the later ones. But it is fair to predict that dialogue reveals even more about the speaker than soliloquy can. Removed from the existential isolation of sonnets like 116 or 121, the speaker emerges as one who, like ourselves, defines his selfhood most fully through encountering another. He illustrates what R. D. Laing has termed "complementarity . . . that feature of relatedness whereby the other is required to fulfill or complete the self."[6] We need not, however, consult modern theorists for a basis that would account for the sonnet-speaker's continued use of dialogue. The idea of complementarity is ever present in Shakespeare's drama, for instance in Achilles' words on the physiology of self-knowledge:

> The beauty that is borne here in the face
> The bearer knows not, but commends itself
> To others' eyes; nor doth the eye itself,
> That most pure spirit of sense, behold itself,
> Not going from itself; but eye to eye opposed,
> Salutes each other with each other's form;
> For speculation turns not to itself,
> Till it hath travell'd and is [mirror'd] there
> Where it may see itself. (*Troilus and Cressida*, 3.3.102–11)

When we study the dialogues in the Fair Youth sequence, we find a variety of patterns that demonstrate intense relatedness. The speaker's eye searches for self-definition by comparison with others: first in the contrast with other poets, but more profoundly in the "speculation" through which he and the youth are foils to each other. Later, in the sonnets that apparently address a woman, a different configuration will emerge; the dialogue declines in quality and becomes less authentic. In other words, relation weakens and gives way to distance.

---

6. *The Self and Others: Further Studies in Sanity and Madness*, p. 71.

II. Four Types of Dialogue

One difficulty in discussing dialogues in the sonnets is that there are so many. These 112 texts must somehow be separated, if only for convenience of reference. The most effective method will be a subdivision, according to the same criteria used before, of the 92 dialogues presumably addressed to the same young man addressed in sonnets 1–126. Four subgroups can be distinguished: (1) using "I" and "thou" pronouns infrequently and with little or no development of a personal relation; (2) referring to "thou" more frequently and with greater emphasis than to "I"; (3) referring more frequently and emphatically to "I" than to "thou"; (4) balancing "I" and "thou" quantitatively while developing a reciprocal relation between them. The first type of dialogue therefore corresponds with the first mode of address, being abstract and impersonal. Just as that first group was the smallest, including only five sonnets, so this is the smallest among the four subgroups. It may be called "marginal" dialogue and consists of sonnets 12, 54, 59, and 60. Each of these poems treats the theme of time, and each appears in the first half of the Fair Youth section. Sonnet 12 has already been discussed in terms of its newly personal approach and its presentation of the speaker's thought process. As a dialogue, it is marginal because it lacks direct address. The speaking "I" recounts his observations and applies them to the auditor: "thou among the wastes of time must go." No other mention of the "thou" occurs, so that he becomes analogous to the trees and flowers. No human dimension is accorded the youth beyond the simply natural functions of the life cycle. The sonnet's implicit dialogue could be paraphrased as: "This is what I have seen; apply the consequences to yourself." Such an attitude does not provide the auditor with many possibilities for response. It sets him at a distance and imposes on him the speaker's own pattern of seeing and inferring, rather than allowing for a different but equally valid set of inferences from the same observed data. Thus sonnet 12, admirable and central as a record of the speaker's mind, scarcely exists as dialogue because it fails to accommodate the mind that it addresses. The same limitation prevails throughout this subgroup of dialogues, although they are effective poems. When dialogue is confined in this way, being condensed and briefly introduced, a heightening of emotion occurs.

In sonnet 54, the process of deferred dialogue again creates a sense that the speaker is forcing his point of view on the auditor. The first quatrain echoes and expands upon "beauty's rose" of sonnet 1:

> O how much more doth beauty beauteous seem,
> By that sweet ornament which truth doth give.
> The rose looks fair, but fairer we it deem
> For that sweet odor which doth in it live.

What follows is a lecture-demonstration pointing out that "canker blooms" cannot be distinguished from roses except in that they are odorless. The only pronouns found before line 13 are "we" referring to public opinion and "they" and "their" referring to the flowers. Both "I" and "thou" make their appearance in the couplet, though Q prints *by* for *my*:

> And so of you, beauteous and lovely youth,
> When that shall vade, my verse distils your truth.

The auditor has now been placed in an elaborate framework of formal imagery. He is the rose, his truth the odor to be preserved by poetry. This is another version of the purely symbolic role he played in sonnet 12. Although the purpose of this analogy now is to praise him rather than to warn of decline, the essential orientation is still that of distance. The "thou" is relegated to passivity: he exerts no more influence on the design of the poem than do flowers on their distillation.

In sonnet 60 we find the most impersonal of these marginal dialogues. Its quatrains set forth the familiar theme of process in a curiously elliptical manner, beginning with the simile

> Like as the waves make towards the pebbled shore,
> So do our minutes hasten to their end,
> Each changing place with that which goes before,
> In sequent toil all forwards do contend.

The speaker's imagination endows "minutes," an invisible abstraction, with a sensuous form; it also links the concept of time with a model of directed movement. The assonance between "waves" as the symbol of time and the two verbs "make" and "hasten" strengthens that correspondence, while the underlying idea is manifest in line 4. The image of wavelike motion, apparently progressive but in fact stationary, becomes a figure for our experience in time.

In quatrains 2 and 3 the same process is reenacted on a larger scale, as the abstraction "nativity" transforms itself to "maturity," only to be destroyed. The speaker reiterates his usual view of natural process, yet the epigrammatic concision of his statements and their subtle associations with imagery keep them from becoming repetitious. Nativity "crawls" like an infant, moving from the "main of light" until it encounters "crooked eclipses." To be sure, time's "scythe" and his destruction of "beauty's brow" have been described before, but sonnet 60 achieves a more philosophical attitude by stating that time "feeds on the rarities of nature's truth." The victims of time, whether flowers or men, have not been considered as a form of "truth" before.

Excluding direct reference to himself and his auditor, the speaker in these lines implies an attitude of detachment and restrained concern. The perspective of cosmic irony does not prevent him from suffusing the description with emotion by means of selective detail. Moreover, it prepares for a belated shift to direct address and personal value, as in the other dialogues of this group. The couplet that effects this shift may therefore seem routine:

> And yet to times in hope my verse shall stand,
> Praising thy worth, despite his cruel hand.

But the closing remains an effective one, primarily because of what it omits. It does not proclaim that personal values can transcend mortality or that there is a dimension to life entirely separate from its timing, yet those ideas are all implied by the phrase "praising thy worth." The preceding discourse on time and the life cycle was confined to the axis of quantity; the length and physical nature of human life were seen through the medium of distance. Now "worth" posits value as a qualitative factor, with "praise" as its concomitant response, so that the vital relation between "my verse" and "thy worth" stands forth as the poem's reason for being. This verse was not written as yet another account of natural process but in order to defeat it; the speaker's true voice is not heard in the impersonal quatrains but emerges in the couplet's brief dialogue. Furthermore, time has been reduced from an all-powerful mythic principle; its personification disappears while the plural form lends it a measure of flexibility. Consonant with that change is the phrase "in hope," another broadly human quality that helps to shatter the desolate sketch that came before. Like "worth" and "praising," "hope" introduces the essentially human realm that resists, and to some extent alters, "nature's truth." Thus the couplet indeed does "stand," opposed at once "to times" and to the narrowly deterministic view of time with which the sonnet began.

A different use of marginal dialogue is demonstrated by sonnet 59. The concept of time persists here, but it has been assimilated to the cultural rather than the physical world. This sonnet does not relegate its dialogue to the couplet, giving it ample expression from quatrain 2 to the end. Nevertheless, its dialogue is marginal, being subordinated to a larger concern with the art of poetry. Instead of commemorating the beloved, poetry exists here as an end in itself. With that thought the sonnet begins, implying that art is not merely the reflector of time:

> If there be nothing new, but that which is
> Hath been before, how are our brains beguiled,
> Which, lab'ring for invention, bear amiss
> The second burthen of a former child!

The speaking voice identifies itself with a group, the poets who strive for "invention" or the discovery of new subject matter. Their striving would be futile if no room for originality remained, if "there be nothing new." But the speaker has a second reason for rejecting the notion of exhaustibility; it detracts from the preeminence he associates with his beloved. He defines himself in a continuum that has two aspects: his affiliation with other poets (who together rack "our brains"), and his liaison with the beloved. The sonnet places more stress on the former relation, which dominates its beginning and end, while the "thou" is present only twice, as "your image" and "your frame" in lines 7 and 9. The pronoun itself is unexceptionable, for in Shakespeare's usage no consistent pattern differentiates "you" from "thou." What does seem noteworthy is that distance now begins to yield to relation, so that there is more reciprocity here than in the other incipient dialogues.

The speaker's wish to see "your image in some antique book" actually combines both relations, poetry and love, perhaps because the auditor addressed is patron as well as friend. The "image" referred to must be a verbal portrait, since the book would be one of poetry comparable to his own. Yet the prevailing purpose in searching through older verse, "since mind at first in character was done," seems to be an evaluation of the speaker's art: "whether we are mended, or where better they." In other words, he now moves away from a natural opportunity for compliment and for more extended dialogue. We would expect an assertion of his beloved's superiority over previous models for poetry. But the initial question remains open, and for that reason the couplet disappoints:

> O sure I am the wits of former days
> To subjects worse have giv'n admiring praise.

The compliment conveyed here is rather anemic; "subjects worse" does not deny that some might also have been better, and "admiring praise" falls short of resolving whether "there be nothing new." Although marginal dialogue succeeds in the three poems dealing with time and nature, its distance precludes effective treatment of the more personal theme of sonnet 59.

The second type of dialogue is no longer marginal but one-directional. These sonnets show a pronounced imbalance in the "I/thou" relation, imparting special stress to the "thou." They are, therefore, "self-effacing" dialogues and can usually be recognized by a simple quantitative factor, the preponderance of second-person pronouns. For an example, with emphasis added, here are the first lines of sonnet 13:

> O that *you* were *yourself*, but love *you* are
> No longer *yours* than *you yourself* here live.

No less than seventeen pronouns based on "you" are distributed throughout this sonnet, while the first person is relegated to a single pronoun in the couplet: "Dear my love you know / You had a father, let your son say so." Clearly, there is little to separate this "I/thou" sonnet from the sonnets of the second mode. Yet the personal appeal suggests an intimate relation. The speaker reveals that relation when he briefly allows himself to enter the picture he paints. In thirteen sonnets of this subgroup, "thou" pronouns outnumber the "I" by at least two to one. These are 10, 16, 17, 18, 38, 41, 58, 73, 79, 82, 93, 96, and 126. That list includes both the first and the last dialogues in the Fair Youth sequence, again suggesting that self-effacement in dialogue is related to the language of polite obeisance. In sonnet 10 the speaker first dared to plead for procreation in his own voice: "Make thee another self, for love of me." In sonnet 126 he expatiates in a cautionary manner on the youth's relation to nature and time. Addressing the youth for the last time, he reverts to being an anonymous spokesman for consensus. He uses the first person only once, in the possessive form "O thou, my lovely boy," then withdraws to a neutral description of nature's ways:

> Yet fear her, O thou minion of her pleasure;
> She may detain but not still keep her treasure.
> Her audit, though delayed, answered must be,
> And her quietus is to render thee.

Ending and beginning this poem with the second person, the speaker concludes his series of dialogues with the youth in the reticent style of address that sonnet 10 had introduced. In returning to self-effacing dialogue, referring nine times to the "thou" and once to himself, he reminds us that this is a sonnet of farewell. Quantity here helps establish tonal quality, especially since the pronouns are augmented by imperatives and other second-person verb forms.

Three more sonnets, in which the two-to-one ratio is not maintained, must still be included in this group of dialogues. In sonnet 57 the "you" is described as "my sovereign" while the speaker characterizes himself as "your slave" and "your servant." The ratio of "I" to "you" pronouns is only seven to twelve, but the "I/you" relation here is as imbalanced as in sonnet 58, where the ratio is four to seventeen. Both poems, with a possible touch of irony, describe an unequal relation in which the reciprocality of "I/thou" has been destroyed. The first person is more conspicuous in 57 than in 58 only because the speaker stresses his own submissiveness rather than the authority of his master. The final sign of submission comes in the couplet, where "I" is replaced by "he":

> So true a fool is love, that in your will,
> Though you do anything, he thinks no ill.

The speaker has become "love" itself; his role playing is ironically defensive in that only "love" is incapable of criticizing his "sovereign." Throughout this sonnet, his pretense of "being your slave" and "your servant" shows how carefully he has dissociated his own identity from the servile behavior he describes. Although he claims all the characteristics of mindless devotion, his awareness prevents him from simply being "so true a fool." Thus the sonnet wavers between the self-effacing mode and some ironic counterassertions. As a dialogue, it recognizes the "thou" but transparently pretends to be overawed by him.

Similarly, in sonnet 99 the dominance of the second person is clear, although its pronouns are not quite twice as many as those of the first person. Here no irony undercuts the speaker's praise, while imagery gives it expression. The violet, lily, marjoram, and rose, he insists, are inferior imitations of the beauty of the "thou." The speaker concludes with a direct tribute:

> More flow'rs I noted, yet I none could see,
> But sweet or colour it had stol'n from thee.

The six-to-four ratio of first-person to second-person pronouns is less significant than the way those pronouns are used. Two first-person pronouns actually refer to the beloved: "my love's breath . . . my love's veins." Elsewhere, the "I" is merely the advocate of the inferiority of all things to the beloved: "thus did I chide," "I condemned," "I none could see." Although the second person appears less frequently, it is always on the receiving end of a compliment, superior to its imitators and to the speaker.

Finally, in sonnet 106, the speaker gathers images—now drawn from art rather than nature—to show his beloved's excellence:

> So all their praises are but prophecies
> Of this our time, all you prefiguring.

This is the unqualified praise that sonnet 59 anticipated but did not provide. The same situation of perusing old books is implied in both poems, each time for the sake of comparison. Unlike sonnet 59, which was so disappointingly noncommittal, 106 soon clarifies its attitude by claiming that earlier poets "would have expressed / Ev'n such a beauty as you master now." The comparison between his work and that of his predecessors is also resolved here:

> For we which now behold these present days,
> Have eyes to wonder, but lack tongues to praise.

As befits this group of self-effacing dialogues, sonnet 106 formulates a decorous judgment, so that the speaker's verse suffers in comparison with the past while the auditor's beauty gains. The compliment rings somewhat hollow because it is so conventional and its dialogue is hindered by the speaker's extroversion. Only two perceptions are reported, "I see descriptions" and "I see their antique pen." In both cases, the verb *to see* refers to the act of reading, although the latter has the sense of "reading into" or judging. Perhaps it is this transposition of seeing, as distinguished from the usual observation of nature, that limits the dialogue. Nothing else is given about the speaker until we reach the couplet. But even here he disappears from us, as he did from his intended auditor. He speaks as "we" in behalf of that same group of contemporary poets and "wits" whose "labouring for invention" had been recounted in sonnet 59. He ends the sonnet as their spokesman rather than as an individual voice, offering a polite compliment whose flattery displaces dialogue.

In many of these self-effacing dialogues, a similar tendency toward praise ranges from the fulsome strategies of sonnet 38 ("be thou the tenth muse, ten times more in worth") to the ironic suggestiveness of sonnets 57 and 58.

These sonnets combine elements of quantity and quality in expressing an imbalance of relation, so that convention and role playing become prominent. Even when the speaker intends to criticize, he is so preoccupied with the other and so oblivious of himself that the mode of address constitutes an unintended compliment. That is the case in sonnet 93, which starts with a definite rebuke: "So shall I live, supposing thou art true, / Like a deceived husband." Almost at once, the speaker hastens to modify what seems to have been too outspoken an opening. He employs a similar syntactic form but replaces the notion of truth with love, which is naturally fickle:

> so love's face
> May still seem love to me, though altered new:
> Thy looks with me, thy heart in other place.

In the other quatrains, criticism is virtually absent as the auditor is praised for his impenetrably fair appearance. There is just a suggestion that this advantage may be misused; heaven is said to have decreed:

> Whate'er thy thoughts or thy heart's workings be,
> Thy looks should nothing thence but sweetness tell.

Simultaneously, the "I" has vanished from the poem; it last appears in the confession made in line 6, "I cannot know thy change." An impersonal discourse begins at this point and continues until the couplet. The speaker has reverted to anonymous wisdom, contrasting "many's looks" with the youth's inscrutability. By dwelling on that trait while avoiding self-reference, he tactfully circumvents the harshness of his own feelings. His remarks continue to lend distance to the "thou" as a unique phenomenon until the couplet finally substitutes a convenient symbol:

> How like Eve's apple doth thy beauty grow,
> If thy sweet virtue answer not thy show.

Besides connoting falsehood, this analogy criticizes the "thou" by depersonalizing him. Likened to the forbidden fruit, he loses his individuality, the uniqueness that heaven gave him, and is reduced to the level of an archetype. Despite the precautionary "if," the likeness is definitely there. Rather than assume a conventional role himself, the speaker now imposes one on the auditor.

The third type of "I/thou" sonnets is analogous to the third mode in that it verges on soliloquy and "speaking of" yet remains in the category of dialogue. The speaker's attention is again turned inward; these sonnets are one-directional in that they tend to efface the other rather than the self. Their introverted quality is reflected in the numerical superiority of "I" over "thou." In nineteen of twenty-seven sonnets, a ratio of at least two to one defines the relation of first to second person. The imbalance can be demonstrated in sonnet 50, which has ten first-person pronouns against "thee" and "thy." This poem about traveling away from the beloved contains a corresponding withdrawal of concern for the other. Not only does the speaker indulge in his feelings, "how heavy do I journey on the way," he also transfers them to the horse that he rides:

> As if by some instinct the wretch did know
> His rider loved not speed, being made from thee.

Quatrain 3 describes the "bloody spur" that the speaker angrily employs until the horse responds by echoing his own mood: "Which heavily he answers with a groan." There is no response to the animal's complaint except one of unfeeling wit, claiming extravagantly that the groan is "more sharp to me than spurring to his side." The couplet explains why:

> For that same groan doth put this in my mind—
> My grief lies onward and my joy behind.

The sonnet therefore is less concerned with dialogue than with giving an account of the speaker's attitudes. Sonnets 30 and 62 take the same approach and reach an even greater imbalance, having a ratio of eight to one. There are only three sonnets of this type—45, 46, and 52—in which the ratio of "I" to "thou" is less than two to one.

Turning to the distribution of these introverted sonnets in the sequence of 1609, we find four clusters that include twenty-two of them. Each of these clusters has a unifying theme: sonnets 26–30 portray the effects of love; 44–47 and 50–52 deal with the theme of absence; 109–15 introduce and resolve a conflict between the lovers; while 76, 85, and 86 (all located within the Rival Poet section) are concerned with the art of poetry. Finally, five of the introverted sonnets do not belong to any of these clusters—numbers 42, 62, 102, 107, and 125. Throughout this type of dialogue, the dominance of the first person should be seen as primarily structural, not psychological. Yet a tension is created between the speaker's self-concern and the self-denying love that he claims to feel. No paradox is involved, since introspection serves to remind him of his complete dependence on another. We find that the "thou" is described only in terms of his influence on the "I." For example, in the sonnets dealing with absence, there is no suggestion that the speaker's sorrow at parting will be reciprocated. The "thou" is merely a place removed in 44 and 45, an object for possession in 46 and 47, and a point of departure and hoped-for return in 50 and 51. Only in sonnet 52, which concludes this cluster, does the second person receive some measure of the imaginative concern that the speaker has lavished on himself:

> So am I as the rich whose blessed key
> Can bring him to his up-locked treasure.

However we analyze this sonnet, it will be impossible to show that the "I" and the "you" are in a relation of equality or reciprocality. Quantitatively, equality may be said to exist because the first- and second-person pronouns both occur twice, but the scarcity of pronouns makes this ratio insignificant. If we consider the placement of "I" and "you" throughout the sonnet, the balance shifts immediately toward the first person, who describes himself by an extended simile throughout the octet. The chest and wardrobe similes in lines 9–10 take "time" as their subject, while "you" remains the object of time's action. Only when "you" reappears in the couplet does it become a grammatical subject:

> Blessed are you whose worthiness gives scope,
> Being had to triumph, being lacked to hope.

Turning to imagery, we find the second person likened to precious objects possessed by the speaker. What is emphasized in the quatrain is this symbolic act of possessing, whose pleasure is enhanced by occasional loss. Yet the final benediction reminds us that the source of all pleasure is the beloved's "worthiness." In thematic terms, the second person remains dominant. However, in structural terms that more closely influence our reading, the "I" holds the key, the treasure, and our attention because his consciousness forms the subject matter of the poem. Sonnet 52, despite its recognition of a debt to the second person, resembles the other soliloquizing dialogues in that it continues their detailed study of the speaker's state of mind.

Many other "I/thou" sonnets that emphasize the "I" dramatically delay the appearance of the "thou." Sonnets 29 and 30 are striking examples of this technique, while the two preceding sonnets use it less obtrusively. The "thou" first appears in line 6 of sonnet 27 and line 8 of 28, while the "I" is present in both opening lines. The speaker's delayed shift of attention from himself to his beloved marks the growth of his awareness in all four poems. That growth also becomes the central theme of sonnet 62: "Sin of self-love possesseth all mine eye." The word "sin" is repeated in line 3, so that (unlike sonnet 29) we realize from the start that the speaker's meditations are false and must be altered. Where 29 had focused on self-hate looking enviously at "this man's art and that man's scope," this poem about self-love offers an inventory of the speaker's own features:

> Methinks no face so gracious is as mine,
> No shape so true, no truth of such account.

After continuing to indulge in self-love throughout the octet, the speaker discovers himself in the mirror "beated and chopped with tanned antiquity." When the "thou" finally makes its appearance, confined again to the couplet, it modifies all that came before:

> 'Tis thee, myself, that for myself I praise,
> Painting my age with beauty of thy days.

The deliberate confusion of "thee" and "myself" suggests reciprocality and thus redeems an otherwise introspective and self-conscious utterance. Similarly, sonnet 125 achieves a complete definition of the speaker's dependence on the other person. As in the previous sonnets, the structural dominance of the "I" (reflected here by seven personal pronouns) does not diminish the psychological dominance of the "thou" (represented by only three). The octet contains a twofold rejection of "outward honoring" by the speaker who has borne the "canopy" himself and seen the fall of other courtiers. The introduction of the "thou" coincides with the traditional turning point: "No, let me be obsequious in thy heart." Finally, a redefinition of the speaker's homage, stressing simple honesty, is epitomized in the phrase "mutual render, only me for thee." The idea of reciprocality, undreamed of in sonnets 26–30 but anticipated in sonnet 62, is expressed clearly here. But the couplet of this sonnet, rebuking another "thou," the "suborned informer," creates a second shift of attention—this time away from the speaker's love:

> Hence, thou suborned informer! A true soul
> When most impeached stands least in thy control.

Whoever the "informer" may be, it is the speaker who asserts himself as a "true soul." In the preceding sonnet he had invoked "the fools of time" to witness the very same truthfulness in love, suggesting that some external opposition is needed as a touchstone to his faith. His primary concern in sonnet 125 is still himself, always located at a tangible distance from the beloved, despite the brief turning to their relation in quatrain 3.

Many dialogue sonnets of this type are entirely introverted, even though they allow for the occasional presence of the "thou." In 109–12, the ratio of "I" to "thou" rises to at least three to one. These sonnets constitute an apology for the speaker's unabashed inconstancy; in contrast to 50–52, he is himself responsible for the absence and separation he now desires to end. Yet his arguments do not encourage us to accept his plea. They are too ego-centric, not only in frequency of self-reference but also in the vapid role they attribute to the other person. Imperative verbs are used, as if to prompt the auditor's words and thoughts:

> O never say that I was false of heart . . . .
> Never believe, though in my nature reigned
> All frailties (109)
>
> Then give me welcome, next my heav'n the best (110)
>
> Pity me then, and wish I were renewed (111)

In an unconvincing attempt to regain credibility, the speaker coins a series of epithets: "my rose" (109), "an older friend . . . / A god in love" (110), and "dear friend" (111). He supposes that such words can cancel the deeds he is professedly guilty of, ascribing either great generosity or obtuseness to his auditor. Sonnet 112 contains a particularly vulnerable overstatement:

> Mark how with my neglect I do dispense:
> You are so strongly in my purpose bred,
> That all the world besides me thinks y'are dead.

What seems objectionable here is the theatrical gesture. The auditor is told to "mark," leading us to expect a new idea or image. Yet all that ensues is an extravagant restatement of what the sonnet has been claiming, that no one else's opinion matters. There is a textual problem in line 14, and the custom-ary emendation ("you are so strongly in my purpose bred / That all the world besides methinks are dead") is probably justified by the overall argu-ment. But the self-dramatization appears excessive, however the last line is read. It is difficult to take the speaker at his word in such dialogues because they fail to actually involve the "thou" who is being so highly praised.

Perhaps their rhetoric was an effective strategy ad hominem, if the person addressed really had the weakness that sonnet 84 charges him with:

> You to your beauteous blessings add a curse,
> Being fond on praise, which makes your praises worse.

Such a low appraisal of the auditor seems to underlie these apologetic dialogues, in which the speaker is really paying compliments to himself. In 113 and 114 he discourses at length on the rivalry between his eye and mind, while 115 undertakes a casuistic study of the sense in which love may be said to "grow." A pervasive ingenuity, coupled with an ability to explain away all that resists easy formulation, lends these poems a rather limited appeal. The same facility that impaired several soliloquies also prevents the "I"-centered dialogues from fully embodying the love they claim to feel. It should be added that in the three dialogues touching on poetry the speaker's self-dramatization and his deliberate analysis of himself by comparison with others go basically unchanged. In 76 and 85 he returns to the stance of Eiron that the first soliloquies had introduced, pretending that his verse is "barren of new pride" and that his "tongue-tied muse" is unable to compete with others. In 86 he complains more seriously of losing favor and with it inspiration:

> But when your countenance filled up his line,
> Then lacked I matter, that enfeebled mine.

Yet our final impression is that the speaker's primary concern is not to establish dialogue for the sake of praising or blaming others but merely to exercise his wit.

Our classification of Shakespeare's sonnets according to four modes, and the division of the largest mode, dialogue, into four types, can now be completed. What remains is the fourth type of dialogue, referring explicitly to "I" and "thou" while keeping a careful balance between them. In these sonnets the speaker avoids the extremes of being too much or too little concerned with himself. He combines self-consciousness with an equally acute awareness of another person's state of being. This subgroup of "I/thou" sonnets is the largest, just as dialogue itself dominates among the four modes. Thus the analogy between the main groups of the sonnets and the subgroups continues in that more than two-thirds of the sonnets take "I/thou" as their mode of address, and more than half of these describe a relation between speaker and auditor in which it is impossible to attribute psychological or structural dominance to either party. The sonnets having an evenly balanced proportion of "I" and "thou" pronouns constitute more than one-third of all the sonnets: 57 of 154. They account for 46 of the 127 sonnets in the Fair Youth section and include a very extensive range of themes. It would be impossible to arrange these poems according to their themes or their place in the sequence. What seems more promising, following the lines of classification set down so far, is an approach that concentrates on the one distinctive feature all of them share: the frequent yet balanced repetition of pronouns referring directly to the speaker and the auditor. Considering the pervasive sense of personal address throughout the sonnets, as well as the numerical preponderance of the "I/ thou" group, it seems fair to say that the changing relations between speaker and auditor create a framework in which specific themes such as time, love, and poetry are incorporated. Yet we also find that these relations can serve a thematic purpose. Dialogue becomes an end in itself, a source of personal knowledge. It provides the speaker's most characteristic and most satisfying response to the challenge of time.

Nowhere does the theme of relationship appear as strikingly as in this final subgroup of "I/thou" sonnets. The numerical balance of "I" and "thou" and the concomitant feelings of intensity and reciprocality make possible a sense of interrelation between the two parties that is stronger than anywhere else in the sonnets. Several examples drawn from these poems support this generalization. They also demonstrate some of the intricate patterns in which Shakespeare's speaker places "I" and "thou." Since each of these poems contains virtually an equal number of "I" and "thou" pronouns, the analysis is based on the order in which these pronouns are introduced and repeated. In some of these sonnets, the structural constellation formed by "I" and "thou" reflects the explicit theme of a personal relation. Sonnet 36, which affirms a union of the two parties despite their separation, begins by stating that two persons must needs be two, although their two loves are always one:

> Let me confess that we two must be twain,
> Although our undivided loves are one.

The paradox is reinforced by the position of "twain" and "one" at the end of these opening lines where they gain emphasis by bearing the final iambic beat. This technique of repeating closely related words in successive lines is employed throughout the octet. In lines 3–4 continuity results from the syntactically parallel phrases, "with me remain . . . by me be borne alone," where the shared appositive is the speaker's "blots." Lines 5 and 6 are joined by the phrases "in our two loves . . . in our lives," which continue the opening paradox, since the former has "but one respect" while the latter has "a separable spite." Finally, the effects of separation are conveyed by the parallel phrases that conclude lines 7–8; "love's sole effect" is unchanged but "love's delight" suffers loss.

Up to this point, despite the use of "we two" and the repetition of "our," the mode of address has not been fully personal. The speaker has referred to himself three times, but only superficially: "Let me confess," "with me," "by me." The "thou" appears only in the phrase "without thy help." Thus the main stress falls neither on "I" nor on "thou" but on an abstract idea, an "it" that is termed "our undivided loves" and "our two loves." The truly personal mode of address, depending on the frequent and balanced repetition of "I" and "thou," makes a dramatic appearance in the opening line of the sestet and dominates the rest of the sonnet:

> I may not evermore acknowledge thee,
> Lest my bewailed guilt should do thee shame;
> Nor thou with public kindness honour me,
> Unless thou take that honour from thy name.
> But do not so; I love thee in such sort,
> As, thou being mine, mine is thy good report.

Like the first two quatrains, lines 9–12 are linked by reiteration. But here the repeated words are "I," "thou," and related pronouns. Furthermore, the placement of these pronouns within lines 9–11 is at the greatest possible distance, so that their pattern echoes the theme of separation. In line 9, "I" and "thee" (the grammatical subject and object) are the first and last syllables. "Thee" is repeated in the next line, now in the penultimate position, while the first-person pronoun is correspondingly the second syllable of the line. In line 11, "thou" and "me" are the second and last syllables. The second person now serves as subject and the first person as object, reversing the pattern of line 9. Just as the speaker may not acknowledge his beloved, so the latter cannot honor the speaker. As the result of this patterning, a rhyme between "thee" and "me" connects lines 9 and 11 and provides a half-link with line 10 where "thou" is the penultimate syllable. In all three lines, "I" and "thou" appear only once and are always separated by at least three iambic feet. Finally, line 12 repeats the "thou" of the previous line, again placing it as the second word while omitting the "I" entirely. The speaker's "blots" have caused a separation that is more than physical, leading to what can be called a pact of nonrecognition. This sense of enforced estrangement is heightened by the pattern of distancing between "I" and "thou" throughout the quatrain.

In the couplet the two persons come together in terms of thought and structure:

> But do not so; I love thee in such sort,
> As, thou being mine, mine is thy good report.

The speaker begins with a command, using the imperative mood for the first time since the opening line of the poem. He unites "I" and "thou" in the phrase "I love thee," where their proximity for the first time in the poem establishes a sense of intimacy. This interrelation of "I" and "thou" receives a more elaborate patterning in the closing line, where two first-person and two second-person pronouns are carefully counterbalanced. The line consists of two syntactic units, each one containing a linked "I" and "thou." Thus the proximity introduced in the first line of the couplet is doubled in the second, enhancing the gradual movement from distance to relation.

Throughout the sonnet there has been a movement from discourse about something ("I/it") in lines 1–8, to discourse to someone ("I/thou") in lines 9–12, culminating in the personal address of the couplet. In the first two quatrains, "I" and "thou" were not brought into direct relation but were linked by reference to a third term, the unity of "our two loves." In the third quatrain, the relation of "I" to "thou" is conveyed directly in a pattern that reflects their separation. Finally, in the last two lines, the structural pattern that unites "I" and "thou" coincides with the explicit statement of their union. The closing line, in which "I" and "thou" pronouns receive four of the five metrical beats, concludes the poem with its strongest claim of an invincible interrelation. The meaning of the line derives from the interdependence of its two syntactic units. The first, "thou being mine," expresses the total possession of one person's being by another. The second, "mine is thy good report," suggests the responsibility that this possession imposes on the speaker. He begs not to be honored publicly because he is more concerned with his beloved's name than with his own. The seeming egoism of "thou being mine" is belied by the self-effacing argument that follows. The reciprocality of the "I/thou" relation, gradually revealed in the sestet and reinforced in the couplet, brings the sonnet to a confident close.

Other dialogues of this type resemble sonnet 36 in their frequent, patterned repetition of the key pronouns. However, the patterns vary considerably and need not reflect the theme of a personal relation. Some of these sonnets, while maintaining the structural combination of "I" and "thou," move in the opposite direction from sonnet 36. Beginning with the union of the two persons, they shift toward dissociation and conclude by establishing the dominance of one person at the other's expense. For example, sonnet 61 leads from the union of "I" and "thou" to their separation, shifting from reciprocality to the dominance of the speaker. Even in the first part of the sonnet, the octet being very clearly demarcated, we find that the interrelation of "I" and "thou" is more a matter of form than of feeling. The patterning of the pronouns imposes from the start a structural, but not a psychological, union. It is a pattern composed of three rhetorical questions, two of two lines and one of four:

> Is it thy will thy image should keep open
> My heavy eyelids to the weary night?
> Dost thou desire my slumbers should be broken,
> While shadows like to thee do mock my sight?
> Is it thy spirit that thou send'st from thee
> So far from home into my deeds to pry,
> To find out shames and idle hours in me,
> The scope and tenor of thy jealousy?

Within this unit we note several characteristic techniques used to express the sense of an "I/thou" relation. The opening counterbalance of "thy" and "my" leads to a larger symmetry of contrastive noun phrases. Thus "thy image" reflecting "thy will" raises "my heavy eyelids," while "thy spirit" and "thy jealousy" observe "my deeds." The passivity of the speaker is reinforced by the phrases "my slumbers" and "my sight," both of which are grammatical objects acted on by the "thou." Another device that establishes the sense of a close interrelation is the rhyme of "thee" and "me" in lines 5 and 7. Again, the formal balance of these personal pronouns reveals the imbalance of the personal relation. In this quatrain, a personal reference ends each line: the "thou" is present at the end of lines 5 and 8, the outer limits of the single question that comprises the quatrain; the "I" is found only at the end of lines 6 and 7, the two inner lines, where it acts as a passive object: "into my deeds to pry" and "idle hours in me." Although "I" and "thou" are reiterated and interrelated throughout the first eight lines, there is a distinct sense of an imbalanced relation in which the "thou" is dominant. On the other hand, the interrogative mood that prevails in this octet serves to qualify that dominance by placing it in the realm of the hypothetical. All that remains certain, so far, is the intimacy of "I" and "thou" and the resultant discomfort of the speaker. At the turning point of the sonnet, the true cause of that discomfort is finally identified, answering the questions of lines 1–8:

> O no, thy love, though much, is not so great.
> It is my love that keeps mine eye awake,
> Mine own true love that doth my rest defeat,
> To play the watchman ever for thy sake.
> For thee watch I, while thou dost wake elsewhere,
> From me far off, with others all too near.

Again, balanced pronominal phrases function to reflect a dynamic personal relation. The speaker states that "thy love" is less active than "my love." He emphasizes the primacy of his own emotion, admitting that it is his own love that disturbs his rest. The repetition in the phrases "my love," "mine eye," "mine own true love," and "my rest" within lines 10–11 reaffirms the independence of the speaker, or at least the responsibility of his own mind for the discomfort of his body. The entire sestet belittles both the love and the fidelity of the "thou." After line 9 the second person appears only once as subject, in the subordinate phrase "whilst thou dost wake elsewhere," and twice in the phrases "for thy sake" and "for thee." Even though the speaker acknowledges the other person as the cause of his suffering, he ends the sonnet by stressing his own course of action. The strength of his love is defined by its persistence in the face of infidelity. The speaker who defeats his own rest and plays the watchman for the sake of an unfaithful love gains a definite triumph of his own. He becomes the main subject of the poem, the center of his own and our attention.

Sonnets 36 and 61 show that even when a numerical balance of "I" and "thou" pronouns exists, the personal relation need not be one of equilibrium. This relation is dynamic and changes fundamentally during the course of the poem, either in the direction of greater union or toward the separation of the two people. The sonnets that contain an almost even number of "I" and "thou" pronouns could be classified along these lines: some follow the pattern of sonnet 36 in moving gradually toward the affirmation of a mutual identity; others resemble sonnet 61 in suggesting the dominance of "I" or of "thou." Yet such a comparative classification leads to superfine distinctions. Each one of the sonnets in this subgroup simply has its own pattern for arranging the key pronouns; each presents a unique interplay between the structural and psychological dominance of "I" and "thou." Furthermore, some of these sonnets intertwine the first- and second-person pronouns so completely that they cannot be placed in either of the patterns illustrated above. They present a different type of arrangement, one that begins and ends with a close conjunction of "I" and "thou." Sonnet 120 furnishes an example of this type, beginning with a personal address: "That you were once unkind befriends me now." Nevertheless, in the first quatrain "I" emerges as the dominant figure. Lines 2–4 are devoted to the speaker's comparison of the sorrow he has felt in the past with that which he now inflicts. The "thou" is absent from these lines, while the "I" admits that his own "transgression" is as serious as the unkindness he had previously received. This comparison "befriends" the speaker in that it leads him to a more mature assessment of his own actions. As a result, the essential relation here is not between "I" and "thou" but rather between "I" as past victim and "I" as present agent. Quatrain 2 begins by substituting a personal mode of address for the previous introversion:

> For if you were by my unkindness shaken,
> As I by yours, y'have passed a hell of time,
> And I, a tyrant, have no leisure taken
> To weigh how once I suffered in your crime.

From this second comparison the speaker draws imaginative sympathy into the other person rather than personal consolation. The sense of a reciprocal relation is brought out by the balanced arrangement of the pronouns in lines 5–6: "if you . . . by my . . . As I by yours." Despite the presence of "if," this relation emerges as real, not conditional, as shown by the indicative verbs "you've passed" and "I . . . have no leisure taken." Furthermore, although in lines 7–8 the speaker is again the central consciousness of the poem, these lines contain another carefully balanced construction that suggests the importance of reciprocality. When he recalls what he had forgotten, "how once I suffered in your crime," he brings us back to the second part of the previous balance, "as I by yours." There is also a parallel between the clause built around "I suffered" and the clause that ends line 6: "you've passed a hell of time." The "I" and the "you" are subjects of the same essential action—the suffering they cause each other.

The speaker makes it explicit that he had suffered "in your crime" while his friend has more recently been "by my unkindness shaken." Throughout this quatrain, "I" and "thou" are interrelated in terms of their infidelity and feelings of guilt.

The third quatrain of sonnet 120 extends this interrelation by introducing the element of compassion. In line 11 the speaker wishes that the memory of his own suffering might have led him to pity his friend. He should have made amends "as soon to you as you to me then." Yet this balanced construction, unlike the previous examples, does not transcend the subjunctive mood of the adjacent verbs, "might have rememb'red . . . tend'red." His desire for reconciliation remains no more than wishful thinking; in fact, he does not return the comfort that he had received but only the anterior injury. The speaker gives no motivation for this withholding of kindness. He does not explain why his "deepest sense" fails to reciprocate or even to remember his friend's example. However, the couplet suggests that this mode of conduct stems from choice, not from an incapacity to feel:

> But that your trespass now becomes a fee;
> Mine ransoms yours, and yours must ransom me.

Not surprisingly, the restraint of emotion has led to the introduction of wit. Yet the censure implied in these two lines is inseparable from the previously established empathy.

III. Sonnet 18 as Dialogue

These explications of dialogue sonnets suggest several possibilities for stylistic criticism that can be derived from a study of the "I/thou" relation. Such a study is helpful in solving both of the major problems that face the reader of Shakespeare's sonnets, giving the entire sequence a coherent and unambiguous structure and furnishing a basis by which the unique structures of individual sonnets can be recognized and compared. An awareness of the possibilities for dialogue, and a study of how far they have been exploited, can lead to new insights regarding even the most familiar of poetic texts. For example, sonnet 18 is perhaps the best known in the cycle, owing its popularity to the plain diction and clear-cut imagery that articulate a simple contrast between natural and eternal beauty. But the same simplicity, which is more apparent than real, has deprived the poem of the commentary it deserves. Some critics are concerned with sources and analogues, tracing the theme of poetic immortality rather than focusing directly on the text.[7] Others agree with Philip Martin that this is the "first full-scale immortalization" in the sonnets.[8] They, too, cite it only as an introduction to that thematic group, dwelling on other, more complicated sonnets.[9] As a result, remarkably little has been written on these fourteen celebrated lines. A glance at Rollins's *Variorum* and at subsequent editions shows how little historical and linguistic gloss the poem has received. The "new" criticism, dominant until recently, has preferred to deal with sonnets that offer greater possibilities for complex meaning.

Newer trends in criticism, which explore less conspicuous features of poetic language, seem capable of giving this famous but neglected poem its due. Yet, here too, sonnet 18 still wanders in the shade. Stephen Booth's study of the sonnets mentions 18 only to comment on its place in the sequence.[10] In his copiously annotated edition, Booth adds several lexical and orthographical notes but does not offer an extended commentary. Some of his readings, moreover, seem to induce unnecessary or nonexistent ambiguities. For example, Booth claims that "temperate" in line 2 derives not only from the Latin *temperatus* but also from *tempus,* that is, time. He concludes, "The word *temperate* thus embodies both of the qualities contrasted in the poem," referring to constancy and change.[11] This derivation could be questioned, since *temperatus* is also the past participle of the verb *temperare,* to mingle or regulate. But granting an etymological connection with *tempus,* in any case, would yield an irrelevant meaning. The beloved's beauty is praised for not having "rough winds" and not being "too hot," so that temperance is directly opposed to temporality. At what subliminal level can the Latin affiliation of the source of an English word actually influence the reader, especially when that affiliation is contrary to the word's explicit sense? Booth's unflagging pursuit of ambiguities misleads him again when he dis-

7. See J. B. Leishman, *Themes and Variations in Shakespeare's Sonnets,* p. 137, and Katharine M. Wilson, *Shakespeare's Sugared Sonnets,* p. 173.

8. *Shakespeare's Sonnets: Self, Love and Art,* p. 146.

9. See Hilton Landry, *Interpretations in Shakespeare's Sonnets,* p. 144; Hallett Smith, *Elizabethan Poetry,* p. 178; James Winny, *The Master-Mistress: A Study of Shakespeare's Sonnets,* p. 31; Ann Ferry, *All in War with Time: Love Poetry of Shakespeare, Donne, Jonson, Marvell,* pp. 10–13. For a different reading of the sonnet, finding an anticlimax in its closing lines, see G. Wilson Knight, *The Mutual Flame: An Interpretation of Shakespeare's Sonnets,* p. 99.

10. *An Essay on Shakespeare's Sonnets,* p. 3.

11. *Shakespeare's Sonnets: Edited with an Analytical Commentary,* pp. 161–62.

cusses the phrase "eternal lines." He suggests, "As he comes upon line 12 . . . a reader may well understand *lines* in its root meaning of 'cords' or 'ropes,' and take *eternal lines* as 'bound eternally.'" He does not explain what is gained by inventing a reader, or misreader, who is capable of such confusion. To suppose that "eternal lines" means "eternally bound" requires that we ignore the overwhelming change of tone in line 8: "But thy eternal summer shall not fade." This affirmation, centered on the word *eternal,* makes it impossible to construe "eternal lines" as a form of bondage. Verbal repetition is an important technique in the poem, and it results in an undeniable clarity of meaning. Booth's comments extend the new-critical approach by insisting on semantic depth rather than analyzing structural features. Yet it is precisely the question of structure that must be considered in evaluating sonnet 18 and describing its actual effects.

One of the few critics to comment on the meaning of this sonnet is Edward Hubler. His remarks, with some modification, offer a starting point for detailed study. He states that although sonnet 18 "is not one of Shakespeare's greatest poems, it approaches perfection. The thing to be noticed is Shakespeare's skillful and varied presentation of its subject matter; and we should note in passing that with the poet's celebration of his friend there is a concomitant disclosure of himself. The more one studies the sonnets in search of the young man, the more one learns of Shakespeare."[12] Hubler's evaluation may also be questioned. If a poem is virtually "perfect," why should it not be "great"? Presumably, the achievement of sonnet 18 is lessened by its limited scope. But the question of value cannot be resolved without a thorough description of the poem's structure. Rather than accepting literally what the sonnet-speaker says, it is important to examine what he does in the context of dialogue. Only in this sense is it true that the sonnet describes his love. The subject matter is therefore not a celebration of the youth but a series of actions and decisions made by the speaker. He ponders making a comparison, then makes it and develops its consequences.

The opening question—"shall I compare thee to a summer's day?"— combines two very different meanings. The first is whether or not to make this comparison. The second is whether the comparison is just. The distinction is useful because the speaker replies affirmatively to the first question and negatively to the second. He finds the comparison worth making, even though his beloved's beauty exceeds that of ordinary nature. It is essential,

12. *The Sense of Shakespeare's Sonnets,* p. 80.

then, that line 1 be recognized as a genuine question rather than a rhetorical formula. The difference helps explain how the sonnet attains a higher threshold of emotion than do its predecessors. Five of sonnets 1–17 begin in the interrogative mood also, but their questions are always put to the youth, not to the speaker himself. Each question implies a specific, inevitable answer. Sonnets 4 and 8 use the question form, preceded by an apostrophe, to convey a complaint about the youth's self-love: "Unthrifty loveliness, why dost thou spend / Upon thyself thy beauty's legacy?" and "Music to hear, why hear'st thou music sadly?" Both queries point out a discrepancy between what the youth is, "loveliness" and "music," and what he does. Both assume the same reply, that his behavior cannot be justified. Similarly, in sonnets 9 and 16 the initial questions have a built-in answer: "Is it for fear to wet a widow's eye / That thou consum'st thyself in single life" and "But wherefore do not you a mightier way / Make war upon this bloody tyrant time"? One question calls for an admission of guilt, while the other denies any course of action but that the speaker prescribes. Even in sonnet 17, which looks ahead to the subsequent breakthrough, the rhetorical answer "no one" is dictated by the opening question: "Who will believe my verse in time to come / If it were filled with your most high deserts?" Only by comparison with other sonnets does this rhetorical question become significant. It touches on the problem of poetic description, which becomes less credible the more it praises. The speaker realizes that a detailed attempt to "number all your graces" will seem hyperbolic. Rather than solving the problem in poetic terms, he takes recourse for the last time to the procreation theme: "But were some child of yours alive that time, / You should live twice in it and in my rhyme."

In another sense, the first line of sonnet 18 continues from the Procreation sonnets and outdoes them. The phrase "a summer's day" combines two recurrent images of natural beauty. "Summer" appeared as one of the emblems in sonnet 12's catalog ("summer's green all girded up in sheaves") and in sonnet 5's brief account of natural process: "For never-resting time leads summer on / To hideous winter and confounds him there." Sonnet 12 also mentioned "brave day sunk in hideous night," while sonnet 15 more emphatically warned that time will "change your day of youth to sullied night." Just as the question form becomes more charged with meaning, so the compound image in sonnet 18 acquires a new intensity. Unlike the earlier allusions to "summer" and "day," there is no immediate decline to hideous winter and night. Instead, "summer's day" stands as an example of beauty whose impermanence has been temporarily forgotten. A contrast is made, but, as the second line shows, it is no longer between youth and age but rather between natural and ideal beauty: "Thou art . . . more temperate."

Taken together, the complex question and image of line 1 suggest that the controlling presence of the speaker will be instrumental in shaping the poem's structure of dialogue. None of the previous sonnets began with so powerful a sense of personality. Shakespeare's speaker, it should be remembered, had first referred to himself only in the modest phrase "for love of me" in sonnet 10. He subsequently appears as an observer of nature in sonnet 12 and in sonnet 14 as an astronomer whose knowledge is derived from his beloved's eyes. The speaker finally identifies himself as a poet in sonnets 15–17, but he remains radically unsure of his powers.[13] The new confidence displayed in sonnet 18, therefore, arises from his awareness of an ability to order the world according to degrees of likeness and unlikeness. There is no concern for the misguided opinions of posterity and no claim that nature's own replication will surpass the poet's art. The lyric art has become autonomous because the technical problem raised in sonnet 17 has been solved; the speaker decides to bypass the self-defeating task of detailed physical description. Instead, he represents the inner meaning of the beauty he perceives and explores its influence on his own mental processes. By concentrating on dramatized response to an ideal beauty, he avoids the danger of drawing an unconvincing portrait. What he stresses is the dynamic interplay of ideas, among which the beloved's beauty functions as a central premise and as a source of meaning.

Although sonnet 18 marks a shift toward greater subjectivity and more sustained introspection, the poem is remarkably free of egoism. Only once, in the opening line, is the speaker's "I" explicitly mentioned. The following lines take "thou" and correlative images of natural beauty as their subject. Were it not for the couplet in which "this" refers to the poem as an eternal artifact, the speaker could be said to retire entirely behind the manifest content of his thoughts. His self-conscious conclusion is an unmistakable reminder of the human identity that has created the poem. It is especially significant that these two allusions to the speaker's self, occurring in the first

13. For a contrasting interpretation of sonnet 15, see Ferry, *All in War with Time,* pp. 3–10. She concludes, "The language of the poem is therefore a demonstration of what the couplet bravely claims, the poet's power through his art to combat destruction by time." Ferry does not mention sonnet 16, which adds a pessimistic continuation to the argument of its predecessor.

and last lines, impose a frame of self-awareness that encloses the subject matter of the poem.

In this way, the abstract entity of framing the two inner strophes of a sonnet by the two outer ones, as pointed out by Jakobson and Jones, takes on a specific psychological dimension.[14] But the framing effect of lines 1 and 14 is not limited to the speaker himself. In both lines we also note the only appearances of the pronoun *thee,* indicating the second person as object of an action: "I compare thee" and "this gives life to thee." The sonnet begins and ends with the speaker (or his poem) acting on the beloved. During the extended absence of the "I," beginning with line 2, the second person functions as subject matter rather than as object: "Thou art more lovely and more temperate." The "thou" does not actively perform but exists statically in contrast to the ever-changing phenomena of nature. Lines 3–8, marking the third and final step toward impersonality, evoke nature's inconsistency without referring to either "I" or "thou." They continue the speaker's basic comparison between his beloved and a summer's day by illustrating the defects of the latter through a series of images. First, the imperfection of natural beauty is shown by the "rough winds" that are no less a part of May than the "darling buds." The winds' action of shaking the buds also suggests the ascendancy of power over beauty. The second image, "summer's lease hath all too short a date," depends on a commercial metaphor to argue that if natural beauty were unblemished it would still be transient. The speaker thereby concedes his first point by uncovering a second, more basic flaw in natural beauty.

If these two images explain why his beloved is "more lovely," the third, more developed image can be seen as an extension of "more temperate." The sun is given the humanizing epithet "the eye of heaven" as well as "gold complexion" in order to remind us of its contrast with the "thou." By shining "too hot" or being "dimm'd," the sun behaves intemperately but in accordance with its place in nature. It is with the universal rule of nature that the speaker is finally concerned. He begins with the small but precise image of shaken buds, progressing to the wider scope of summer and the sun. He concludes on the broadest level of generality:

> And every fair from fair sometime declines,
> By chance or nature's changing course untrimmed.

14. *Shakespeare's Verbal Art in "Th'Expense of Spirit,"* pp. 23–24.

The images in lines 3–8 have all been metonymic, drawn from the customary associations of "a summer's day." But the last two define the innate limita- tions of all that exists merely on the order of nature. The repetition of "fair" quickly separates the particular and the temporary from the universal, for each fair creature declines from its fair condition while the idea of beauty remains. And the alliteration of "chance" and "changing" underscores the inevitability of such a decline, if not by accident then by the predetermined pattern of growth and decay.

That repeated "ch" sound, bringing the octet to a close, is the most striking example of alliteration within any of these fourteen lines. Indeed, alliteration and other forms of purely auditory repetition are not prominent in sonnet 18. What has replaced them is a different technique of repetition that gives the sonnet its unique quality: the reiteration of whole words rather than sounds. The process begins rather inconspicuously in line 2: "more lovely and more temperate." Although this semantic repetition may not appear significant, it is soon precisely balanced by "too short" and "too hot" in lines 4–5. The doubling of "more" emphasizes the beloved's virtues, while the repetition of "too" serves to heighten our sense of nature's excesses. The idea of instability is reinforced by the reiteration of "some- time" in line 5, where it is interwoven with yet another repetition: "every fair from fair sometime declines." Repeated words thus establish the son- net's texture of apparent clarity, which conceals a network of complex pat- terning. Engaged in making a comparison, the speaker is concerned primarily with distinguishing likeness from unlikeness. By reiterating words, and modifying their meanings in different contexts, he links physical and emotional similarities throughout the sonnet and arranges a system of correspondence parallel to that of the external world.

Sonnet 18's octet features another type of meaningful repetition, depend- ing not on the same word or sound but rather on the same grammatical relation. In these eight lines there are no less than six possessive construc- tions; together, they contribute directly to the poem's thematic develop- ment. The series, like the series of images, begins with the phrase "a summer's day." It continues with the rhyme-link the "buds of May" and ends with the repetition of the key word in "summer's lease." The next genitive phrase, "the eye of heaven," is exactly parallel with the second and leads to the corollary, "his gold complexion." Finally, "nature's changing course" indicates the most inclusive network of ownership. The series of possessive phrases has set out a hierarchy of natural beauty from which the speaker deliberately excludes his beloved. He now creates a separate, opposing level of beauty that belongs solely to the "thou." Line 9 furnishes the traditional turning point: "But thy eternal summer shall not fade." The line is strikingly effective because it combines a series of transformations from the patterns established before. The reentry of the second person makes a bridge between line 2 and lines 10–12, in which the "thou" figures as subject of an action. In the *volta* of line 9, however, the pronoun is genitive: "thy eternal summer" implies a reversal of the previous order since "summer" is now an object possessed rather than a possessor of beauty. Both techniques of repetition, the grammatical and the verbal, are employed here. The beloved's ownership of beauty has been substituted for that of nature. Summer continues to represent the idea of beauty, but it has been assimilated to a personal vision, hence the change from "summer's" to "summer." Despite the use of "thy" instead of "thou," we realize that the speaker has abandoned the natural, impersonal universe of lines 3–8 and turned to a uniquely human conception of reality.

Although the line that marks this turning point has structural affinities to those that came before, it nevertheless makes a clear departure. Throughout the octet the speaker used the simple present tense, placing a single verb in each line. By introducing the future in "shall not fade," he shifts from the ordinary world to an anticipation of the ideal state that is preexistent in his mind. The phrase "thy eternal summer" represents an unprecedented act of imagination when compared to the rather passive and conventionally associated images that adumbrate "a summer's day." It is a metaphor rather than a metonymy, being based on a personal insight instead of a common or necessary association. The speaker is no longer content with recording reality and seeks to transform it in this line and throughout the third quatrain. The centrality of the beloved as the possessor of beauty is reinforced by line 10: "Nor lose possession of that fair thou ow'st." As in lines 9 and 11, the speaker makes his point by negation in contrast to the assertions of the previous quatrain.

The second and third quatrains are quite similar in structure; both consist of an opening statement followed by two lines of development. In quatrain 2, both of the amplifying lines began with "and," whereas in quatrain 3 they begin negatively with "nor." There is also a corresponding contrast of imagery. The personification of death and "his shade" balances the earlier picture of the sun and "his gold complexion" as an emblem of life. Again, the use of a possessive construction denotes a hierarchy of power. Death's sovereignty concludes in absolute terms the speaker's definition of the realm of mortality. It provides a background from which the beloved's "eternal summer" is exempted. The actions of the "thou" remain static. They are either negations, such as not losing beauty and not wandering in the shadows of death, or modes of existence—owning and growing being the actions that link lines 10 and 12 by rhyme. The speaker's central contrast is fulfilled once again by the use of repeated words. The "fair" owned by the beloved defies the rule that "every fair from fair sometime declines." The distinction between two levels of beauty is expressed further in the "eternal summer," which is opposed to nature's summer and allied with the "eternal lines" that will stand against time. The quatrain is unified by this reiteration of "eternal" in its opening and closing lines. By uniting the beloved's "summer" and his own "lines" through the repeated adjective, the speaker subtly alludes to his own creative role. He chooses only to imply his possession of the ideal love and its poetic expression, which are equally his inventions. Sonnet 19 will be the first to use the possessive phrase "my love," while also mentioning (without ironic deprecation) the corresponding phrase "my verse."

The eternity alluded to in line 12 is explicitly defined by the couplet, which stands apart from the central comparison and explores its consequences:

> So long as men can breathe or eyes can see,
> So long lives this, and this gives life to thee.

The closely parallel structure of the couplet represents a more condensed version of the sonnet's organizing technique. Its basic symmetry derives from the repetition of "so long," which serves to coordinate the separate actions of each line. The first line in itself repeats the auxiliary "can" in order to link two related actions that stand for life itself. These actions of breathing and seeing are further linked by assonance. The second line is similarly divided into two corresponding actions through which "this," the entire sonnet, both "lives" and "gives life." Two tendencies that were developed earlier in the sonnet, toward longer sentences and increased frequency of verbs, culminate in the couplet. Every line until the eighth is grammatically complete, containing a subject and a single verb. Although three of these seven lines begin with "and," the conjunction is needed for stylistic rather than grammatical purposes. Line 8, however, is unquestionably less than a sentence: "By chance, or nature's changing course untrimmed." In quatrain 3, lines 10 and 12 are likewise subordinated to the lines that precede them, so that the speaker has moved toward lengthier, more complex statements. He also lends emphasis to these statements by doubling the verbs. Lines 10 and 11 are the first to include two verbs instead of one; thereafter, four of the sonnet's last five lines contain two active verbs, giving a final sense of purposeful activity.

The intent of the couplet's intricate symmetry is to set forth a relation of condition and result. If human life continues, so that people can read and recite the poem, then the poem, too, will live and confer a kind of immortality on the object of its praise. The speaker's promise to eternalize his beloved is thus carefully qualified. His sonnet is not a stone that simply endures the elements but a human monument that exists only as long as mankind chooses to read. A threefold relation of interdependence is now established. Just as the beloved's immortality depends on "this," the poem itself requires that life and literacy continue. The basic relation between the sonnet-speaker and his ideal love yields in the couplet to a wider dimension of human interaction. The reader himself, as one who breathes and sees, must complete the process of eternalization that the speaker began.

This reading of the sonnet verifies its closing prediction, even though our knowledge of the speaker and his beloved remains negligible. No description of their particular identities has been given; nonetheless, we are content to understand, and perhaps to emulate, the speaker's essential act of comparison. The sonnet's world is divided between the contemporary present that nature provides and the eternity created by poetry. It passively and impersonally renders the former realm but involves us in actively creating the latter. From the opening, and open, question of line 1 we are allowed to share in the poetic performance. In the interpersonal framework of lines 1 and 14, the act of immortalization is carried out by the speaker's "I" and by "this," the poem itself. Lines 2–13 lack any reference to the speaker, enhancing our sense of being "in" the poem, where a clearly defined dramatic speaker would have excluded us. We identify with the speaker, who is playing an active role, in contrast to the passivity of the beloved, who is merely the object of the action. Moreover, the complex patterning within these lines, beginning with the doublings of "more" and "too" in the first quatrain, encourages us to recognize how poetic artifice, subsuming a hierarchy of images and of semantic and grammatical repetition, reflects the beauty of nature but transcends it by virtue of its constancy. Finally, our human presence, as those who breathe and see, validates the poet's claim that our participation is a necessary component of poetic immortalization. It is the reader's task as co-maker of the poet's pledge that accounts for the distinctive and continuing appeal of sonnet 18. Dialogue has been extended here, beyond the dramatic "I" and "thou" toward the vital participation of all humanity.

4 *Awareness Lost*

Let us define 'man' as a poet perpetually conspiring against himself.

—Laurence Durrell,
Clea

To separate the last twenty-eight sonnets from all the others is a vulnerable but by no means arbitrary decision. It is impossible to prove that sonnets 127–54 do revolve on one sustained relation without obtaining a signed, notarized statement by the poet, yet the traditional view that these sonnets deal with a "Dark Lady," real or imaginary, has much to recommend it. Eight of these sonnets do explicitly address a woman, while many others refer to feminine features, and five mention her emblematic coloring. In the absence of contrary evidence, it is reasonable to assume that the other poems continue to address the same person. Sonnet 144 directly supports such an assumption: "Two loves I have of comfort and despair." And sonnets 133 and 134 draw the same love triangle. Therefore, the loves, the "man right fair" and the "woman coloured ill," may be regarded as the only auditors addressed by Shakespeare's speaker. They define two distinct areas of experience, creating two discrete bodies of poetry. As Hyder Rollins points out, the theme of time that has been so pervasive throughout the sequence does not appear after 126.[1] It should be added that two other themes, ideal love and poetic immortality, are also absent from sonnets 127–54. Just as the speaker never returns to the procreation theme after sonnet 17, he also drops the basic contrast of natural process against eternal love and poetry, establishing a thematic distinction that corresponds to the change in the quality of his dialogue.

The twenty-eight poems addressed to a woman maintain a single, nearly obsessive train of thought and in that respect resemble the opening group of sonnets 1–17. An exact contrast can be drawn here: Shakespeare's sonnets begin with an insistence on nature and fertility, but end by reiterating the opposite themes—sterility and frustration. The two smaller groups of the 1609 sequence thus define antithetical extremes. Just as continence is the speaker's main target in the Procreation group, promiscuity becomes his

---

1. "It seems worth noting that the word *time* is used seventy-eight times in sonnets 1–126 and not once in the remaining ones. Rearrangers have not always observed this fact," *Variorum*, 1:52–3.

subject in the closing section. The difference, however, is more than thematic because he has by now abandoned sententious preaching and is concerned with the dramatic rendering of his own experience. Although his depiction of destructive sex might be said to confirm conventional morality, what most impresses us in these sonnets is the authenticity with which they represent one man's ordeal. This quality made the Dark Lady sonnets repugnant to Victorian taste, but questions of morality, however we respond to them, are not crucial to these poems. Our interest focuses on the speaker, his inner life, and the modes of self-expression that he develops out of a new, often distressing liaison. The ideal love that had evolved around the figure of the youth now disappears as completely as the ideal of procreation had vanished before.

The last group of sonnets is no less distinctive in tone than in its thematic range. Again, we observe a gradual development in which the speaker discovers and defines himself through interaction with the object of his love. Dividing these sonnets into soliloquies and dialogues, we find that only eighteen out of twenty-eight actually address the woman by using various forms of "thou" or "you." Dialogue has fallen to a lower proportion than in the Fair Youth section, suggesting that the decrease will be accompanied by a lessening in the intensity of dialogue. Even those sonnets that directly address the mistress fail to establish anything like the closely felt reciprocity of an "I/ thou" relation. She remains remote from the speaker, alien to what he considers his best self. Her alleged lack of integrity or moral "worth" may well reflect the speaker's own dissatisfaction with what he has become. Such a sense of personal limitation, if not failure, is most clearly defined in the ten soliloquies. Addressing himself, as well as personifications of love and of his soul, the speaker probes the familiar yet unresolved questions of identity and self-knowledge. In addressing the young man, as we have seen, he underwent a process of testing and reaffirming the personal values that hinge on ideal love. Now, with that form of love entirely excluded, he must pursue some other, equally stable basis on which to build his poetic structures of personal affirmation. A comparative reading of these sonnets will determine whether such an alternative has been found.

I. Soliloquies

A gradual curve, rather than a strictly linear progression, is formed by the ten soliloquies. They begin and end with sonnets that are highly stylized rather than personal. The first, sonnet 127, furnishes a compliment to the woman's unconventional beauty: "my mistress' eyes are raven black." The last, sonnets 153 and 154, are narratives rather than lyrics and scarcely portray the speaker's state of mind. They are minor poems, setting up a definite (perhaps intentional) anticlimax at the end of the sonnets, and they have often been dismissed as spurious. But it is preferable to regard the first and last poems of this group as coordinating points between which a distinct pattern can be traced. The speaker moves from convention to self-disclosure, from wit to pathos, only to revert to a cryptically impersonal style at the end. In structural terms, we note a resemblance to the Fair Youth group, which also began and ended with the highly formalized statements of sonnets 1 and 126. Moreover, the first soliloquies, sonnets 127 and 130, say little if anything about the speaker. They seem to be preparatory exercises that take the beloved as their subject rather than the lover himself. Introspection in these poems begins late and yields relatively little insight. The speaker will not travel far or deep into the interior realm assumed by self-address. His central statements, 138 and 144, to some extent correspond to the final affirmations at the end of the Fair Youth section. But they differ radically in their content and in the speaker's strategies for self-presentation. Sonnet 145, intervening between two major poems, is yet another reminder of the limited world of artifice to which we return reluctantly in 153 and 154.

The first soliloquy in the Dark Lady group is remarkably similar in tone and in tactics of persuasion to the first sonnet of the 1609 sequence. Sonnet 127 recalls sonnet 1, as if to inform us that a new beginning is being made. It appeals at once to consensus instead of provoking our own opinions or reflecting the poet's: "In the old age black was not counted fair." The qualification that follows in line 2 does not fundamentally change the sense: "Or if it were it bore not beauty's name." One may wonder at the discrepancy of black being fair yet not named as beauty. But the underlying idea is perfectly consistent: black had always been considered at best an illegitimate offspring of beauty. Lines 3–4 show that the relation has been reversed so that true beauty is now "slandered with a bastard shame." The same concern for personified beauty is shown in sonnet 1, where "beauty's rose" is preserved by its "tender heir." However, the natural order has been altered now that black is made "beauty's successive heir."

Other verbal echoes show a similar displacement of emphasis, while the imaginative connection remains unmistakable. Both poems single out eyes as symbols of beauty; the youth is "contracted to thine own bright eyes," while the "mistress' eyes are raven black . . . and they mourners seem." The youth is thus unconventional in his behavior, the mistress in her beauty. Although the speaker praises one and condemns the other, his perspective is equally remote. Sonnet 1 uses "we" rather than "I," while in sonnet 127 the phrase "my mistress' eyes" marks the only sign of the first person. The "world" is cited twice in the former poem, corresponding to "every tongue" in the latter; both expressions delineate received opinion. The broad frame of reference shared by the two sonnets further strengthens their similarity. The opening sonnet speaks of "fairest creatures" rather than human beings, while 127 sees false beauty as "sland'ring creation." Finally, in both sonnets a reminder of death, the grave in 1 and the mourners in 127, serves to place beauty in a wider context of nature. The difference here is that the grave is real whereas "mourners" is merely a conceit for the mistress's eyes. The earlier tone of moral earnestness, reflecting concern for the continuity of life and beauty, has given way to a much less solemn attitude. The force of paradox in the opening poem was used to attack the youth's disregard for natural process: "Thyself thy foe . . . makest waste in niggarding." In sonnet 127 the contradiction of "fairing the foul" cannot be taken seriously, even if "every tongue says that beauty should look so." The ouster of true beauty by "art's false borrowed face" does not violate nature. It is so widespread a fault that it merely echoes human weakness: "each hand hath put on nature's pow'r." The speaker's stance becomes accommodating rather than indignant. He does not claim, as he did in the Fair Youth section, that his love possesses true beauty as opposed to worldly artifice. He states that his mistress mourns out of sympathy for beauty's exile, yet the contradictory result is that a form of false, black beauty is admired by the world. His wit thus gets the better of his initially moral protest. The paradox is not controlled by the speaker, who does not even seem aware of it. Throughout the Dark Lady sonnets he repeatedly brings himself to this quandary as he excoriates "the world" yet finds himself sharing its frailty. Appropriately, sonnet 127 begins the sequence by hinting at a vast uncertainty beneath the surface of an extempore conceit. The speaker attacks "each hand" that deceives appearance but finally agrees with "every tongue" that ascribes beauty to his own beloved.

After dialogue is introduced by sonnet 128, the next poem returns to "speaking of" and illustrates more explicitly how the speaker has begun to qualify some seemingly absolute ideas about nature. Sonnet 129 is entirely in the impersonal mode of address; no first- or second-person forms appear. It is not a soliloquy but can be read as a veiled self-portrait in which personal feelings are projected through a network of anonymous generalizations: "Th'expense of spirit in a waste of shame / Is lust in action." "Is" recurs symmetrically at the start of line 3: "Is perjured, murd'rous, bloody, full of blame." As the sonnet continues, it constantly implies that verb as a means of affixing attributes to "lust" or "it." The insistent statement "it is" must be understood as preceding the various adjectives and labels, so that when we encounter chains of modifiers or linked epithets we have no doubt as to what they refer. What we do not know is who is speaking in this strange way and why. The result is poetry of sheer distance and no discernible relation, a sonnet of pure "it."

The sonnet's intricate structure of repeated forms has often been analyzed, most painstakingly by Roman Jakobson and Laurence Jones. Their inventory of linguistic and structural features need not be considered here except as leading to their much less authoritative interpretation. The crux comes in the couplet and its connection to the entire design:

All this the world well knows, yet none knows well
To shun the heav'n that leads men to this hell.

Jakobson and Jones claim that the final line "brings the exposure of the malevolent culprit, *the heaven that leads men to this hell,* and thus discloses by what perjurer the joy was proposed and the bait laid."[2] That view, however plausible, lays bare the unbridgeable gap between descriptive linguistics and evaluative criticism. There is no basis in their elaborate anatomy of strophes and syllables for the idea that line 14 "seems to allude to the ultimate persona, the celestial condemner of mankind."[3] The conclusion is based on two things: the insight that "taker" and "men" are "the only animate nouns of the sonnet" and the assumption that both these nouns indicate victims of "heav'n" or God. But as Jonathan Culler points out, "Whatever makes the taker mad should be related to what leads men to this hell. . . . The natural interpretation is thus to take 'heaven' as the vision of 'bliss' and 'joy proposed' which baits the taker and not as a trope for 'heaven's sovereign.'"[4] One might question what Culler means by "the natural interpretation," but his reading does seem to follow the poem's connotative language more

2. *Shakespeare's Verbal Art in Th'Expense of Spirit,* p. 18.
3. Ibid., p. 27.
4. *Structuralist Poetics,* p. 73.

closely. Just as the "taker" and "men" represent humanity, so "lust" or the pursuit of "bliss" are the no less human qualities by which man defeats himself. In sonnet 129 humanity is both agent as Culler points out and victim as Jakobson and Jones assume. In fact, the word *lust* does not appear in any other sonnet, making this poem unusually outspoken. Elsewhere the speaker employs circumlocutions like "plague," "madness" and "use." Here he states his theme directly but uses an impersonal and indirect point of view. It is this combination of plain speaking and uncertain perspective that has so stimulated the commentators.

The eclipse of the speaker behind a facade of sententia is necessitated by his aim of seeing through all the stages of wanton sex: "had, having and in quest to have." That ability to reverse the normal sequence of expectation and fulfillment marks his extratemporal position. So detached a perspective could not have been maintained except by removing the speaker from the poem. No less impersonally, sonnet 5 defined the pattern of "hideous winter" undoing all beauty, while 67, 68, and 94 contemplated an equally chilling pattern of moral decay. Having once again distanced himself from his subject, the speaker can describe a pattern of human self-destruction through a series of mirror-like images: "hunted . . . had . . . hated." The sonnet lacks the customary turning point, or *volta,* because it has absorbed this psychological structure of hunger and satiety into its basic form. The pivotal point becomes the act itself, dividing promise from performance, and that act is repeatedly reflected in lines 1–12. Sonnet 129 may seem far removed from 127 by virtue of its more intense emotion and wider scope, yet the first two monologues are linked in a number of undeniable ways. Both are "minimal," revealing little if anything that can be identified as the speaker's own experience. Both have close analogies, sonnets 1 and 5 respectively. Finally, both poems take a similarly ambivalent position toward received opinion. The first soliloquy subtly shifted away from righteous anger at false beauty, admitting that beauty might indeed be black. And the impersonal poem is even more drastic in revising its initial morality.

Sonnet 129 seems at first no more than a "palinode," condemning and abjuring the power of love. Ralegh's "A Farewell to false Love," for example, effects an impassioned denunciation by listing a series of derisive epithets. Some of these have affinities to Shakespeare:

> A schole of guile, a net of deepe deceit,
> A guilded hooke, that holds a poysoned bayte.

A fortress foyld, which reason did defend,
A syren song, a feauer of the minde.[5]

The epithets characterize the abstracted essence of false love, whereas sonnet 129 defines the effects of lust on its victim. Ralegh's list is potentially endless; monolithic in thought, it leads to a consistent, predictable conclusion:

False Loue, Desyre; and Bewty frayll adewe
Dead is the roote whence all these fancyes grewe.

In the Shakespeare sonnet there is no farewell, only a rather surprising accommodation to what has been portrayed in lines 1–12 as deplorable reality. The couplet's role is to qualify deeply, if not contradict, all that has been said before. Once again, the device of paradox works toward increased complexity:

All this the world well knows, yet none knows well
To shun the heav'n that leads men to this hell.

The speaker concedes that his moralizing anger is very much beside the point. His efforts till now had all been directed into denunciation through the use of highly charged modifiers; the couplet, however, has not a single adjective. It attempts to state a fact, not a judgment, about man's behavior: there is a gap between theory and practice in human affairs because men fail to apply their abstract knowledge. More specifically, the phenomenon known and condemned as *lust* has attributes of heaven as well as of hell. Time and human experience must resolve the paradox, eventually reaffirming that only the infernal aspect of lust is authentic. Yet the "knowledge" gained, with a hint of biblical knowing, remains valuable. That recognition constitutes a broad extension of the speaker's thinking. At first his ironic wisdom had resided in perceiving that what people seek as "bliss" becomes "a very woe." Now, in the couplet, he admits that the entire process of pursuit and disappointment has the benefit of teaching people what they might not otherwise understand. He does not deny morality but simply confirms the value of human experience as a means of acquiring it. This deeply humanistic attitude, defined in sonnet 129 in universal terms, will underlie the speaker's attempt to articulate his own bewildering experience. At the end of sonnet 141, for example, he summarizes in a way that could easily be misconstrued as masochistic:

5. *The Poems of Sir Walter Ralegh*, ed. A. M. C. Latham, p. 8.

> Only my plague thus far I count my gain,
> That she that makes me sin awards me pain.

The affirmation of experience, however sinful, as a valid path to morality has now been applied by the speaker in reference to his own condition. There is no enjoyment of pain, only the elemental awareness that knowledge grows out of suffering.

A more familiar reversal of conventional opinion is performed by the next soliloquy: "My mistress' eyes are nothing like the sun." Questions of morality yield here to the lesser issue of describing and praising the beloved. Yet the basic structure, twelve highly repetitive lines contradicted by the couplet, is congruent with sonnet 129. Instead of an extended attack reversed by a two-line reassessment, the first twelve lines reject the dubious praises of poetic convention, while the last two bestow a more acceptable compliment:

> And yet by heav'n I think my love as rare
> As any she belied with false compare.

Swearing by "heav'n," the speaker may well recall the previous sonnet's apparition of "the heav'n that leads men to this hell." He has been itemizing at some length the reasons for not seeing, hearing, and smelling natural beauty in the mistress. In the brief affirmation that follows, he gives no sensual or rational evidence for thinking that his love is "rare." Despite its wry descriptions, sonnet 130 depicts a speaker who is "past reason" and not essentially different from the "taker" in 129. What he portrays now is the "swallowed bait" that has caused him to ignore his own perceptions. His underlying seriousness is further established by "well I know" in the ninth line. That confession echoes the couplet of sonnet 129, "all this the world well knows," while it also belongs to the series of deliberate contrasts presented by the speaker in this poem. What he well knows is that music is more pleasing than his mistress's voice, yet he admits "I love to hear her speak." Similarly, he knows the difference between her appearance and ideal beauty: "I have seen roses damasked, red and white, / But no such roses see I in her cheeks." Such awareness, again, does not deter him from loving and praising the lady. The speaker's irrationality, which will become the serious, possibly tragic, theme of the sonnets, still goes unrealized. He prefers to explore the comic implications of mocking both the mistress and the hollower commonplaces of poetic praise. But if anything suggests the speaker's latent uncertainty, it is the tentative quality of the verb *think* in the couplet. Coming after the concrete, sensory images of dissociation, after verbs of seeing, hearing, and knowing, his affirmation "I think my love as rare" lacks inner conviction as well as external evidence. Finally, his oath "by heav'n" fails to reinforce the claim because we have seen the ambivalence of that heaven in the preceding sonnet.

Like 127 and 129, sonnet 130 has a distinct companion piece in the Fair Youth sequence. Many critics have discerned echoes of sonnet 21 because both poems reject excessive compliments and present the speaker as a plain-speaking, truthful poet. As Hyder Rollins observes, "the ridicule of contemporary sonnet writing" is their common concern.[6] But when we compare sonnets 21 and 130 we discover some of the major differences in the Fair Youth and Dark Lady soliloquies. Sonnet 21, as has been noted, is the speaker's first attempt at self-representation. By contrasting himself against "that muse," he emerges as an Eiron who exploits the very conventions he protests against, infusing them with a new vitality. There is no such self-portrait in sonnet 130, where all the speaker's energies are devoted to the gap between his mistress and the ideal lady of the love sonnet tradition. As a soliloquy, 130 is far less revealing than 21. The speaker's presence is conveyed three times by the merely possessive phrases "my mistress' eyes" and "my mistress," while the subject in lines 1, 8, and 12 is always the woman, not the lover's response to her. When the couplet adds a personal evaluation it refers to her more seriously as "my love," yet its closing comparison in terms of "any she" remains disappointingly impersonal. The earlier poem's imperatives implied a personal address without using second-person forms: "O let me true in love but truly write, / And then believe me." But sonnet 130 has no suggestion that the mistress is even implicitly addressed. Readers have often sensed that the poem would insult rather than amuse a real "she" were it presented to her. Even if we read it as a satirical tour de force, whose target is empty poetic conventions, there is still something less than good-natured in its anatomy of the lady's flaws; she cannot be redeemed by the couplet's belated gesture of praise. In contrast, the youth in 21 fares better; his compliment in lines 10–11 is introduced earlier and strengthened by the closing lines:

> my love is as fair
> As any mother's child, though not so bright

6. *Variorum*, 1:334.

As those gold candles fixed in heaven's air.
Let them say more that like of hearsay well;
I will not praise that purpose not to sell.

Here poetic praise and self-defense are smoothly integrated. A more modest comparison is set against a "proud compare" to the stars. A closing gibe at the expense of other poets reinforces the bond between the speaker and his love as opposed to "that muse" and its "painted beauty." No such reciprocality can be detected at the end of sonnet 130. Its modest comparison is lacking in force: "as rare / As any she belied with false compare." The "she" seems to be no more than the artificial beauties derided in both poems, and the qualifying phrase "belied with false compare" limits this small compliment even further. In contrast, note the sweeping confidence of the earlier poem: "as fair / As any mother's child." Thus the soliloquy about the woman is less discriminating in its use of irony. Her appearance and the speaker's integrity are tinged by the implications of his mockery.

The differences between sonnets 21 and 130 suggest what the final soliloquies will confirm. There is less revelation and less presentation of the speaker in the Dark Lady poems because his concern for the beloved is correspondingly reduced. Since the woman remains an "it" rather than a fully realized "thou" (even when so addressed in the dialogues), she cannot provide the poet with a true reflection of himself. Sonnets 127, 129, and 130 show an unwillingness or inability to engage in genuine introspection. If the following soliloquies do move toward self-awareness, they never quite achieve it. The speaker's incipient but unsuccessful search for selfhood in relation to the woman thus continues in the next soliloquy.

Sonnet 138 is unique as an anatomy of interpersonal behavior:

When my love swears that she is made of truth,
I do believe her though I know she lies.

Its focus is no longer on the solitary speaker but on a series of postures by which he and the lady pretend to deceive each other. These opening lines suggest that her protestations serve as the stimulus to his rather passive response. His stance recalls the honest rogue in the drama, who forthrightly explains to the audience how he tricks his fellows. Such an attitude might be engaging enough onstage; we simply acknowledge the rogue's honesty and look forward to the eventual frustration of his design. In the sonnets, however, it is inappropriate to the speaker's character. We cannot forget his stress on the constancy of love throughout the Fair Youth sequence. If we grant that the woman's "love" is a wholly different affair, some unpleasant implications regarding the speaker still remain. He sanctions lying and even raises falsehood to a universal principle:

> O love's best habit is in seeming trust,
> And age in love loves not to have years told.

The sonnet sequence does not contain a coherent plot that will put such principles to a protracted test, nor is the speaker a rogue whom we expect to be put down.

Fortunately, sonnet 138 does not quite succeed in its attempt to evade the newly begun process of introspection. Attempts of this kind have often been characteristic of Shakespeare's speaker. They usually take place when he dodges unpleasant realities by chop-logic, or neutralizes them with a pun. Yet it is also typical that such evasions ring hollow. The speaker's circumvenient wit does not convince himself or the reader who is attentive to his tone. In this case, the most revealing evidence of underlying integrity comes in the couplet:

> Therefore I lie with her, and she with me,
> And in our faults by lies we flattered be.

As if faults and lies were not enough, the speaker admits that the entire relation is an exercise in flattery, that is, in mutual self-deceit. The term *flattered,* highly charged with echoes from the history plays, has a double application to the text. We have been reading the demonstration of a method that is ostensibly a self-defense. But "flattered" is a sure sign of criticism leveled against what the speaker has written, as well as what he has done. The same word at the end of sonnet 87 shows his emergence from illusion:

> Thus have I had thee as a dream doth flatter:
> In sleep a king, but waking no such matter.

In sonnet 42, flattery appears in the couplet, marking the speaker's awareness of a specious but pleasant argument:

> But here's the joy, my friend and I are one;
> Sweet flatt'ry, then she loves but me alone.

In sonnet 138, the sustained pretenses are another comfortable illusion from which the speaker awakes in the couplet. His recognition is anticipated by earlier criticisms: the lady "lies" and has a "false-speaking tongue," while his own dissimulation admittedly fails, "vainly thinking that she thinks me young." All this deceit would be pardonable if we accepted the claim of lines 11–12, that dishonesty is the way of the world, or at least of worldly lovers. But when we come to the closing lines, we realize together with the speaker that his self-defense is a further self-deception. Like his attempt to pass as "an untutored youth," his excuses are a transparent mask. His epigram that "love's best habit is in seeming trust" denies the value of the very love that is being defended. Neither that saying nor its companion, "age in love loves not to have years told," really answers the questions posed in quatrain 3:

> But wherefore says she not she is unjust?
> And wherefore say not I that I am old?

Since the lovers see through each other's lies, why do they keep up their pretense; why is "simple truth suppressed"? Presumably, they prefer not to acknowledge what they already know, their own falsity. In other words, they retain an awareness of what truth is even as they consciously collude to ignore it.

That the speaker should justify his own actions by claiming a normal human weakness is quite revealing. Lying with and to his lady, he suggests through the pun itself that the "lie" is a source of sensual pleasure while love as "lying" is fundamentally dishonest. He imposes a logical-sounding veneer on this cynicism by twice using "wherefore" in the questions of lines 11–12 and by neatly replying with "therefore" in line 13. Nevertheless, his moral uncertainty appears in the substitution of frailty for virtue and in the recognition that the entire argument is flattery. Describing real people, he reduces them to role-playing abstractions; "love" and "age in love" sound very much like figures in an allegory. He admits "our faults" or natural failings in the couplet, only to give a pseudo-objective existence to "lies" (not "*our* lies") in the ensuing statement: "in our faults by lies we flattered be." Again, the tendency is to resist self-scrutiny and personal accountability. Sonnet 138 thus continues from its predecessor, rather than marking a change of direction. The speaker no longer blames Cupid for his inner corruption as he did in sonnet 137; he pleads guilty with the extenuation that all lovers are as dishonest as himself. In this way, an attempt to change value judgments replaces the appeal to a mythic force. Both of these sonnets offer alternative escape routes from valid self-knowledge. Sonnet 138 might represent a slight advance in that it avoids myth and is confined to purely human experience.

Having no scapegoat, the speaker becomes increasingly uncertain and uncomfortable. He cannot succeed in transforming the pleasures of "lying" into a basis for personal values.

Perhaps the greatest shortcoming of this exercise in acquiescence lies in its inability to fully and accurately represent the speaker. As a soliloquy, sonnet 138 does not speculate on what might or should occur; its focus is narrowly confined to what is. This refusal to consider possibilities other than the immediately apparent points to a lessening of the speaker's imaginative resources. The flights of memory, imagination, and association that gave a dramatic dimension to the Fair Youth soliloquies are missing. There is none of the self-division or analysis that marked the speaker's earlier, more probing essays in introspection. And his role playing as "age in love" provides no substitute for self-knowledge. By thinking of things (not ideas) strictly as they are, he has reduced the lady and himself to objects rather than independent and freely functioning people. The results of this shift are felt in the unimaginative texture of the poem's language. Its diction is everywhere colloquial and threadbare, while figurative expressions have been entirely excluded. The well-worn epithet "false-speaking tongue" is as close as this sonnet comes to a metaphor. An underlying monotony thus resides in the poem's thought and is not dispelled by its half-hearted sallies of wit: "But wherefore says she not. . . . And wherefore say not I?" This persistent note of dullness describes an emotional state that the puns can only partially conceal. It is his own conscience, and with it a full awareness of himself, that the speaker has begun to deny.

The last significant soliloquy is 144, which gives a full exposition of the speaker's predicament. It should be noted that sonnets 145, 153, and 154, the weakest soliloquies in the sequence, add nothing, although they show a touch of the wit and irony that characterize Shakespeare's speaker. In sonnet 145 he uses four-beat lines to relate how his mistress "saved my life" when she added "not you" to the words "I hate." The lady's completed sentence is compared with deliberate exaggeration to day pursuing night, "who like a fiend / From heav'n to hell is flown away." The poem crudely employs the same technique of delayed reversal of extremes that succeeds elsewhere, notably in sonnets 29 and 30. The effect is reduced in 145 because it gives no account of the speaker's inner feelings, his supposedly "woeful state." Sonnets 153 and 154 are even further removed from any psychological experience. They recount the origin of a hot spring by telling how Cupid's fiery brand was immersed in it. Another extreme contrast, this time between desire and chastity, serves as their logical basis. The conflict is illustrated mythologically by Cupid and Diana, and symbolically by fire and water. Out of such opposition emerges the anomaly of waters whose "dateless lively heat" is said to cure venereal disease. The speaker concludes rather lamely with the paradox that, although "love's fire heats water, water cools not love."

The same vision of contraries is embodied far more dramatically in 144 by comfort and despair, that is, by the friend and the woman who vie to possess the speaker. Since both are his "loves," their rivalry also represents an inner division:

> Two loves I have of comfort and despair,
> Which like two spirits do suggest me still.

The poem is usually grouped among the six sonnets in which the speaker acknowledges a liaison between his friend and his mistress. But all the other "triangle" sonnets are dialogues. Sonnets 40, 41, and 42 are clearly addressed to the youth, the "gentle thief" who is forgiven for his robbery almost as soon as he is accused. Sonnets 133 and 134 turn to the woman instead, berating her as a temptress who has struck a "deep wound" to "my friend and me." In these five poems the speaker's double betrayal is a foregone conclusion; he is intent on formulating a proper attitude toward those who have betrayed him. Yet in 144 he still doubts "whether that my angel be turn'd fiend" and is less than sure that the betrayal has occurred. Despite its later place in the sequence, the soliloquy seems to precede the five related sonnets. However, its purpose may be to allow the speaker to reconsider. Speaking to others in the "triangle" sonnets, he must exaggerate for rhetorical purposes while concealing some part of his own feelings. Speaking (or thinking) to himself in 144, he can pause to define his predicament more precisely. In the first eight lines, of course, he describes his two loves, not himself. Yet as a result of his situation between "comfort" and "despair" he, too, is characterized in symbolic terms. His situation is that of every rational soul, influenced by good and evil and forced to choose between them.

Quatrain 1 of sonnet 144 depends on the simile "like two spirits" to set out this symbolic scene. It uses simile rather than metaphor to prevent the complete conversion of an amorous predicament to religious allegory. What makes the analogy possible from the speaker's point of view is an absolutely clear distinction between morality and immorality. He chooses simple diction and a balanced syntax to link the analogous systems of orthodox morality and a peculiarly human love triangle:

The better angel is a man right fair,
The worser spirit a woman coloured ill.

The language is so highly charged that we may forget that a comparison rather than an equation is being made. However, quatrain 2 begins to lead us out of the static framework of theology. The change is brought about as "my female evil / Tempteth my better angel from my side," a development that makes little sense in allegorical terms. The epithet "my better angel," found in line 3, is now replaced by "my saint," reminding us that this angelic being is after all a man, pursued by a temptress who would corrupt him "to be a devil, / Wooing his purity with her foul pride." This neat antithesis echoes the opening scheme of absolute good versus evil. But there now exists the danger that this sharp distinction is fading. We recognize a shift from the ideal order of allegory to the confused, inconstant world of human entanglements. For example, the woman's purpose in corrupting the speaker's friend is unclear. Although the meaning of "to win me soon to hell" seems religious, the pun on "hell" as the woman's sexual organ is already operative. With apparently motiveless malignity, the "worser spirit" contrives the speaker's ruin by corrupting his ideal love. Her strategy can only be to keep his affection by arousing his jealousy. The "saint" is wooed not because of the needs of a morality play but because a real woman uses him as a stalking horse.

After the first four lines, it becomes evident that sonnet 144 is anything but a solemn disquisition. The subject is not the traditional contrast of divine and profane love; that commonplace functions only as a source of imagery, while the speaker's mind is concerned with the far more earthly matter of human behavior—his own and that of his friends—in the game of love. His clearly defined attitude, especially in the sestet, reflects the poem's real theme. It is comparable to the "wait and see" speeches interspersed in the comedies:

And, whether that my angel be turn'd fiend,
Suspect I may, yet not directly tell,
But being both from me both to each friend,
I guess one angel in another's hell.

There is no denouement to resolve the speaker's doubts. The couplet only presents an imaginary resolution that is also incomplete. If we accept circumstantial evidence (as the speaker evidently would), the friend's infection with venereal disease will prove his corruption by the "female evil." But what then? We know only that the speaker must "live in doubt" until that event takes place. There is no clue as to what his response will be. Perhaps it is a sufficiently clear sign of the speaker's sensibility that he can endure such a state of affairs. His suspicion is well grounded ("both from me both to each friend"), not the fruit of a jealous disposition. He is able to admit his lack of proof ("yet not directly tell") while continuing to suspect. This tolerance of ambiguity marks the speaker as a character quite unlike Claudio in *Much Ado*, let alone Othello and Leontes. He is an Eiron who can remain inconspicuous while observing the follies of mankind. He can even pun coolly on what is traditionally the most outrageous of betrayals: "I guess one angel in another's hell." Here the austerely religious vocabulary of the poem undergoes its final, most complete translation into the worldly idiom of passion.

Further evidence of the speaker's ironic sensibility lies in his reconciliation of disparate concepts within so small a space. Sonnet 144 begins entirely in the mode of traditional Christian thought. It ends with a ribald pun that alludes to the unpredictability of human affairs. So extensive a transition is rare, and it points to a definite decline in the speaker's use of irony. This is not the cosmic irony from which his awareness of the nature of things originated. Neither is it the rhetorical irony that, ever since the procreation sonnets, has served as an instrument to prod and instruct the auditor. This irony belongs to the third type, dramatic irony, since the speaker is concerned with registering the change that occurs in his own mind. But there can be no self-discovery through a turning to the other, since sonnet 144 is a soliloquy. The kind of solitary affirmation achieved in soliloquies like 65 or 124 is not found here because the orientation toward distance, inherent to soliloquy, has become more absolute. In fact, throughout the soliloquies whose context is the relation with the woman we cannot unearth any assertion of an ideal or value that goes unscathed by the speaker's irony. Her beauty, faintly praised in sonnets 127 and 130, gets more criticism than defense. Her love, excoriated in 144 but acknowledged in 138, has no more worth than "foul pride," or a series of "faults" and "lies." Such corrosive ironies leave the speaker without a coherent identity; they undercut the interpersonal background against which he defines himself. He is now using what Wayne Booth calls "unstable irony," in which "all statements are subject to ironic undermining. No statement can really 'mean what it says.'"[7]

7. *A Rhetoric of Irony*, pp. 240.

In sonnet 144 we can specify some aspects of the final decline of soliloquy. The speaker does not act, or think of acting, according to his ideals of love and art, or any other value. His situation is a static one, between two persons whom he has idealized as contrary forces, without being able to exert an influence on either. He can affirm nothing in himself or the external world because he has come to question the youth who had embodied all real value. Irony, which earlier in the sequence had challenged others' pretensions while establishing a framework of values, now yields to a self-destructive cynicism that is deadlier than time's scythe.

II. Initial Dialogues

It would be oversimplifying to call sonnets 1–126 a dialogue of comfort, as the idealized youth cannot sustain the image that is imposed upon him. But one need have little hesitation in viewing sonnets 127–54 as a dialogue of despair. If the youth has disappointed the speaker by resembling the festering lilies of 94, the woman who is seen as merely a "weed" offers less joy and a deeper sense of disillusion. Just as the soliloquies of this section show a reduced depth of introspection, the dialogues indicate that the essential process of interrelation is no longer viable. Like the soliloquies again, the dialogues addressed to a woman have a definite pattern of distribution. Sonnet 128 stands apart as an introduction, while the other dialogues fall into three consecutively numbered groups: 131–37, 139–43, and 146–52. Each of these clusters marks a phase in the overall pattern of the speaker's decline. The Dark Lady dialogues are even more emphatic than the soliloquies in their exposure of a gradual weakening. The speaker, having grown from a detached observer of nature to an active participant in the experience of ideal love, reaches an impasse in his continued attempt to define himself. His ability to sustain a relation of dialogue will be impaired, not by the partner he blames but by his own failure to achieve a satisfactory understanding of himself.

The opening of sonnet 128 is distinguished by its elaborately subordinated syntax. Lines 1–8 compose a suspended sentence that can be typographically arranged:

> How oft, when thou my music play'st
>   Upon that blessed wood
>   Whose motion sounds with thy sweet fingers
>   When thou gently sway'st the wiry concord

That my ear confounds,
Do I envy those jacks
That nimbly leap
To kiss the tender inward of thy hand,
Whilst my poor lips,
Which should that harvest reap,
At the wood's boldness
By thee blushing stand.

This outline of parallel structure calls attention to the poem's extremely artificial language. Although such a style conforms to Elizabethan taste, the pattern seems rigid and monotonous for Shakespeare. Within eight lines we find three temporal clauses ("when" twice and "whilst") and four relative clauses that begin with "whose," "that" twice, and "which." The total effect is one of strained, mechanical ingenuity. Furthermore, the repeated couplings of adjective and noun reinforce the impression that the poet (perhaps imitating his lady at the keyboard) is plodding through a five-finger exercise; "blessed wood," "sweet fingers," "wiry concord," "tender inward," and "poor lips" all are placed within the octet. However well she may perform on the virginal, his verbal playing remains uninspired.

The opening line suggests this analogy and prepares us for the manneristic wit that follows: "Thou, my music, music play'st." At the center of the poem's conceit is the lady who is identified with the music she performs. She serves as the subject of the speaker's praise, "my music," and the object of her own performance. The "jacks" of the keyboard instrument provide another opportunity for facile punning, with the nursery-song echo of jacks being "nimble" contributing to a gamelike atmosphere. Personification is carried on relentlessly in the speaker's description of his envious lips, as well as the "dancing chips" or "saucy jacks" and the lady's fingers that "walk with gentle gait." But no sense of personality or of personal relation emerges from this series of compliments and conceits. The lady functions only as a stimulus to the speaker's hearing and his wit. Beneath his polite flattery lies a scarcely concealed concern for his own pleasures and an indifference to the other's experience. Thus in the couplet he proposes dividing her between himself and his wooden rivals: "Give them thy fingers, me thy lips to kiss." The division is facetious, just as the entire sonnet attempts to be. But it is precisely this evasion of serious contact that limits dialogue in the Dark Lady sequence. One has only to recall the last line of sonnet 20, where a comparable division appears: "Mine be thy love, and thy love's use their treasure."

There the speaker had asked for no less than a full interchange of affection, with merely sexual "use" reserved for women. The refusal to grant women the same seriousness accorded to his friend underlies sonnet 128 and the dialogues it introduces.

Contrasting 128 with an analogous sonnet will further illustrate the new, more restricted relation. Sonnet 8 is the only other that absorbs music into its central theme: "music to hear, why hear'st thou music sadly?" The similarity is enhanced as both opening lines turn "music" into an epithet for the person addressed. The youth, however, is told to listen, enjoy, and understand what he hears. Although the music will modulate to yet another image of procreation, the speaker is still concerned with what the other person thinks and feels. Correspondingly, the youth can be said to establish his own presence in the text as a real, contradictory human being. That he is chastised for self-love, instead receiving empty compliments, only increases his worth in our eyes. We are led to share what the speaker discovers in music's "speechless song," the fear that "thou single wilt prove none." No such involvement is conveyed by the speaker's address to the "thou" of sonnet 128. The poem serves as an overture to all these dialogues by suggesting that the speaker's interest in the woman is confined to her influence on himself.

Sonnets 131–36, the first continuum of dialogue, set forth the initial phase of the speaker's relation to his mistress. Polite compliment still abounds here but does not conceal intermittent feelings of resentment. The tendency to avoid direct and intimate encounter manifests itself in the "triangle" situation that is elaborated in 133 and 134 as well as in the puns on "Will" in 135 and 136. Both pairs of sonnets allow a third party to intervene between the lovers; the youth and "Will" (who is not simply the poet) are impediments to a stable union of "I" and "thou." Even in sonnets 131 and 132, where the lovers are alone, the speaker shows exaggerated interest in the opinions of those who criticize his lady: "some say . . . / Thy face hath not the pow'r to make love groan." He can reply to the doubters only by swearing, but in 131 he swears "to myself alone," and in 132 he promises to refute them only on condition that the lady show him her favor: "Then will I swear beauty herself is black, / And all they foul that thy complexion lack." Such an urge to verify the lady's beauty by making a formal declaration is a peculiar feature of these dialogues. The speaker's aim is really to convince himself by means of a legally binding statement to others. He never considers what the "thou" feels and whether she requires such testimony. By the end of the sequence, in sonnet 152, he will confess to a lack of good faith in all his swearing: "For all my vows are oaths but to misuse thee." The absence of real affection can be traced throughout these poems in the very texture of their dialogue.

In sonnet 131 the speaker admits for the first time that he is dissatisfied with the beloved: "Thou art tyrannous, so as thou art." The opening line and its repetition of "thou art" set up the basic structure of the dialogue in which the speaker probes for the lady's essence, what she truly is. By calling her "tyrannous," he praises ambiguously: she has the cruelty that belongs to the courtly-love tradition but not the beauty that should go with it. She is set apart from those "whose beauties proudly make them cruel." The speaker then employs the formula "thou art" to justify his continued love for one who is neither fair nor kind: "to my dear doting heart / Thou art the fairest and most precious jewel." The lady is therefore one thing to the impartial world and another in the speaker's view. No attempt to ease the contradiction is made; nor is the overfamiliar jewel metaphor helpful in giving poetic force to the speaker's subjective feelings. Instead of pursuing his argument, he tells of an imaginary debate with his lady's detractors. For unspecified reasons, he dares not defy them openly and swears to himself "to say they err." He reinforces his case by invoking "a thousand groans but thinking on thy face." Since such a private demonstration will convince no one, its only function is to prove the speaker's faithfulness. Yet there is something suspicious about these quasi-legal proceedings in which he reiterates to himself what he cannot maintain in public. His referring twice to "thy face" suggests an unwillingness to accept the "thou" as a person rather than a collection of specific parts or attributes. Whatever the woman is, she should be more than a face. The other attributes mentioned in this sonnet, "thy black" and "thy deeds," only strengthen our suspicion that the speaker's attitude toward her is far less enthusiastic than he pretends. His personified groans are said to testify that "thy black is fairest in my judgment's place," but the compliment could reflect his own defective judgment rather than the lady's beauty. Any doubts as to the highly critical perspective in which he sees and judges her are finally dispelled by the couplet:

> In nothing art thou black save in thy deeds,
> And thence this slander as I think proceeds.

Using "black" here in its pejorative sense undercuts the speaker's previous defense of his lady's coloring. Again, since the significance of "thy deeds" outweighs that of "thy face," it is evident that all the compliments (if such they really were) have been nullified.

Sonnet 131, then, addresses the lady directly but does not truly function as a dialogue. The speaker seems to be thinking aloud about his mistress, evaluating her much as one would appraise the "precious jewel" to which she is likened. He is nearly oblivious to her living presence, and when he does acknowledge it the results are bitterly ironic. He resorts to the interjection "yet in good faith" to prepare her for the unpleasant things that supposedly "some say." But good faith is the very element missing in this interrelation. By choosing the phrase he attempts to compensate for what he senses to be a tangible lack of respect for the woman. The speaker thus protests too much, leaving the inescapable impression that the harsh opinions of others are also his own. When he inserts the ingenuous "as I think" in line 14, he is not refuting the "slander" but implicitly defending it. An obvious condescension is shown here, as if the lady were obtuse enough to accept so damming a defense. The dialogue situation could therefore be defined as one of "speaking through" the auditor; the speaker directs his words to her but not his ultimate meanings. The orientation is egocentric in a way the Fair Youth dialogues never were. As a result of the unrealized dialogue, the speaker's self-portrayal also becomes rather shallow. He is condemned to role playing as the conventional lover ruled by his "dear doting heart" and sighing no less than "a thousand groans." It may sound anachronistic to say that Shakespeare's speaker in this section has given us dialogues that are "inauthentic" in an existential sense, but we have already seen how the dialogues involving the youth, no less artificial in their format, achieve a dramatic interdepedence of two people, a "marriage of true minds." In Dark Lady dialogues like sonnet 131, the lovers are never together, although they are alone with each other.

Sonnet 132 continues from its predecessor by performing another anatomy of the "thou." Again, we find "thy face" as well as "eyes" and "complexion." To those purely physical features are added "thy heart" and "thy pity." Nothing is said about the speaker after line 1: "Thine eyes I love, and they, as pitying me." He is presented as merely a victim of the lady's disdain, so that the "I" reappears only in the couplet promising to swear "beauty herself is black." This reticence, combined with an entirely conventionalized representation of the "thou," creates a highly attenuated form of dialogue. It recalls the introductory sonnet 127 by using the conceit of her dark eyes as "mourners." But now the speaker's "pain" (not counterfeit beauty) has made her eyes "put on black, and loving mourners be." An inner division is projected onto the woman. For if her eyes are dark "as pitying me," her heart continues to "torment me with disdain." The main argument is thus a supplication; her heart should "mourn for me, since mourning doth thee grace." The speaker links "mourning" to "morning" by loose association rather than by a pun. At the center of the poem he devises an epic simile: just as the "morning sun" and evening star suit the beauty of the sky, so "those two mourning eyes become thy face." It is not immediately clear what this "proud compare" has to do with the speaker's request for favor. He connects black (via mourning) with sympathy, so that the mistress whose eyes are charitable should now "suit thy pity like in every part." Not only is the reasoning convoluted, the imagery itself lacks energy:

> And truly not the morning sun of heav'n
> Better becomes the gray cheeks of the east,
> Nor that full star that ushers in the ev'n
> Doth half that glory to the sober west—
> As those two mourning eyes become thy face.

When compared to sonnet 33, "Full many a glorious morning have I seen," 132 reflects a substantial decline of imagination. The "heav'nly alchemy" seen in the earlier poem had an equivalent in the speaker's own transformation of language through his art. In 132 his vision has subsided from metaphor to meek comparisons. There is but one slight metaphor in the five lines quoted above, "the grey cheeks of the east." The rest is merely the rhetoric of plain statement buttressed by padding modifiers: "The morning sun," "full star," and "sober west." The speaker is no longer an active part of the scene he describes. Instead of integrating nature into his own experience, he conveys an impersonal account of heavenly beauty. The picture is passively recorded, suggesting a familiar source of aesthetic pleasure without making it fully visual. Perhaps the weakness stems from a circularity in the images; no transformation can occur when we see two aspects of the same form, the "cheeks" and "face" of heaven compared to the woman's.

A general tendency has been illustrated here, for these poems are almost totally lacking in nature imagery. It should be remembered that the sonnets began with a vision of physical nature as background to the themes of procreation, ideal love, and poetic eternity. The last sonnet to convincingly invoke the workings of natural process was 104, with its retrospect of "three beauteous springs to yellow autumn turned." Subsequent sonnets anticipate the Dark Lady group by avoiding direct observation of the natural world.

After 126, we note only a few images drawn from natural phenomena, and these are always subordinated to the dominant context of human relations. Sonnet 132 departs from this trend by attempting to revive the perspective of natural beauty. What emerges, however, is the type of hollow praise that was ridiculed in sonnets 21 and 130. This mistress's eyes are suddenly like "the morning sun," so that the speaker now resembles the muse "stirred by a painted beauty" to a similarly bombastic style. Perhaps an element of personal concern can be found in the closing injunctions to "let it . . . beseem thy heart" and "suit thy pity." But the couplet betrays the speaker's remote and calculating attitude. He will not swear to the lady's beauty unless she grants him favor; in other words, he will not unconditionally take the first step toward asserting her worth. Even the promised oath is weakened by abstraction and overstatement. Rather than defend the woman, he bypasses her entirely and arrives at the unnecessary generalization that "beauty herself is black." The closing line shies away from direct encounter with the mistress through a process of reversal: "And all they foul that thy complexion lack." Somewhere between the abstract "beauty herself" and the inclusive "all they," the person in question has been ignored. An authentic confrontation of "I" and "thou" has still not taken place.

The remaining sonnets in this first phase are no less disappointing if we look for depth of dialogue. What they do give us is a sketch of the speaker's unresolved attitudes expressing themselves through wit rather than feeling. Sonnets 133 and 134 deal primarily with a situation and only secondarily with the persons who compose it. The same love triangle, or at least a congruent one, had been set out in sonnets 40–42, chiding the friend for the speaker's double betrayal. Now in 133 it is the lady's turn to be blamed, with none of the forgiveness that was so quickly granted to the youth: "Beshrew that heart that makes my heart to groan." The plea of the preceding sonnet has apparently been denied, for there is now a consistency between the lady's heart and her "cruel eye." The first four lines, however, do not even mention her. They speak of "that heart" and "it" rather than "thy heart" and "thou." Impersonal diction also implies the absence of a personal subject in the rhetorical questions of lines 3–4:

> Is't not enough to torture me alone,
> But slave to slavery my sweet'st friend must be?

The actions of torture and enslavement are carried out as if automatically because the speaker's concern lies not with the woman herself but with the consequences of the actions he imputes to her. In quatrain 2 he is forced finally to acknowledge her existence by "thy cruel eye" and then more directly: "And my next self thou harder hast engrossed." But the passive verbs that follow, "I am forsaken" and "thus to be crossed," still exemplify his tendency to avoid contact.

The speaker's central strategy for avoiding dialogue is to portray himself as the victim of a higher force. In grammatical terms, this often means functioning as object rather than as subject. The nominal "I" appears only twice, each time entrapped by passive constructions: "I being pent" as well as "I am forsaken." Such syntax corresponds to the conventional imagery that highlights his weakness and dependency. For example, the causative form "that makes my heart" is combined with the groaning that sonnet 131 had cited as the epitome of love's effects. The "tyrannous" behavior countenanced there is now demonstrated with no apology. Other familiar images that follow from this opening are concentrated in the first quatrain: "wound," "torture," and "slavery." Each prescribes a passive, helpless role for the speaker; it is the syndrome of Petrarchan love, from which the Fair Youth sonnets had been relatively free. All that prevents this dialogue, and several others, from becoming entirely stereotyped is the three-sided relationship. In dramatic terms, the speaker's emphasis has shifted from character to plot, since he, the woman, and the friend are not free to modify their roles. An ironic disparity thus arises, since his images of Petrarchan dependence are very much out of place. This woman's cruelty is not customary chastity but its exact opposite. The "slavery" she provokes is not courtly service but a humiliation shared by the speaker and his friend "whom thou harder hast engrossed."

Sonnet 133 sets the stage and introduces the people of this drama without showing how they will speak to each other, if at all. At its center, the speaker maps out his threefold loss of "myself," "my next self," and "thee." The only escape he can devise is a fantasy derived from poetic convention. He turns the interchange of lovers' hearts into a metaphor of mutual imprisonment:

> Prison my heart in thy steel bosom's ward,
> But then my friend's heart let my poor heart bail.

The "thou" has been reduced to an allegorical symbol; her "steel bosom" differentiates her from the living hearts of the two men. In proposing an exchange, the speaker forgets that as a captive he cannot ransom his fellow prisoner. The unusual inversion in line 10, which is entirely monosyllabic, reflects his uncertainty as to the subject-object relation. We expect "my friend's heart" to perform an action but find it to be an object. Inevitably, there is some confusion; who is bailing out whom? The second proposal made by the speaker is similarly obscure: "Whoe'er keeps me, let my heart be his guard." He uses "whoe'er" as a means of evading the lady once again. It implies that his love for her is neither lasting nor exclusive. Moreover, "his" could refer ambiguously to "whoe'er" or to the friend. In this confusing array of pronouns, the ostensible idea is that the speaker will function as an intermediary; he will be kept by the lady or "whoe'er" while he keeps his beloved friend. The pattern of possession here is one of three concentric circles, with the speaker's love for his friend as a cell within the larger jail of his own captivity. All his conceits attempt to control imaginatively what is uncontrollable, the lady's sovereignty over him: "Thou canst not then use rigor in my jail." Nevertheless, the couplet returns to inescapable reality:

> And yet thou wilt; for I being pent in thee,
> Perforce am thine, and all that is in me.

This closing stresses the speaker's role as object and victim. Yet it is he who defines the triangle from its focal point, determining what the lady can and cannot do. He takes refuge in his own articulateness, controlling not reality but its verbal representation. In that sense, he dominates the poem and the situation it describes. Not surprisingly, there are seventeen "I" pronouns as opposed to eight references to "thou." The imbalance in quantity suggests an egocentric orientation on the speaker's part. His closing words, "all that is in me," may therefore carry a secondary sense that qualifies their overt surrender of autonomy. All that the speaker has created in this sonnet, even his depiction of the lady's power, belongs to him.

Sonnet 134 opens with a direct link to the situation defined in the previous poem: "So now I have confessed that he is thine." The first-person verb here begins a series that reflects the speaker through the first three lines: "I have confessed," "I myself am mortgaged," "myself I'll forfeit." These verbs progress in their tenses from perfect to present to future, creating a sense of finality and completeness; the main possibilities for the timing of actions have been accounted for. It is virtually the same effect as that of the more compressed sequence in sonnet 129: "had, having, and in quest to have," although three different verbs now are used. The speaker tries to extricate himself from his present captivity by setting up an imaginary future. He will make a forfeit of his own self "so that other mine / Thou wilt restore." He

soon realizes that character traits that determine the future make this projected escape impossible: "But thou wilt not . . . / For thou art covetous,
and he is kind." The sonnet concludes with another patterned repetition of
first-person verbs: "So him I lose . . . Him have I lost." Emphasis has been
gained by using the same verb twice while the sequence of tenses has been
reversed, moving from present to perfect and excluding the future. The
triangular situation attains a timeless stasis when the simple present tense is
finally reiterated: "Thou hast both him and me; / He pays the whole; and
yet am I not free."

Although the speaker's attention still centers on the situation, he does
consider the human factors that keep it in alignment. The underlying metaphor has changed from the jail of 133 to a courtroom in which the lady holds
her "bond" or "statute" of beauty against both men. She is represented as a
"usurer" rather than merely a "steel bosom," closely corresponding to
Shylock in the trial scene of *The Merchant of Venice* when his character has
devolved to a mythic stereotype. She, too, is attacked for taking needless
advantages by putting forth "all to use." The specific reference here is to the
friend, who like Antonio in the play "came debtor·for my sake." However,
the speaker's own debt to the usuress, and her exploitation of it, do not
provoke his complaint. Those two corners of the triangle are presented as
accomplished facts, while the friend's involvement is inveighed against.
Worst of all, the youth's complicity deprives the speaker of his "comfort."
So great is his self-centeredness he displays no more interest in his friend's
feelings than in those of his mistress. He assumes that loving her must
simply be a punishment for the youth, although he mentions her beauty
explicitly. He sees the usury of love as an abuse, even thou this love convention is traditionally beneficent, as in sonnet 6:

> That use is not forbidden usury
> Which happies those that pay the willing loan.

We cannot determine whether the speaker is justified in making his
"dark" assertions about the lady. But the formulaic, abstract quality of his
thought cannot be denied. His tendency to reduce all three people to one-
dimensional figures works against her, since she (however arbitrarily) is
given the villain's role. No margin for judgmental error has been provided.
The speaker rejects outright the possibility that the "thou" he addresses
could be capable of change; nor does it occur to him that his own schematic
view of things could be mistaken. Enjoying his narrow certainty, he tries to

establish simple facts rather than coming to terms with complex, uncomfortable feelings. There are no questions in this sonnet and no commands; all the sentences are simply declarative. There is no appeal to the two lovers who have betrayed him, only an objective-sounding inventory of events and consequences. The language of the sonnet remains spare and "factual," containing a total of only four adjectives: "free" is repeated as a rhyme word; "kind," with "covetous" as its opposite, reappears in "unkind." Each person has been neatly labeled, the woman being "covetous," the youth "kind," and the speaker "not free." This last modifier, shared by both men, is highlighted by the parallel between the two end-stopped phrases "nor he will not be free" and "and yet am I not free." The lack of adjectives throughout this sonnet reflects the speaker's reluctance to qualify in any way his basic assumptions about the love triangle he has plotted. Although sonnet 134 does grant human motivations to all three people, it reduces them to stereotypes. In following out the ramifications of this scheme, the speaker's imagination is confined to an uncharacteristic rigidity. Figurative language has been harnessed completely to a single "conceit," so that four related terms—"will," "bond," "statute," and "use"—represent the relationship of both men to the lady. No room is left for spontaneous exercise of the imagination, for ornamental or sensuous metaphor. The friend has "suretylike" become the speaker's "debtor," while he is "mortgaged" and "forfeit." His mind is just as tightly "bound" to the scheme he has created, making him the victim not of others' actions but of his own desire to simplify human relations by means of self-fulfilling predictions about them.

In the two "Will" sonnets that continue this initial phase of dialogues, the speaker succeeds brilliantly in avoiding a direct confrontation with the woman. The higher force that he interposes between them is expressed in the various meanings of the word *Will*, until the speaker's identity fades behind a semantic screen. Unlike the pun on "lie" in sonnet 138, no suggestion exists here of any dissatisfaction beneath the surface of cleverness. "Will" is mentioned thirteen times in sonnet 135, six times in 136. Yet the constant equivocations go untouched by any feeling other than wit for wit's sake. Perhaps the imaginative germ for these poems lies in the phrase "mortgaged to thy will" in sonnet 134, where a pun had already combined the legal term with the psychological "will" (volition or power of choice), as well as its slang sense of "sexual organ." Another origin may be the use of "will" and "wilt" as auxiliary verbs in sonnet 133 ("and yet thou wilt") and 134 ("but thou wilt not, nor he will not"), anticipating "wilt thou" in 135.

Whatever their immediate source, these two sonnets project the speaker's persistent tendency to escape the consequences of the erotic relationship. This getaway is flawless because its statements are polysemously perverse; they can be variously and endlessly deciphered while the grossly physical sense of "Will" is never far away. For example, sonnet 136 begins by assuaging the lady's conscience, "if thy soul check thee." Its argument depends on the pun "I was thy will / And will thy soul knows is admitted there." Although the primary movement is from the man named "Will" to "will" as a faculty of the soul, we are reminded of the underlying sexual symbolism by the verb "admitted." On other occasions, the physicality is explicit, as in the speaker's request in 135 "to hide my will in thine." Yet even here the secondary, spiritual sense should not be overlooked. The speaker indeed does hide or lose his will in the sense of an ability to make decisions for himself. His identity and the woman's have been submerged in the lowest and most common denominator, so conveniently a homonym for his name. Both sonnets exploit unlimited possibilities for punning, so that the speaker appears a most willing victim. The second sonnet is the weaker; "Will" appears less frequently and with less effect because the puns and equivocations have become familiar. A similar decline occurs in other pairs of sonnets, such as 29 and 30 or 113 and 114, where the second derives from and repeats an initial inspiration.

In this case, the central argument scarcely merits repetition because its implications are damaging to the speaker. In sonnet 135, quatrain 3 demonstrates by analogy that as the sea adds rain to its water, "so thou being rich in will, add to thy will / One will of mine." Although analogies between love and the sea (in terms of infinite extent) need not be derogative, this one is. The "thou" is reduced to elemental nature, after the opening line had already brought her down to the status of anonymous, generalized womanhood: "Whoever hath her wish, thou hast thy will." But the plea for indifference, rather than exclusive love, slights the speaker no less than the woman. In "making addition thus," he surrenders any claims he may have had to an individuality achieved through love. He is content to let her think "all but one, and me in that one will." The second version of this belittling argument is significantly more extreme. The nature imagery, however conventional, is replaced by the simple arithmetic of reduction. The analogy this time takes in lines 7–8 as well as the third quatrain:

> In things of great receipt with ease we prove,
> Among a number one is reckoned none.

The woman therefore corresponds to a thing "of great receipt" while the speaker is merely one "among a number." According to the axiom given here, his love for her adds nothing to her "store." Being "reckoned none," the speaker imputes a loss of value to himself and to the idea of love. When he asks to "pass untold" and pleads "for nothing hold me," his self-annihilation is complete. All that remains of him, at best, is "a something sweet to thee," while the couplet substitutes a name for his actual selfhood: "and then thou lov'st me for my name is Will." This reductive arithmetic needs to be taken seriously, despite the amusingly evasive action of the puns. Nowhere else in the sonnets can Hamlet's words be applied so tellingly: "reason panders will." The application of quantitative terms, together with the sterile imagery, precludes the emotional depth of an "I/thou" relation. Through both sonnets, imperatives abound as the speaker tells his beloved to "add," "think," "swear," and "love." He functions as the commanding subject whereas she, having a "blind soul," is no more than the object of his cajoling. Yet the mask of "Will" has a restrictive influence on the speaker too. He can no longer present himself through an inclusive "I" that organizes his experience directly. He has objectified part of himself as "Will" and is forced to speak in the third person about this new and partial image: "Will will fulfill the treasure of thy love." The triumphant wit of these two sonnets is literally self-defeating. They continue the first phase of dialogues, in which the speaker admits his dependence on the woman, by successfully ignoring all the unwelcome implications of that dependence.

Sonnet 137 ends this cluster of dialogues and marks the speaker's first attempt to define his experience in order to come to terms with it:

> Thou blind fool love, what dost thou to mine eyes,
> That they behold and see not what they see?

He has now become aware of the inner contradictions that were implied before. The alteration of beauty, reproved and then condoned in 127, has now begun to cause intense suffering since his eyes "know what beauty is, see where it lies, / Yet what the best is take the worst to be." Beauty, despite the speaker's previous claims, has not really changed; its constant qualities, he admits, have been distorted through his subjective error. Although this new awareness marks a dramatic growth, it is channeled into a highly restrictive scheme. The fault supposedly lies not in the speaker but in Cupid. In effect, using this outmoded personification provides a convenient label for what Jakobson and Jones termed "the malevolent culprit" by whom "the joy was proposed and the bait laid. "[8] As in sonnet 129, knowing true love does not prevent one from choosing its counterfeit. As in Ralegh's "A Farewell to false Love," sonnet 137 contains "hooks" that trap the victim. Shakespeare's version, however, internalizes the image: "Why of eyes' falsehood hast thou forged hooks, / Whereto the judgement of my heart is tied?" The fatal link is located between the faculties of sight and judgment, rather than between the external world and himself.

Poetic convention is thus subverted by the speaker's self-anatomy; he presents himself as the object of a mythic, external force. Blaming the "blind fool" Cupid for his own faulty vision, he unwittingly points to the psychological origin of his decline. From the beginning of the sonnets, he had been a reliable observer sketching nature, the youth, and himself with unquestioned accuracy. Now, by calling his own perception into doubt, he undermines the basis on which his understanding of the world depends. The process of seeing, pondering, and making sense of things can no longer function effectively. Sonnet 137, with its repeated rhetorical questions, illustrates the static quality of uncertain perception:

> Why should my heart think that a several plot,
> Which my heart knows the wide world's common place?
> Or mine eyes, seeing this, say this is not,
> To put fair truth upon so foul a face?

When these questions are answered definitively in the couplet, the speaker has at last forgotten Cupid and forthrightly blames his own inconstancy:

> In things right true my heart and eyes have erred,
> And to this false plague are they now transferred.

The "things right true" may simply be ideal love and beauty, or perhaps the speaker's pursuit of those ideals in his friendship with the youth. The "plague," as in sonnet 151, is the mistress herself. Suffering at her hands comes as a deserved punishment, much as real plagues were religiously ascribed to God's wrath. A rigid morality operates here, one that resembles Edgar's view at the end of *King Lear*:

> The gods are just, and of our pleasant vices
> Make instruments to plague us:

8. *Shakespeare's Verbal Art,* p. 18.

The dark and vicious place where thee he got
Cost him his eyes. (5.3.171–74)

Cupid in sonnet 137 serves as the mere agent of an unnamed internal force by
which the speaker's eyes "are transferred." Given the basic scheme of self-
division in which sight and judgment are corrupted, it must be his rational
soul that censures them. That soul, as sonnet 146 will stress, also owes its
allegiance to a higher force. Sonnet 137 in this way anticipates the later, more
powerful invocation: "Poor soul, the center of my sinful earth." It marks a
breakthrough in the speaker's introspective quest, although it fails to isolate
in his own soul the actual causes of his error.

III. Later Dialogues: The Final Breakdown

At this point, when roughly a third of the sonnets to a woman have been
examined, a definite turning point appears. Sonnets 137 and 138, a dialogue
and a soliloquy, uncover in different ways the very lack of self-confidence that
the "Will" sonnets have camouflaged so well. The speaker is therefore more
open about himself when he returns to another unbroken chain of dialogues,
139–43. This second phase is marked by persistent attempts to define and
control what he now acknowledges as an unbalanced, corrosive relation. His
style remains weakly unimaginative, suggesting a broader spiritual decline.
His syntax contains an unusually high proportion of imperatives rather than
statements or questions. Finally, the essential thought of these sonnets is
conveyed through block-like structures of cause and effect, very often in the
form of "if/then." In these ways, the speaker carries on his search for an
understanding of himself in relation to his mistress. He has advanced considerably beyond the sugared wit of sonnets 131–36. In particular, the intensity
of dialogue has increased. However, the second series of "I/thou" sonnets
comes to a disappointing end: sonnet 143 revives the pun on "Will," a
gambit that cannot work effectively in this new context of greater self-
disclosure.

The opening line of sonnet 139 sets the tone for this section: "O call me
not to justify the wrong." Its strategy is counterattack, which at least
implies a newfound mutuality between both people. But the speaker has by
no means abandoned his role of helpless victim; he insists that the lady's
might "is more than my o'erpressed defense can bide." What he seeks is a
measure of restraint that would qualify her supposed control over him. He
does not deny the wrong done by her "unkindness . . . upon my heart" but

protests being asked to apologize for her misdeeds. Throughout the first eight lines he assents to being a victim so long as certain vestigial rights are not infringed. He can tolerate the lady's infidelity ("Tell me thou lov'st elsewhere") but cannot bear to see evidence of what he already knows: "in my sight, / Dear heart, forbear to glance thine eye aside." This sensitivity as regards visual experience is highly characteristic. Earlier in the sonnets, the speaker's observations of time and change in nature were firmly based on his personal insight. Now, in choosing to suppress or ignore what he knows, he risks a self-imposed censorship of his eyes. He assumes that words, at least the woman's, count for less than looks: "Wound me not with thine eye but with thy tongue." Such an assumption has its dangers, especially in the context of a dialogue poem. It implies that what the lady says is of no real consequence. What she does, loving elsewhere, has similarly been ignored. All that remains is false appearance, a syndrome that Shakespeare habitually scorns. Yet the speaker of his sonnets at this point asks for nothing more.

From this awkward position the speaker abruptly retreats in line 9. Having insisted that he will not justify the lady, he proceeds to do just that: "let me excuse thee." The loss of meaning ascribed to her words now operates through his own self-contradiction. Moreover, the speaker's fear of dialogue shows most glaringly as his excuse unfolds: "ah, my love well knows, / Her pretty looks have been mine enemies." The person who had been addressed directly, as "thou" and "dear heart" in lines 1–8, is no longer recognized as a partner in dialogue. She has been so fully encapsulated as part of the speaker's being, as "my love" and merely "she," that the "thou" pronouns never reappear. The effect is not simply formal but also points to the speaker's increasing sense of detachment from the lady. Since he is speaking *of* her and not *to* her in this third quatrain, it is unclear to whom his justification is addressed. Presumably, he speaks to some imaginary tribunal in his mind. The soliloquy mode, as in sonnet 30's "sessions of sweet silent thought," has often created the metaphor of an introspective courtroom. Now the same technique is at work in dialogue, although the summoned thoughts are far from sweet and the speaker makes a much less probing examination of them. Posing as defense attorney, he speaks of his love in the third person as if she were his client. His case, distinguishing the lady from her "looks," posits an inner division in her soul no less than in his own: "Therefore from my face she turns my foes, / That they elsewhere might dart their injuries." Such stale imagery, the darting looks being outmoded weapons of Petrarchanism, testifies to the speaker's less than serious intention. "Therefore" adds the familiar stamp of pseudo logic. However, the transition from complaint to humorous reconciliation has not been convincingly achieved. The two modes remain incompatible because the speaker's position lies vaguely between passion and jest. Either the jesting of quatrain 3 undercuts the earlier complaints of mistreatment, or a reverse modification occurs. Whatever the case, a consistent and controlled range of attitudes does not exist. It follows that the relation to the woman addressed (and evaded) is in demonstrably bad faith. The speaker's confusion is only complicated further when he attempts to renew the previous sense of dialogue:

> Yet do not so, but since I am near slain,
> Kill me outright with looks, and rid my pain.

The game of "kill me-kill me not" thus concludes with yet another reversal, again in the form of mock submission. Although mixed feelings are generally a source of psychological depth, especially in introspective poems, the speaker in sonnet 139 has simply and regrettably failed to make up his mind. He slights the lady and undermines the dialogue situation on which the poem is based when he assumes that she can be teased indefinitely and does not deserve a consistently personal orientation.

In sonnet 140 the speaker continues to impute an inner division to the woman while presuming his own integrity. This time the split is between her eyes and heart rather than her eyes and tongue. The advice given does not relate to two modes of expression, looks and words, but separates outer and inner qualities. The speaker begins his analysis by conjoining seemingly opposite traits: "Be wise as thou art cruel." He will conclude this sonnet by revising the request of sonnet 139: "Bear thine eyes straight, though thy proud heart go wide." Between those opening and concluding commands he poses a series of somewhat denigrating directives. If the cruel one is to become "wise," she must first moderate her abuse by avoiding "too much disdain." However, the subjunctive mood in line 5 implies that her betterment is impossible: "If I might teach thee wit." The speaker is not merely polite here, since he goes on to define his condition as contrary to fact: "Better it were, / Though not to love, to tell me so." His proffered wisdom involves deception, and its hypothetical benefit would be no more than lying. As in 138, seeming replaces being, if only as a means of coexisting with what is known to be false. The speaker tries to alleviate his suffering through this unlikely compromise rather than delivering a mock-defense of the woman. He asks for clemency, but his plea has distinctly threatening overtones:

> Lest sorrow lend me words, and words express
> The manner of my pity-wanting pain.

The archly rhetorical device of *anadiplosis* or *reduplicatio,* the repetition of a key word in one phrase at the beginning of the next, heightens the intrinsic artificiality of their thought. The repetition of "words" as the link between "sorrow" and "manner" seems especially appropriate, since it calls attention to the speaker's self-conscious rhetoric. If the mistress refuses to be manipulated, the consequences will be no more real than if she agrees.

In quatrain 3, another chain reaction is sketched out with a slightly less formulaic quality. The speaker warns that he could "grow mad" and "might speak ill of thee" so that the world's "mad ears" would believe him. Again the underlying concern is with self-expression, while the ends of the chain are connected by the repetition of "mad." A subtle blackmail is at work in both rhetorical schemes; in fact the speaker is threatening to slander the woman, perhaps with these sonnets. His language here is characteristic of the blackmailer in that it projects unpleasant events that might result if his demands are not met. Lines 11–12 then bridge the gap between a hypothetical situation and the real world:

> Now this ill-wresting world is grown so bad,
> Mad sland'rers by mad ears believed be.

It is another way of saying that the speaker is not mad at all, at least no more than the rest of the world. He and society are joined not only by the epithet *mad* but also by being modified by some of the "compounds strange" that sonnet 76 had vowed to expunge. He has "tongue-tied patience" and "pity-wanting pain" the world itself is "ill-wresting." Another correspondence between the speaker and the world emerges in lines 7–8, which contain the sonnet's only significant image, an extended simile that appears as an afterthought rather than introducing its idea.

After the speaker has insisted on being told, however falsely, that he is loved, he describes his deception by appending an image:

> As testy sick men, when their deaths be near,
> No news but health from their physicians know.

Perhaps this is no more than another demand for convenient dishonesty;

what is disturbing is the misleading analogy between personal and professional relations. The speaker has forgotten the intimacy implied by "I" and "thou," even though he continues to use that form of address. He chooses for himself the role of "it," the terminal case who can only be comforted and from whom a truthful encounter must be withheld. Such a role is clearly at odds with the attempt to present himself elsewhere in this sonnet as a knowing and capable guide. Again, his basic uncertainty about himself can be inferred, an uncertainty that vitiates this relation. What he asks of her, to temper cruelty with wisdom, must remain a contradiction even granting that the cruelty works against him while the wisdom serves her interest. The speaker is in fact projecting onto the woman his own duality as victim and instructor. He expects her to respond simultaneously to two contrary aspects of his own being. Yet the couplet suggests an awareness that all these conditions cannot be met. It formulates a structure of cause and effect in which the lady will control only one aspect of herself:

> That I may not be so, nor thou belied,
> Bear thine eyes straight, though thy proud heart go wide.

Because quatrain 3 implies that the speaker is desperate, since the woman has already been described as "cruel," "proud," and wanting "wit," there is little point to this plea to leave things as they are. The situation is intolerable, yet the speaker argues doggedly for its preservation because he is not prepared to express openly the feelings that he implies. Nonetheless, throughout sonnet 140 a sharpening of attitudes can be traced by comparing its tone with that of 139. For example, "dear heart" in the earlier poem yields to the critical phrase "thy proud heart" in line 14. At one point, the speaker does employ a term of endearment, but the context is devastating in its irony. It is better, he claims, "not to love, yet, love, to tell me so." Where love does not exist, the title *love* becomes a reminder to the "thou" of her failings. There is no veneer of humor in 140 but a consistently plaintive and querulous tone. No attempt is made to defend the woman or to become reconciled to her shortcomings. Instead, the speaker concentrates on making the best, which is clearly not good enough, of a bad thing. He chafes at "too much disdain" without resisting disdain itself.

A more extreme example of the decline of dialogue is sonnet 141. In its tonal implications this is a soliloquy, although it preserves, almost to the end, an outward form of address between "I" and "thou." The speaker has begun to focus on self-analysis, discarding his earlier interest in a conflict between the lady's warring faculties. He begins by turning his attention inward, using the starkly monosyllabic diction that often appears at this stage of the sequence: "In faith, I do not love thee with mine eyes." What he discovers is an asymmetrical division of his own parts. His heart opposes his eyes and his other powers of perception ("my five senses") and understanding ("my five wits"). Outnumbered and seemingly overwhelmed, his "one foolish heart" still prevails, causing him to become "thy proud heart's slave and vassal wretch." By "serving thee," the speaker's heart betrays him to the lady's besieging forces, and thereby to the well-worn paths of Petrarchan imitation. Sonnet 141, however, becomes more interesting when considered in the context of gradually declining dialogue. It should be recognized as the exact equivalent of 130, in which the speaker swears that his love for the woman was unaffected by her less-than-godlike appearance. That claim, as we have seen, was unconvincing, and sonnet 141 will show exactly why. The woman's role was necessarily passive; her unflattering portrait served primarily as evidence of poetic honesty. As a soliloquy, sonnet 130 also conveyed an internal monologue in which the speaker reviewed his attraction to the lady. Now in 141 the same structure of mental privacy has been transposed into the less compatible form of dialogue. The "thou" continues to be catalyst to a complex set of reactions in the "I." A one-directional flow of sensations leads to ideas that are never expressed as dialogue, for example:

> Nor are mine ears with thy tongue's tune delighted;
> Nor tender feeling to base touches prone,
> Nor taste, nor smell, desire to be invited
> To any sensual feast with thee alone.

The question of whether the woman should be at all interested in these personal ruminations, and how she should reply to them, never occurs. She affects the speaker while he merely studies her effect on him. No suggestion of his exerting a counterinfluence and causing a response in her can be found.

This lack of reciprocation would be appropriate to soliloquy but becomes a serious flaw in a poem built on direct address. It brings down "thou" to the level of "it," something that is perceived, understood, and finally controlled. In fact, the nominal "thou" never enters this sonnet. What we do find is "thee" and "thy," accusative and possessive forms showing that her function is never that of an autonomous subject. As "thee" she is studied and served, the creature in whom "a thousand errors" are noted. She is also referred to as target of the speaker's eyes, namely "what they despise." Her parts are

inventoried with the possessive form as in "thy tongue's tune" or merely
listed as sensory phenomena, "tender feeling" and "base touches." She
offers a "sensuous feast" that appeals inexplicably to the speaker's heart so
that she can be said to embody the "swallowed bait" of sonnet 129. The
couplet of 141 ruthlessly extends this process of depersonalization. Even
"thee" and "thy" disappear as the third person replaces the second:

> Only my plague thus far I count my gain,
> That she that makes me sin awards me pain.

This is the same radical displacement of "thou" as in sonnet 139, which
substituted "my love" and "she" for "thou"; it is the more extreme example
because the speaker's orientation has become entirely introverted. He abandons his pretense of carrying on a dialogue when he refers to his auditor as
"she." Making her at last an active subject, he at once denies her even the
formal basis of a dialogue relation. Line 13 anticipates this rejection of the
other person when it assimilates her into the speaker's mind. She is "my
plague" and "my gain" but nothing more; her existence has been absorbed
into the speaker's imperial self. Yet the process at work here has a double
edge. In depersonalizing the woman, in isolating her parts under the cover
of dialogue, the speaker unwittingly undermines his own integrity and
"leaves unswayed the likeness of a man." A comparison with other sonnets
employing similar schemes of self-division will show a reintegration that is
lacking here. Sonnets 46 and 47 described a "mortal war" between eye and
heart that is settled by a "league" for sharing the sight and thought of their
ideal love. Interestingly, the speaker's eye there took in exactly what it rejects
in sonnet 141: "my eye doth feast, / And to the painted banquet bids my
heart." That internal rivalry did not stem from a conflict of values; each part
had affirmed the youth's worth and desired a larger portion of it. Such is
clearly not the case in 141, where an uncertain value system causes an over-
simplified scheme of self-division. The heart as scapegoat for all the speaker's
vacillations is an inadequate and overfamiliar symbol. Moreover, he does not
notice the correspondence between his own self-division and his dismem-
bered vision of the woman. His one-sidedness has dramatic value but makes
the sonnet disappointing, since we have come to expect a far greater
awareness.

The decline of dialogue, the dissociation of "I" and "thou," and the
speaker's attempt to dominate the other are further illustrated by the frequent, patterned repetition of pronouns in sonnet 142. Its opening line

places "I" and "thou" in a balanced, antithetical construction: "Love is my sin, and thy dear virtue hate." Three separate antitheses are combined here, between "love" and "hate," "sin" and "virtue," and "my" and "thy." Yet the equality between "I" and "thou" is suggested by a paradox: the speaker's "sin" of "love" cannot be worse than the auditor's "virtue" of "hate." This balance is articulated in line 3: "O but with mine compare thou thine own state." It is reinforced by both the parallel syntax and the rhyme of lines 5 and 7, in which the speaker accuses "those lips of thine" of being faithless "as oft as mine." Finally, in lines 9–10, "I" and "thou" are brought together for the last time:

> Be it lawful I love thee as thou lov'st those
> Whom thine eyes woo as mine importune thee.

All the structural devices of balance merely have illustrated a relation devoid of reciprocality. The "I" and "thou" may be equally unfaithful, but the speaker's "sinful loving" still outvalues the beloved's virtuous hate, being more comprehensive and less self-righteous. The request that "I love thee as thou lov'st those" makes clear the one-sided nature of the relation, since the "I" must importune a "thou" whose attention is bestowed elsewhere. After this line, the "I" disappears while the "thou" recurs five times in the last four lines. The lack of structural parity emphasizes the imbalance within the personal relation. The speaker must remonstrate with his beloved, "root pity in thy heart," following this plea with a mild threat:

> If thou dost seek to have what thou dost hide,
> By self-example mayst thou be denied.

Presumably, it is the speaker who will later withhold the pity now denied him. The sonnet, which demonstrates the breakdown of shared affection, ends with the promise that unkindness, at least, will be mutual.

Not only have "I" and "thou" become dissociated, the speaker has ceased to occupy the dramatic center of the poem. He ends this cluster of dialogues on a hapless note as sonnet 143 portrays him as an infant neglected by its keeper:

> Lo, as a careful housewife runs to catch
> One of her feathered creatures broke away,
> Sets down her babe, and makes all swift dispatch
> In pursuit of the thing she would have stay.

This simile is overextended through twelve lines, creating a parodic effect by the disparity of form and content. At the *volta*, the speaker studiously works out his application of the image:

> So run'st thou after that which flies from thee,
> Whilst I, thy babe, chase thee afar behind;
> But if thou catch thy hope, turn back to me,
> And play the mother's part, kiss me, be kind.

It would be pointless to pursue psychological significance in these images; the woman's figuring as a mother carries no more import than that of the friend as a runaway fowl. What appears to be most meaningful in this rather trivial sonnet is the triviality itself. It deliberately plays down the same neglect and suffering that 139–43 so heavily inveighed against. The speaker has returned to wit as an antidote to feeling, seeking refuge in the miniature mock-epic of lines 1–12 and finally reverting to the mask of Will:

> So will I pray that thou mayst have thy will,
> If thou turn back and my loud crying still.

Thus the fourth and last dialogue in this series employs anticlimax as a temporary respite from the emerging tensions that will become uncontrollable as the entire sequence nears its end.

Throughout the sonnets addressed to a woman we discern a definite tendency in the speaker to conceal himself behind a series of psychological masks. In the soliloquies, we traced his decline from an equivocating lover in 127 and 130 to "age in love" in 138 and a wryly suspicious cuckold in 144. Although he remains an Eiron, the irony turns inconsistent; he appears to speak as the "taker" of 129 yet also as the knowing "world." In the dialogues examined so far, he becomes a conventional Petrarchan victim, the man who is "testy sick" and growing mad, the helpless babe and the ever-ready Will. All these masks serve as camouflage, for the speaker can no longer give an honest answer to the questions of identity that have continually concerned him. The last cluster of dialogues, sonnets 146–52, shows his psychological disintegration in extremis; these seven poems actually close the 1609 sequence, since the final soliloquies 153 and 154 do no more than repeat the familiar escape from feeling into easy wit. The closing phase begins with 146, the last great sonnet in the sequence and one that is often singled out as a uniquely religious, possibly Christian poem:

Poor soul, the center of my sinful earth,
Thrall to these rebel pow'rs that thee array,
Why dost thou pine within and suffer dearth,
Painting thy outward walls so costly gay?[9]

There is nothing unique about this simple separation of body and soul. Sonnet 74 employed it as a means of resolving the conflict between permanence and change:

The earth can have but earth, which is his due;
My spirit is thine, the better part of me.

Again in sonnet 151, scarcely a companion piece for "Shakespeare's Christian sonnet," we find the same dichotomy:

For thou betraying me, I do betray
My nobler part to my gross body's treason;
My soul doth tell my body that he may
Triumph in love.

Like the separation of body and soul, the dramatic gesture of invocation has its precedents: the speaker apostrophizes time in sonnets 19 and 123, the muse in 100 and 101, and Cupid in 137. What makes sonnet 146 different from those dialogues is that one part of the speaker is invoking another; the soul or "thou" is merely an aspect of the speaking "I." Who then, or exactly what entity, speaks the poem? It is clear that we need not limit ourselves exactly to the dramatic character whose development we have been studying. He has somehow divided himself without indicating along what lines. One solution, suggested by Michael West, is to see the situation as continuing the medieval tradition of an internal dialogue between the body and the soul.[10] However, it is implausible either that the soul should invoke itself or that the body should refer to itself as "my sinful earth" and "thy outward walls." The voice heard in this sonnet comprehends both body and soul, whereas the tradition adduced by West is argumentative with a clear differentiation between the corporal and spiritual voices:

9. "Thrall to" in the second line is the emendation of B. G. Kinnear, replacing the repetition of "my sinful earth" that appears in Q, and is retained by Stephen Booth in his edition. For other emendations, see *Variorum*, 1:374.
10. "The Internal Dialogue of Shakespeare's Sonnet 146."

Soule: Thou art the meanes, by which I fall to sin
Body: Thou art the cause that set'st this means awork
Soule: No part of thee that hath not faultie bin
Body: I shew the poyson that in thee doth lurke.[11]

While sonnet 146 does owe something to this conventional opposition, its structure still is not a debate but an expostulation with no reply. As a dialogue, it must be considered self-effacing, belonging to the second of the four types defined earlier. It refers to the "I" only once, in the phrase "my sinful earth," so that the speaker (or whatever aspect of him is delivering this apostrophe) disappears after the opening line while various forms of "thou" occur ten times. Self-effacing dialogues, like 18 and 126, tend to assume an authoritative air, using consensus rather than personal knowledge. In this case, the soul is given a series of directives whose origins go beyond the mind of any personal speaker. Quatrain 3 consists entirely of such commands:

Then, soul, live thou upon thy servant's loss,
And let that pine to aggravate thy store:
Buy terms divine in selling hours of dross;
Within be fed, without be rich no more.

Rhetorical questions, another feature of the self-effacing mode, have already contributed to the establishment of an artificial consensus:

Shall worms, inheritors of this excess,
Eat up thy charge? Is this thy body's end?

Thus the soul, like the reluctant youth in the Procreation sonnets, is urged to shun an unthinkable, worm-eaten end. The self-effacing voice of this sonnet may be best understood as a wishful projection of the dramatic speaker; it is an articulation of himself as he would like to be, his "better part" or reason in Renaissance terms. A comparable act of transcendence was accomplished in sonnet 116, which insisted on giving an ideal definition of love despite the confessions and accusations of adjacent sonnets.

Sonnet 147 helps define the speaker of 146:

My reason, the physician to my love,
Angry that his prescriptions are not kept,
Hath left me.

11. An Anonymous "Dialogue between the Soule and the Body" printed in Francis Davison's *Poetical Rhapsody* (1602) and quoted by West, "Internal Dialogue," p. 112.

In this poem the speaker endeavors to become just that, the voice of pure reason, prescribing for his own benefit an impossibly rigorous regime. Whether his assumptions are pagan or Christian cannot be determined, since the central metaphor of the body housing the soul has so many possible origins:

> Why so large cost, having so short a lease,
> Dost thou upon thy fading mansion spend?

Commentators on the sonnet do not offer a convincing source for that image, but one can be found in Plutarch's *Moralia*. Appropriately enough, the relevant passages come as part of a debate on the conflict of body and soul. In "Advice about Keeping Well," Plutarch quotes Theophrastus' saying that "the soul pays a high rental to the body." He then adds a remark attributed to Democritus, that the body could successfully sue the soul.[12] In "Desire and Grief—Physical or Bodily Phenomena," the first quotation is expanded: "Theophrastus, on the contrary, said that the soul's lodging in the body was an expensive one; that for a *short tenancy* it paid a *heavy price* for its pains and fears, desires and jealousies"[13] (italics mine). The description corresponds exactly to Shakespeare's contrast between "so short a lease" and "so large cost." However, the use of Plutarch by no means excludes a Christian orientation; nowhere in the sonnets does the body-soul dichotomy imply a particular creed.

The crucial question raised by this sonnet is why the speaker chooses to address his soul at all. His passionate advice is never repeated elsewhere, nor is there any evidence of its being adopted. Only the gesture of self-division performed here will be sustained through all the final dialogues; sonnets 147–52 postulate such varied schemes of self-analysis that the woman's felt presence virtually disappears. Sonnet 146 marks a turning away from the human "thou," who has become superfluous because the speaker's attention is so concentrated on himself. The poem is a mask of reason, assuming that real problems can be solved by the eloquent reiteration of an ideal. We are reminded of the King's extravagant words at the beginning of *Love's Labor's Lost*, vowing a "war against . . . affections / And the huge army of the world's desires" (I.i.9–10). When Longaville subscribes to that campaign, he provides a very close echo to line 10 of the sonnet:

12. Plutarch, *Moralia*, 2:283.
13. Ibid., 15:43.

I am resolved, 'tis but a three years' fast:
The mind shall banquet, though the body pine. (I.I.24–25)

He is echoed at once by his comrade Dumain:

To love, to wealth, to pomp, I pine and die,
With all these living in philosophy. (I.I.31–32)

What these gallants do not realize is that their task is simply not feasible. They are quickly disabused by Biron and by the plot of the play. In sonnet 146 the speaker has made a brief, no less utopian resolution. To ascribe ironic overtones to his exhortation is to deprive the poem of its desperate pathos.

Any suspicion that this appeal to the soul results in a change of attitude or alleviates the speaker's plight is dispelled by sonnet 151, whose sharp division between body and soul confirms the former's absolute supremacy. Yet the central term is "conscience," joining both morality and awareness no less fully than in Hamlet's conclusion: "Thus conscience does make cowards of us all" (3.1.82):

Love is too young to know what conscience is,
Yet who knows not conscience is born of love?

These lines are consonant with other sonnets, especially 129, in asserting a tangible value in sensual experience. Passion may be unconscionable in its actions and influence, but as a result we gain an awareness of ourselves and others, together with a beneficial sense of guilt. That, at any rate, is precisely the development that has occurred in the speaker's relation with the woman, for the next lines apply the opening generalization to them:

Then, gentle cheater, urge not my amiss,
Lest guilty of my faults thy sweet self prove.

The argument, or rather the plea, is that the woman ought not either reprimand him or tempt him to further misdeeds. But at this point, where the balanced "my" and "thy" begin to suggest a measure of complementarity, the speaker again withdraws into himself. His elaborate conceit of body and soul, by which "flesh" is reduced to its purely sexual function, now displaces his relation with the "thou." It occupies lines 5–12, after which there is no return from distance to relation:

No want of conscience hold it that I call
Her love for whose dear love I rise and fall.

The couplet shows a characteristic touch of depersonalization, so that "thou" becomes "her" and "love." The moral sense of "conscience" has been overthrown, since here the word can only mean an awareness of desire.

Similarly, sonnet 147 is totally devoted to the exposition of a scheme for self-analysis. It expands the image of disease and madness introduced in sonnet 140:

> My love is as a fever, longing still
> For that which longer nurseth the disease,
> Feeding on that which doth preserve the ill,
> Th' uncertain sickly appetite to please.

The speaker has returned to the role of delirious patient, a most convenient mask that externalizes inner conflict and eliminates responsibility. He acknowledges the self-destructive nature of his illness, which has banished the physician and indulges its own appetite. The origins of his suffering are placed as if beyond his control because of the autonomous existence granted to his reason and appetite. The verb *to be* (stated and understood) figures throughout the poem as an expression of this static yet fragmented reality: "My love is as a fever," "My reason, the physician to my love," "Desire is death, which physic did except," "Past cure I am, now reason is past care," "My thoughts and my discourse as madmen's are." Not surprisingly, as the speaker becomes entirely concerned with his inner faculties, granting them a being of their own, he retains little concern for the other person. In fact, the "thou" is absent throughout this dialogue with the exception of line 13:

> For I have sworn thee fair, and thought thee bright,
> Who art as black as hell, as dark as night.

Even here, her function is an impersonal one. She is the etiology of his disease, the catalyst to a series of emotional reactions that the speaker finds so intriguing. Sonnet 147 thus continues from its predecessor in following out a scheme of self-division. It also defines the two central motifs with which all the final dialogues are concerned, the speaker's unreliable vision and the falsity of his vows. Its couplet juxtaposes an irresolvable tension between what he thinks and what really is. As in sonnet 137, a breakdown in his ability to see things accurately will undermine the very core of his identity.

Such a breakdown now occurs, as sonnets 148–50 repeatedly complain of blindness:

> O me! what eyes hath love put in my head,
> Which have no correspondence with true sight!
> Or if they have, where is my judgment fled,
> That censures falsely what they see aright?

This initial uncertainty, as to whether perception or judgment is at fault, persists until the end of the sequence. At first, the resultant split is between the speaker and other men:

> If that be fair whereon my false eyes dote,
> What means the world to say it is not so?

The disparity is sharpened by a play of wit: "Love's eye is not so true as all men's: no. / How can it?" Then, in sonnets 149 and 150 the division becomes internal. The speaker protests, "I against myself with thee partake," using a formulation that appeared in sonnets 88 and 89. There he had willingly vowed to act against his own interests, but now the submission is accompanied by bitter regret.

In sonnet 150, another anatomy involving sight, heart, and mind is performed. As in all these complaints, the style is marked by frequent, querulous questions whose parallel syntax and thought lead to oppressive monotony:

> O from what pow'r hast thou this pow'rful might,
> With insufficiency my heart to sway? . . .
> Whence hast thou this becoming of things ill . . . ?
> Who taught thee how to make me love thee more,
> The more I hear and see just cause of hate?

These unanswerable questions, if nothing else, indicate the speaker's need to find a culprit. He cannot blame himself, having become a collection of parts rather than a whole, and when none of his parts can be fairly indicted he turns to the woman. In sonnet 148, after twelve lines of unmediated soliloquy, he invokes her only for the sake of blame:

> O cunning love, with tears thou keep'st me blind,
> Lest eyes, well seeing, thy foul faults should find.

Since "love" has been described throughout this poem as a personified force, as Cupid, "cunning love" suggests that the woman is seen in mythic rather than human terms. Similarly, sonnet 149 begins its dialogue with the stereotyped epithet "O cruel" and ends with another salvo of blame:

> But, love, hate on, for now I know thy mind;
> Those that can see thou lov'st, and I am blind.

These last, strangely obsessive dialogues show in the plainest language and in highly regular structures of thought that their speaker is no longer in control of his imaginative powers. Perhaps the cause lies not only in his frailty but in the intellectual categories at his disposal. His bewildering sensations and behavior cannot be adequately explained in terms of received morality and its psychological presuppositions. Again and again, he constructs patterns of antithesis and rudimentary "either/or" divisions in an attempt to clarify his state of mind. But these patterns do not succeed in resolving the essential conflict. As in the soliloquies, especially 144, he returns to a static situation as uncomfortable as it is inescapable. Sonnet 152 concludes the downward trend but has a confessional quality that to some extent redeems the speaker's earlier evasions:

> But why of two oaths' breach do I accuse thee,
> When I break twenty? I am perjured most,
> For all my vows are oaths but to misuse thee,
> And all my honest faith in thee is lost.
> For I have sworn deep oaths of thy deep kindness.

The phrase "for I have sworn" is carried over from the couplet of 147; it also recurs in the couplet of this sonnet:

> For I have sworn thee fair: more perjured eye,
> To swear against the truth so foul a lie.

This striking pun on "eye" and "I" cannot be disregarded; it epitomizes the speaker's character as a seer whose essential faculty has been corrupted. Moreover, it gains prominence by contrast with the sonnet's starkly colloquial diction and the absence of any other figurative language.

Perhaps we can best summarize the speaker's progress by recalling the extensive reference he has made to sight and insight, beginning with sonnets 12 and 15. His discovery of cosmic process in the natural world was counterbalanced by the evolving ideals of procreation, eternal poetry, and love itself. His perceptions of inconstancy on the human level were likewise assimilated into a larger framework of abiding personal value. But in the sonnets addressed to a woman, the irony of process infiltrates the speaker's mind instead of being observed from the vantage point of emotional detachment. Awareness has become so complex and so pervasive as to constitute an intolerable ordeal, leading the speaker to mix unanswerable questions with explanations that explain nothing. It is this slow development and final collapse of a personal identity portrayed throughout the 1609 quarto that gives so enduring a value to Shakespeare's sonnets. The universality of that experience, dealing with elemental issues of orienting oneself in space and time and among other people, is aided rather than harmed by the paucity of our historical knowledge. We cannot know who the youth and the woman were, or if they were, but in the speaker's anxious questionings and shifts of mood, in his persistent explorations of true and false identity, in his pursuit and loss of dialogue, we cannot fail to recognize ourselves.

Appendix

The Sonnets Classified by Modes of Address

Note: The dotted line in each group separates sonnets 1–126 from sonnets 127–54.

I. The Impersonal Mode
5   67–68   94

129

II. The Self-Effacing Mode
1–2–3–4   6–7–8–9   11
53   55–56   69–70   77
84   95

III. Soliloquy
21 23 25   33
63–64–65–66   105   116 119 121
124

-----

127 130   138   144–145
153–154

IV. Dialogue
A. Impersonal
12   54   59–60

B. Self-Effacing
10   13   16–17 18   38 41
57–58   73 79 82   93 96
126

131–132   142

C. Introverted
26–27–28–29–30   42
44–45–46–47   50–51–52
62   76   85–86   102 107
109–110–111–112–113–114–115   125

-----

133   141   147–148

D. Balanced
14–15 19–20 22 24   31–32
34–35–36–37 39–40 43
48–49   61   71–72 74–75 78
80–81 83 87–88–89–90–91–92
97–98–99–100–101–103–104 106
108   117–118 120 122–123

-----

128   134–135–136–137
139–140   143   146
149–150–151–152

Bibliography

Note: This list includes works cited and other book-length studies of the sonnets since 1950.

Bacon, Francis. *Essays, Advancement of Learning, New Atlantis.* Edited by R. F. Jones. New York: Odyssey Press, 1937.

Baldwin, T. W. *On the Literary Genetics of Shakespeare's Poems and Sonnets.* Urbana: University of Illinois Press, 1951.

Booth, Stephen. *An Essay on Shakespeare's Sonnets.* New Haven: Yale University Press, 1969.

Booth, Stephen, ed. *Shakespeare's Sonnets: Edited with an Analytical Commentary.* New Haven: Yale University Press, 1977.

Booth, Wayne C. *A Rhetoric of Irony.* Chicago: University of Chicago Press, 1974.

Buber, Martin. *The Knowledge of Man.* Edited by M. Friedman. New York: Harper and Row, 1965.

Burckhardt, Jacob. *The Civilization of the Renaissance in Italy.* Translated by S. G. G. Middlemore. Oxford: Phaidon Press, 1945.

Campbell, S. C. *Only Begotten Sonnets: A Reconstruction of Shakespeare's Sonnet Sequence.* London: Bell and Hyman, 1978.

Chapman, George. *The Plays of George Chapman, the Comedies: A Critical Edition.* Edited by Allan Holaday. Urbana: University of Illinois Press, 1970.

Culler, Jonathan. *Structuralist Poetics.* London: Routledge and Kegan Paul, 1975.

Daniel, Samuel. *Poems and a Defence of Rhyme.* Edited by A. C. Sprague. Cambridge: Harvard University Press, 1930.

Davies, John. *The Poems of John Davies.* Facsimile edition. New York: Columbia University Press, 1941.

Drayton, Michael. *The Works of Michael Drayton.* Edited by J. W. Hebel. 5 vols. Oxford: Oxford University Press, 1931–1941.

Evans, G. Blakemore, ed. *The Riverside Shakespeare.* Boston: Houghton Mifflin, 1974.

Ferry, Ann. *All in War with Time: Love Poetry of Shakespeare, Donne, Jonson, Marvell.* Cambridge: Harvard University Press, 1975.

Fineman, Joel. *Shakespeare's Perjured Eye: The Invention of Poetic Subjectivity in the Sonnets.* Berkeley: University of California Press, 1986.

Furnivall, F. J., and W. R. Morfill, eds. *Ballads from Manuscripts.* Vol. 2. London: The Ballad Society, 1863-1873.

Giroux, Robert. *The Book Known as Q: A Consideration of Shakespeare's Sonnets.* New York: Atheneum, 1982.

Green, Martin. *The Labyrinth of Shakespeare's Sonnets: An Examination of Sexual Elements in Shakespeare's Language.* London: Charles Skilton, 1974.

Hammond, Gerald. *The Reader and Shakespeare's Young Man Sonnets.* London: Macmillan, 1981.

Herrnstein [Smith], Barbara, ed. *Discussions of Shakespeare's Sonnets.* Boston: D. C. Heath, 1964.

Hopkins, Gerard M. *The Letters of Gerard Manley Hopkins.* Edited by C. C. Abbott. London: Oxford University Press, 1935.

Hotson, Leslie. *Mr. W. H.* New York: A. A. Knopf, 1964.

Hubler, Edward. *The Sense of Shakespeare's Sonnets.* New York: Hill and Wang, 1952.

Ingram, W. G., and Theodore Redpath, eds. *Shakespeare's Sonnets.* London: University of London Press, 1964.

Jakobson, Roman, and Laurence Jones. *Shakespeare's Verbal Art in Th'Expense of Spirit.* The Hague: Mouton, 1970.

Jespersen, Otto. *The Growth and Structure of the English Language.* New York: G. E. Stechert, 1905; Anchor Books, 1955.

Johnson, Samuel. *The Yale Edition of the Works of Samuel Johnson.* Vol. 6. New Haven: Yale University Press, 1958.

Knight, G. W. *The Mutual Flame: An Interpretation of Shakespeare's Sonnets.* London: Methuen, 1955.

Krieger, Murray. *A Window to Criticism: Shakespeare's Sonnets and Modern Poetics.* Princeton: Princeton University Press, 1964.

Laing, R. D. *The Self and Others: Further Studies in Sanity and Madness.* London: Tavistock, 1969.

Landry, Hilton. *Interpretations in Shakespeare's Sonnets.* Berkeley: University of California Press, 1963.

———. "The Marriage of True Minds: Truth and Error in Sonnet 116." *Shakespeare Studies* 3 (1967):98–110.

Latham, J. E. M. Shakespeare's Sonnet 21." *Notes and Queries,* n.s. 25 (1978):110–12.

Leishman, J. B. *Themes and Variations in Shakespeare's Sonnets.* London: Hutchinson, 1961.

Lever, J. W. *The Elizabethan Love Sonnet.* London: Methuen, 1966.

Lewis, C. S. *English Literature in the Sixteenth Century Excluding Drama.* Oxford: Oxford University Press, 1954.

Mahood, M. M. *Shakespeare's Wordplay.* London: Methuen, 1957.

Mann, Thomas. *The Magic Mountain.* Translated by H. T. Lowe-Porter. New York: A. A. Knopf, 1927. 2 vols.

Martin, Philip. *Shakespeare's Sonnets: Self, Love and Art.* Cambridge: Cambridge University Press, 1972.

Melchiori, Giorgio. *Shakespeare's Dramatic Meditations: An Experiment in Criticism.* Oxford: Oxford University Press, 1976.

Muecke, D. C. *The Compass of Irony.* London: Methuen, 1969.

Muir, Kenneth. *Shakespeare's Sonnets.* London: Allen and Unwin, 1979.

Pequigney, Joseph. *Such Is My Love: A Study of Shakespeare's Sonnets.* Chicago: University of Chicago Press, 1985.

Plato. *The Works of Plato.* Translated by B. Jowett. New York: Dial Press, 1937.

Plutarch. *Moralia.* Vol. 2. Cambridge: The Loeb Classical Library of Harvard University Press, 1927–1969.

Polanyi, Michael. *Personal Knowledge: Towards a Post-Critical Philosophy.* New York: Harper and Row, 1964.

Pooler, C. Knox, ed. *The Works of Shakespeare: Sonnets.* 3d ed. London: Methuen and Co., 1943.

Ralegh, Walter. *The Poems of Sir Walter Ralegh.* Edited by A. M. C. Latham. London: The Muses Library, 1926; 1951.

Ramsey, Paul. *The Fickle Glass: A Study of Shakespeare's Sonnets.* New York: AMS Press, 1979.

Richards, I. A. *Poetries: Their Media and Ends.* Edited by Trevor Eaton. The Hague: Mouton, 1974.

Rollins, Hyder E., ed. *A New Variorum Edition of Shakespeare: The Sonnets.* 2 vols. Philadelphia: J. B. Lippincott, 1944.

———. *Tottel's Miscellany.* 2 vols. Cambridge: Harvard University Press, 1926.

Rosmarin, Adena. "Hermeneutics Versus Erotics: Shakespeare's Sonnets and Interpretative History." *PMLA* 100 (1985) : 20-37.

Schaar, Claes. *An Elizabethan Sonnet Problem: Shakespeare's Sonnets, Daniel's Delia and Their Literary Background.* Lund Studies in English, no. 28. Lund, Sweden: C. W. K. Gleerup, 1960.

———. *Elizabethan Sonnet Themes and the Dating of Shakespeare's Sonnets.* Lund Studies in English, no. 32. Lund, Sweden: C. W. K. Gleerup, 1962.

Schmidt, Alexander. *Shakespeare Lexicon.* 2 vols. Berlin: Walter de Gruyter, 1962.

Sengupta, Satyaprasad. *Some Aspects of Shakespeare's Sonnets.* Calcutta: Vidyodaya Library, 1966.

Sethna, K. D. *"Two Loves" and "A Worthier Pen": An Identification through a New Approach.* New Delhi: Arnold-Heinemann, 1984.

Smith, Hallett. *Elizabethan Poetry.* Cambridge: Harvard University Press, 1966.
————. *The Tension of the Lyre: Poetry in Shakespeare's Sonnets.* San Marino: Huntington Library, 1981.
Spenser, Edmund. *The Poetical Works of Edmund Spenser.* Edited by J. C. Smith and E. de Selincourt. Oxford: Oxford University Press, 1912; 1963.
Stirling, Brents. *The Shakespeare Sonnet Order: Poems and Groups.* Berkeley: University of California Press, 1968.

Thompson, Alan R. *The Dry Mock: A Study of Irony in Drama.* Berkeley: University of California Press, 1948.
Tilley, M. P. *A Dictionary of the Proverbs in England in the Sixteenth and Seventeenth Centuries.* Ann Arbor: University of Michigan Press, 1950.

Wait, R. J. C. *The Background to Shakespeare's Sonnets.* New York: Schocken Books, 1972.
West, Michael. "The Internal Dialogue of Shakespeare's Sonnet 146." *Shakespeare Quarterly* 25 (1974):109–22.
Wilson, Katharine M. *Shakespeare's Sugared Sonnets.* London: Allen and Unwin, 1974.
Wilson, John Dover. *An Introduction to Shakespeare's Sonnets for the Use of Historians and Others.* Cambridge: Cambridge University Press, 1964.
Winny, James. *The Master-Mistress: A Study of Shakespeare's Sonnets.* London: Chatto and Windus, 1969.
Wyatt, Thomas. *The Collected Poems of Thomas Wyatt.* Edited by K. Muir. London: Routledge and Kegan Paul, 1949.

General Index

Address, modes of, 99–108
Alazon character, 47, 55, 57
Alden, R. M., 84n
All's Well That Ends Well, 25–26
Arnold, Matthew, 26
As You Like It, 1

Bacon, Sir Francis, 27
Barnes, Barnabe, xi
Blake, William, 44
Booth, Stephen, viii–ix, 11, 17n, 46, 50n, 61n, 84, 92, 93, 129–30, 178n
Booth, Wayne C., 154
Buber, Martin, 107
Burckhardt, Jacob, xi
Butler, Samuel, viii

Chapman, George, 7n
Coriolanus, 28
Culler, Jonathan, 143–44
Cymbeline, 22n, 36

Daniel, Samuel, 53, 102, 105, 106
Dante, 44
Dark Lady group, xiii, 42, 101, 140–85
Davies, Sir John, 93–94
Dialogue, xii–xiii, 99, 106–9; marginal, 109–13; self-effacing, 113–16, 179, 128–38; introverted, 116–21, 163, 173–75, 182; balanced, 121–28; in Dark Lady group, 139–40, 142, 148, 152, 155–85
Drayton, Michael, 56n, 105, 106

Erasmus, 26–27
Evans, G. Blakemore, 14n

Fair Youth group, 60, 108, 109–28, 140, 141, 147–48, 149, 151, 159, 162
Falstaff, 14, 32, 37, 62
Ferry, Ann, 129n, 132n
Frost, Robert, 61–62
Furnivall, E. J., and W. R. Morfill, 95n

Hamlet, 1, 34, 41, 42, 73, 91, 167, 181
Hammond, Gerald, 40, 81, 84

Herrnstein [Smith], Barbara, 78n
Hopkins, Gerard Manley, 37n
Hubler, Edward, viii, 38, 130

I/thou relation, 106, 107–8, 109–28, 132–33, 137–38, 140, 148, 157–59, 161–63, 164, 167, 170–71, 173–76, 178, 181
Imagery: of seeing, x, 15–18, 28, 38, 60–61, 97, 108, 167–69, 174, 183–85; of natural process, 4–6, 10, 12–13, 16–17, 19, 28–29, 38–39, 47, 56, 60–61, 63–64, 72, 131–32, 133–34, 160–61, 166; of family, 8–11; of music, 8, 23, 155–57; religious, 36, 97, 152–53, 178–81; legal, 72, 81, 158, 165, 170; Petrarchan, 147, 162, 170, 174; absence of, 151, 160–61
Impersonal address, 69–70, 99–101, 106, 142–45
Ingram, W. G., and Theodore Redpath, 45, 50n
Irony, xii, 37; in Shakespeare's drama, 1–2, 20; cosmic, 2–20, 31, 43, 64, 71, 111, 154; rhetorical, 20–31, 43, 154; dramatic, 31–43, 54, 68–69; unstable, 154, 173, 177

Jakobson, Roman, and Laurence Jones, x, 133, 143–44, 167–68
Jespersen, Otto, 1n
Johnson, Samuel, 103
Joyce, James, viii
Julius Caesar, 25, 57

King Lear, 2, 55, 98, 168–69
Kinnear, B. G., 178n
Knight, G. Wilson, 84, 89, 129n

Laing, R. D., 108
Landry, Hilton, 78n, 91–92, 92–93, 94, 97n, 129n
Latham, J. E. M., 44–45
Lee, Sidney, 27, 81n
Leishman, J. B., 129n
Lever, J. W., 44
Lewis, C. S., 44, 45, 85
Love's Labor's Lost, 2, 180–81

Index to the Sonnets

Note: numbers in italics indicate extended discussions

194